GRADUATE REVIEW
OF TONAL THEORY

GRADUATE REVIEW OF TONAL THEORY

A RECASTING OF COMMON-PRACTICE HARMONY, FORM, AND COUNTERPOINT

Steven G. Laitz
Eastman School of Music

Christopher Bartlette
Baylor University

New York   Oxford
OXFORD UNIVERSITY PRESS
2010

Oxford University Press, Inc., publishes works that further Oxford University's
objective of excellence in research, scholarship, and education.

Oxford New York
Auckland   Cape Town   Dar es Salaam   Hong Kong   Karachi
Kuala Lumpur   Madrid   Melbourne   Mexico City   Nairobi
New Delhi   Shanghai   Taipei   Toronto

With offices in
Argentina   Austria   Brazil   Chile   Czech Republic   France   Greece
Guatemala   Hungary   Italy   Japan   Poland   Portugal   Singapore
South Korea   Switzerland   Thailand   Turkey   Ukraine   Vietnam

Copyright © 2010 by Oxford University Press, Inc.

Published by Oxford University Press, Inc.
198 Madison Avenue, New York, New York 10016
http://www.oup.com

Oxford is a registered trademark of Oxford University Press

Library of Congress Cataloging-in-Publication Data

Laitz, Steven G. (Steven Geoffrey)
    Graduate review of tonal theory : a recasting of common-practice
    harmony, form, and counterpoint / Steven G. Laitz ; Christopher
    Bartlette.
      p. cm.
    Includes index.
    ISBN 978-0-19-537698-2
    1. Music theory.   2. Harmony.   3. Counterpoint.   4. Musical form.
I. Bartlette, Christopher A.   II. Title.
    MT6.L136G73 2010
    781.2—dc22

                                                          2008048611

Printing number: 15 14 13

Printed in the United States of America
on acid-free paper

CONTENTS

PART 3   ELABORATING THE PHRASE MODEL AND COMBINING PHRASES

7   Six-Four Chords, Nondominant Seventh Chords, and Refining the Phrase Model   88

8   The Submediant and Mediant Harmonies   102

PREFACE

The vast majority of American colleges and universities that have graduate programs in music offer a one-semester review course in tonal harmony. In spite of the fact that such courses are commonplace, no published text has been designed for the special needs of these graduate-level harmony review courses. The dearth of graduate review texts often leads an instructor to adopt the undergraduate theory textbook used at their institution, the result of which is often problematic. For example, undergraduate texts often assume little or no knowledge of fundamentals. However, most graduate students do not need to begin at this point or, if they do, will not require the detail and drill presented in these sources. Another problem with using an undergraduate text stems from the amount of information offered about every topic, which even the most determined instructor can never cover in a single semester. Further, graduate students are often expected to "unlearn" their previous study, replacing terminology, underlying philosophy (e.g., moving from a more vertical, third-stacking approach to a more linear approach), and often even hard-and-fast rules (e.g., variation in the treatment of hidden fifths). Such a reorientation takes time and is difficult to accomplish with a text designed for first-time users. Finally, graduate students can often be challenged to think about, test, and develop the theory themselves. This is rarely discussed in undergraduate texts.

Of course, an instructor can also choose to provide self-developed materials for the class. This will always enrich the experience for the students and instructor, but it is time consuming for the instructor to find appropriate materials for every discussion topic. The materials can supplement an undergraduate textbook, but then the students are asked to purchase books that they will hardly use. Clearly, there is a need for a concise, musical, entertaining, challenging, relevant, and inexpensive text geared to the specific requirements of graduate music students.

Approach

Graduate Review of Tonal Theory is appropriate for a graduate student's re-engagement with music theory and analysis. It is intended for students who have a grasp of musical fundamentals, basic voice leading, and roman numeral analysis but may need to fill in gaps.

The text provides a means by which we can discuss the perception and cognition, the analysis and performance, and the composition and reception of common-practice tonal music. The theory has as its core the assumption that music has structure. If music did not have structure, it would be difficult to conceive of it as anything other than a wash of sound. Structure allows us to latch onto elements of music that either fulfill or deny expectations; both scenarios provide psychological cues through which we can grasp similarities and differences among different musical excerpts.

There are numerous ways in which music can have structure, three of which form the primary focus of *Graduate Review of Tonal Theory:* melody, harmony, and form. All are hierarchical, and the text's analytical foundation is based on the relative weight of harmonies, given their function within a given musical context.

Application

Graduate review courses take many shapes and sizes: The number of meetings per week, the number of weeks per semester, the number of semesters, and the specific content of the courses vary greatly from institution to institution. It is impossible to provide a clearinghouse for all of the approaches taken in these courses—it is therefore not the goal of this text to be a chameleon that assumes a confusing array of perspectives and terminologies in order to fit into every possible analytical style. Rather, the text offers a linear, cohesive presentation of tonal theory while allowing for different trajectories through the material. Since differences in terminology, labeling, and presentation exist, we include references to these other approaches in the appendixes and the Index of Terms and Concepts. We encourage the instructor to connect students' former studies with the material in this text; however, in order to avoid confusion, we suggest that the labels and terms given in the body of the text be used in the review course. It will be easiest to speak with one approach than continually to refer to the divergent approaches brought to the course by the students.

The 15 chapters of *Graduate Review of Tonal Theory* are organized so that they can be covered approximately one per week in a graduate review course. The text progresses from context and fundamentals to chromaticism and forms:

- A prologue, "Setting the Stage," provides a reorientation and whets the appetite by revealing music theory and analysis to be an activity that depends on human cognition, musical instincts, and personal choice.
- Fundamentals (Chapters 1–3) unfold quickly and include higher-level topics such as accent in music, metrical disturbance, melody and species counterpoint, tonal hierarchy, and melodic fluency.
- Beginning with Chapter 4, each chapter closes with an "Analytical Extension," in which an additional analytical topic is introduced and explored. If the instructor wishes to move more quickly through chapters, he or she may omit one or more of the analytical extensions without harming the text's pedagogy or organization.
- A hierarchic approach undergirds the presentation of both diatonic harmonies (Chapters 4–8 and Chapter 10) and chromatic harmony (Chapters 11–14), all of which is introduced through a *phrase model.*
- Musical context is central to the text. To that end, complete formal components are introduced early on (Chapter 6) and unfold throughout the text, including phrase, period, and sentence (Chapter 9) and binary, ternary, and sonata forms (Chapters 12 and 15).

It is possible to adapt the organization of the book—along with sections of Appendix A—to focus on other elements of tonal theory. In general, if there is too much material to cover, some or all of the analytical extensions can be omitted. If there is not enough material, items from Appendix A or supplemental discussions (provided by the instructor) can be added. The following scenarios provide examples of alternate paths.

- If one wishes to skip the discussion of form, the following could be omitted:
  - Chapters 9 and 15
  - The discussion of binary form in Chapter 12

- If one wishes to include a deeper discussion of form, analytical extensions could be omitted, and some or all of the following could be added from the appendix:
  - "Subphrases and composite phrases": after Chapter 6
  - "Variation techniques": after Chapter 12
  - "Ternary form and the nineteenth-century character piece": in Chapter 15, after ternary form
  - "Rondo": in Chapter 15, after ternary form
  - "Further characteristics of sonata form": after Chapter 15

- If one wishes to cover fugue, a supplementary discussion can be inserted after Chapter 5.

- If one wishes to cover more extended chromatic techniques, a supplementary discussion can be placed after Chapter 14.

Accompanying Workbook

We encourage the use of the separately sold workbook to support the text and its included DVD of recordings. The workbook is organized into discrete assignments, with approximately four assignments per chapter. Each assignment contains a mix of activities that progress from short, introductory analytical and writing exercises to more involved tasks. Marginal icons indicate that corresponding exercises are available in the workbook.

The Recordings

The majority of musical examples from both the textbook and the workbook are recorded on a single music DVD, which is included in the textbook. The recordings are played by students and faculty from the Eastman School of Music. Icons in the text and workbook indicate which examples are recorded as well as their locations on the DVD. You'll find a track listing of all examples in the back of this book. The nearly four hours of excerpts and complete pieces will provide you with instant access to hundreds of examples drawn from over three centuries of music.

The DVD presents the music in CD-quality format. In addition, high-quality MP3 files are available by accessing the following website: www.oup.com/us/Laitz. (Note: A standard CD player will not play the DVD.)

Accessing the Recordings

Insert the DVD into your computer; you should see a screen with:

1. Title of book
2. Text Examples
3. Workbook Examples

To access Textbook Examples:

1. Select "Textbook Examples"
2. Select the desired textbook chapter (or "Setting the Stage" or Appendix)
3. Select a specific example within the desired chapter

To access Workbook Examples:

1. Select "Workbook Exercises"
2. Select the desired workbook chapter
3. Select a specific exercise within the desired chapter
4. Select a specific example within the selected exercise

Acknowledgments

We would like to thank the students in our graduate review courses at the Eastman School of Music. It is because of our experiences in the classroom that we saw the need for, and the application of, this book.

We are grateful for the support of our colleagues at the Eastman School of Music and Baylor University School of Music, particularly Robert Wason and William Marvin, for their ideas and support of this project. We would also like to thank Douglas Lowry, Dean and Director, and Jamal Rossi, Senior Associate Dean. The reviewers, many of whom made more than one pass through various versions of the manuscript, provided both musical insights and pedagogical advice. They include: Andrew Davis, University of Houston; David Garner, San Francisco Conservatory of Music; Roman Ivanovitch, Indiana University; Philip Lambert, Baruch College; Neil Minturn, University of Missouri; Samuel Ng, Louisiana State University; Jeffrey Perry, Louisiana State University; Stephen Slottow, University of North Texas; Gordon Sly, Michigan State University; Ken Stephenson, University of Oklahoma; and Kristin Wendland, Emory University.

We wish to thank the staff at Oxford University Press for their support and encouragement in the development of this project. Jan Beatty, Executive Editor and visionary, was terrific throughout the process. Cory Schneider, Assistant Editor, worked tirelessly on all aspects of the project. Lisa Grzan, Senior Production Editor, and Mary Araneo, Managing Editor, oversaw each stage of the production.

We also wish to express our gratitude to Mike Farrington, the recording engineer and supervisory editor, who is a model of professionalism. And many thanks to Helen Smith, Director of Eastman's Recording Services, for her help and support. Lastly, we thank our families—Anne-Marie, Madeleine, Kathy, and Arica—for the central role that they play in our lives.

GRADUATE REVIEW
OF TONAL THEORY

Setting the Stage

When we pay attention to something or someone, we observe, analyze, interpret, and decide whether (and how) to act. These actions are based on our abilities, our experience, our traditions, and our knowledge. Our actions are also based on hierarchy. Every moment of our lives is filled with an overwhelming amount of information. We choose what will get our attention: Is it safe to turn on the red light? Does the multivitamin supplement have enough calcium or too much vitamin B_1? How will I improve a flagging relationship?

In music performance, many choices are made every second, most of which are subconscious, but plenty of which are conscious. In a moment of a clarinet piece, for example, there is an extraordinary number of simultaneous mechanical considerations. Lip pressure, articulation, breathing speed and pressure, finger placement, intonation, balance, color, and countless other considerations all come into play to effect tempo, phrasing, and pacing. There are many other types of analysis that accompany these mechanical elements and require study of the score itself, in order to consider the relationship between individual parts and the overall structure, as well as historical context and style, performance practice, and so on.

How do we learn and memorize music? We analyze the score. We begin by grouping events and looking for patterns and their repetitions. We categorize and simplify in an effort to latch onto something we already know. If we were pianists and, while sight-reading, we encountered a long series of pitches in a single hand, what would we do? We might look for changes in contour, or we might consider the overall motion—if it is stepwise, it could form a scale. If it is a scale, then—in a fraction of a second—we observe accidentals and the beginning and ending points of the scale.

Some abilities are hardwired, such as seeing a line of pitches and knowing that if there are no gaps, then every consecutive step is to be played. When sight-reading, we do not stop and determine the name of each notated pitch and then find its corresponding location on the piano; instead, we group the pitches into a single, logical shape. We know from experience that when such lines of pitches occur, they are nearly always identifiable scales; we expect another example of a scale and play it immediately as such. If the pitches have unusual chromaticism, then we would return to the passage later and practice it. Another aspect of sight-reading is the ability to determine a hierarchy. For example, we might leave out less important—or "nonstructural"—notes in order

1

to play only the notes that are necessary. Examples include removing octave doublings in the piano and thinning out a texture while maintaining a given sonority. These important abilities come from analysis and interpretation.

Analysis encourages us to attend actively to the music; we reflect and then make choices based on our reflection, which we then apply to performance. Undergraduate studies of music theory and analysis typically involve a regular regimen of activities that includes labeling harmonies with roman numerals and figured bass symbols. The aim of this text is to go further, to reveal how analysis is an active, process-oriented, and goal-directed enterprise, including—but *much deeper* than—the mechanical and descriptive. Analysis should illuminate a work's unique structure on the one hand and place that artwork within the wider musical context, comparing and revealing its underlying structure as conforming to more general and consistent tonal principles. This requires musicianship, opinion, creativity, and decisiveness. Analysis matures us, because active attention to a work's structure reveals subtle connections between phrases, sections, and movements. We can also consider important deviations from expectation that are marked in our consciousness and rendered expressively in performance.

The following four examples illustrate these issues:

- The more we know about a musical work, the more we understand its context, narrative, and meaning.
- Composers can create countless artworks based on just a few underlying structures.
- Something we do not expect can lead us to investigate whether events are part of a larger compositional process.
- Attending to the way the musical elements of melody, harmony, and motive converge—even in a commonplace musical passage—can reveal elegant subsurface structures.

Deeper Understanding: Narrative in Brahms' "Edward Ballade"

A young Brahms wrote a series of Ballades for piano. The first ballade, subtitled the "Edward Ballade," was apparently influenced by a Scottish ballad entitled "Edward," for which the German translation was newly published. As pianists, we will dig into the work, finding a suitable walking tempo (*Andante*) and attempting to reconcile the wild mood swings, large climaxes, and brooding ending into a unified interpretation of the piece. Although we might make this attempt without consulting the poem, let us take an extra step and look at what Brahms cites as his motivation for the Ballade.

The Edward Ballade is a narrative, and it details the arrival home of a grief-stricken youth—with blood-drenched sword—and the ensuing dialogue with his mother. Naturally, she is consumed with learning what has happened. She asks, "Where did this blood come from?" to which the youth replies, "I killed a hawk." Doubting this is the case, the mother says, "Your hawk's blood was never so red." The youth changes his story, shifting the death to his horse, to which the mother responds, "That horse was old and you have plenty of others. What really happened that would explain your grief?" The youth blurts out that the blood belongs to his father, whom he has just murdered. The mother, in apparent shock, asks what he will do now; the youth answers, "I will run away alone, never to return, and that my wife and children would become beggars." The mother asks, "What will ye leave to your own Mother dear?" The youth responds, "The curse of Hell from me shall ye bear, Mother, since it was you who bid me to do this thing."

Having read this dark and tragic tale, and already knowing that it influenced Brahms' composition of the Ballade (a word which means "story"), it would seem impossible not to consider how such knowledge might influence our interpretation of the piece. Might there be a literal correspondence between the unfolding of the poem and that of the piece, perhaps explaining the wild mood swings? Knowing the story behind the piece, would our initial tempo, pedaling, voicing, coloring and general mood be changed? Clearly the more we know about a piece of music, the more rich, varied, and inspiring our interpretations will be.

Underlying Structures: A Deeper Level of Melodic Organization in Two Folk Songs

Let's start with the most basic musical element: melody.

EXAMPLE 1 "Clementine"

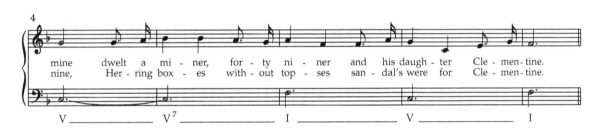

Example 1 is in F major, and the controlling harmonies are written below each measure. The lengthy pause on the G in m. 4, which provides a natural place to breathe, divides the example into two four-measure phrases. In the first phrase, the melody leisurely ascends to the C in m. 3, using a series of melodic leaps. After attaining a melodic high point, the melody quickly descends to the G in m. 4, completing the melodic shape of an arch.

In order to show this structure more clearly, we will "peel away" layers of music—that is, we will remove parts of the music so that the underlying skeleton will be revealed. Take the initial ascent to the C in m. 3. The descending leaps at the beginning of the first two measures are subordinate to the upward leaps at the downbeats of each measure. The notation in Example 2 reflects the relative importance of pitches to the melodic shape of an arch: More important notes have stems and beams, and less important notes have only noteheads and are connected to important notes with slurs. We see the stemmed notes F–A–C, which form an arpeggiation of the F major triad in the first three measures.

EXAMPLE 2   Structural Analysis of "Clementine"

The stepwise descent that leads to m. 4 stops short of returning to F, which gives rise to a phrase ending that is somewhat unsettled and incomplete. The second phrase begins on G and ascends to B♭, and melodic leaps return in mm. 6 and 7. As in the first phrase, the emphasized downbeats of mm. 5–8 reveal a melodic pattern—this time a stepwise descent from B♭ to F. The F at the end of the second phrase "resolves" the G "left hanging" at the end of the first phrase. These larger motions are revealed in Example 2.

Having analyzed the long-range pitch structure of "Clementine," it may be illustrative to compare it to "God Save the King" (Example 3). This piece is also in the key of F major and has two phrases. The first phrase contains six measures, and the second phrase contains eight.

EXAMPLE 3   "God Save the King"

For the most part, the melody moves in stepwise motion. The first phrase has a melodic arch, from F (m. 1) to A (mm. 3–4), and back to F (m. 6). The second phrase begins on C and includes a repeated pattern ("sequence") in mm. 7–8 and 9–10. These patterns lead from C (mm. 7–8), through B♭ (mm. 9–10), to A (mm. 11–12). After a brief upward motion (mm. 12–13), the melody descends from A to F (mm. 13–14). These shapes—the arch in the first phrase and the descending stepwise motion in the second phrase—are summarized in Example 4.

EXAMPLE 4   Structural Analysis of "God Save the King"

Note that although the end of the first phrase descends to F, the larger melodic shape of both phrases combined has a different structure: an ascent through F–A–C, followed by a descending stepwise line. If we compare "Clementine" and "God Save the King," we see that the songs have different numbers of measures, different rhythms, and different pitches. However, through our analyses, we now see that these two tunes are embellishments of the same basic melodic shape.

Surprise and Discovery: An Emergent Tone in Haydn's op. 74 Quartets

Early in the Minuet of Haydn's op. 74, no. 2 String Quartet, there is a C♯ that is accented (by its duration and volume) and abrupt. Although it is part of an ascending chromatic line (C–C♯–D in mm. 3–5), it jumps out of its context and surprises the listener. This C♯ seems out of place until we consider the following Trio, in the distant chromatic key of D♭. The single C♯ in m. 4 foreshadows the upcoming D♭ in the Trio (Example 5).

EXAMPLE 5   Haydn, String Quartet in F major, op. 74, no. 2, *Menuetto*

A.   Minuet: Measures 1–8

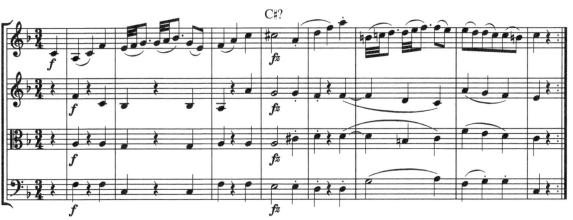

B.   Trio: Measures 42–47

It turns out there is a similar musical process in the first op. 74 quartet (Example 6). In spite of the quartet's different key (C major instead of F major), the very same chromatic C♯ appears early in the Minuet as part of the same chromatic line encountered in the other quartet: C–C♯–D. The Trio reveals another distant chromatic key (A major), and sure enough, the C♯ is once again developed—this time as a member of the A major scale. These relationships are clearly more than coincidental—and a look at the other movements of the first and second op. 74 quartets reveals multiple occurrences of C♯ and D♭. C–C♯–D emerges as a crucial motive—and C♯ as the main note—that ties the two quartets together.

EXAMPLE 6   **Haydn, String Quartet in C major, op. 74, no. 1,** *Menuetto*

A.   Minuet

B.   Trio

Elegance in the Commonplace: A Deeper Level
of Melody, Harmony, and Motive in Beethoven's op. 110

We will use the opening passage of one of Beethoven's late piano sonatas, op. 110 in A♭ major, as a final springboard to launch our studies (Example 7).

EXAMPLE 7   **Beethoven, Piano Sonata in A♭ major, op. 110,**
Moderato cantabile molto espressivo

Consider the analysis provided in the example. The roman numerals describe the quality and inversions of chords, which notes are members of the chords, and how chords relate hierarchically to the tonic (A♭). Let's look beyond the roman numerals and consider how melodic shape, repetition and parallelism, and harmony intertwine in this excerpt.

The highest and lowest "voices" in the excerpt—which we will label the soprano and bass voices, respectively—present the interval of a third as the main motive. The underlying bass line for the first three measures is the ascending line A♭–B♭–C; at the same time, the soprano melody ascends from C to E♭. Example 8 summarizes the bass motion for this passage.

EXAMPLE 8

Thirds appear in the opening measure: A♭–C in the bass and C–A♭ in the soprano form a "voice exchange" between the parts. This occurs again in the second measure, with B♭–D♭ in the bass and D♭–B♭ in the soprano. In fact, the
eighth notes at the end of m. 3 also outline thirds: F–E♭–D♭ in the bass and
D♭–E♭–F in the soprano. Example 9 shows all of these third relationships within
voices and between voices, within measures and among measures. (Xs indicate voice exchanges in the example.)

EXAMPLE 9

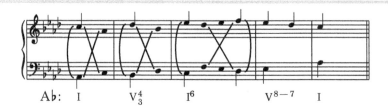

Measures 4–5 have a stepwise descent in the soprano. The E♭ on the downbeat
of m. 4 and the D♭ on the fermata lead to the C on the downbeat of m. 5. Thus,
the overall melodic structure for the excerpt is a melodic arch. Notice what has
occurred here: Through our discussion of melodic structure, we have made
decisions about important notes, which in turn have led us to identify important chords in the progression. For example, the I^6 in m. 1 and the V$^4_2$ in m. 2—
although important for establishing the interval of a third—do not participate
in the overall melodic arch.

But we are not done yet! We have skirted over the short cadenza-like flourish
in m. 4. Indeed, pianists are often baffled by this curious figure. However, if we
review the structural contents of the melodic line in Example 9, we see a note-for-
note correspondence between this line, which unfolds over four measures, and
the thirty-second-note flourish (Example 10). Beethoven even summarizes the
proportional relationship between the slowly moving line that begins the piece
and the more quickly rising third (D♭–E♭–F) that occurs in m. 3 by his notation:
The D♭-E♭-F figure is notated at a more quickly moving grace-note figure in the
flourish in m. 4. Indeed, it seems as if Beethoven has provided us with a
summary of exactly what took place in the first four measures of the piece.

EXAMPLE 10

Finally, lest we think that Beethoven limits the use of this flourish to one
movement, let us look at the theme for the last movement of the piano sonata
(Example 11).

EXAMPLE 11 Beethoven, Piano Sonata in A♭ major, op. 110, *Allegro ma non troppo*

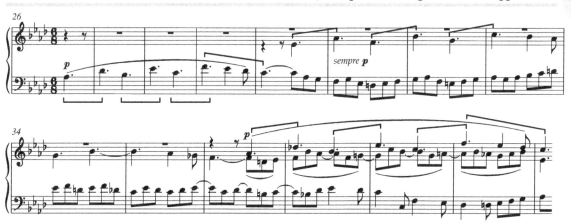

Comparing this theme to the theme in Example 7, we see that they are highly contrasting in their rhythms and metrical placement. In addition, the first movement is all about thirds, while the last movement projects rising fourths. However, comparing their pitch content, we see a note-for-note correspondence between the two themes: The beamed notes in the bass line of Example 12 are the same as the soprano theme in Example 7.

EXAMPLE 12

    The last movement's theme can be considered a recomposition of the first movement's. Beethoven has omitted the initial C, beginning the last movement's theme on A♭, which allows the unarticulated fourths of the first movement's theme to emerge as the controlling interval. To cinch the connection between movements, both the high point of the first movement's theme— the F—and its stepwise return to C recur in the last movement.

    In this discussion, we have seen the crucial role that analysis plays in illuminating the rich fabric of music. Therefore, we must always consider the function and interaction of all musical elements. We must attend to the details in music, since analysis can reveal important musical correspondences that will help us to gain insight into a work's inner logic and structure and to develop our own performance interpretations.

CHAPTER 1

Musical Time and Space

This chapter presents a reorientation of important concepts and terminology related to temporality and pitch. We review meter and then explore the issue of accent in music. Next, we review pitch and intervals. In Chapter 2, we observe the interaction of consonance and dissonance, which leads to the presentation of two-voice counterpoint. Finally, we review the building blocks of tonal harmony—triads and seventh chords—and explore their various representations in analysis.

The Metrical Realm

Undifferentiated and equally spaced clicks or taps are called **pulses**. A series of identical pulses does not group into larger units but remains an undistinguished stream that simply punctuates the passage of time. When pulses are differentiated through accent, they become **accented beats** and **unaccented beats**. **Meter** refers to the grouping of accented and unaccented beats into recurring patterns. There are three basic types of meter:

- **duple** (strong–weak, strong–weak, strong–weak, *etc.*)
- **triple** (strong–weak–weak, strong–weak–weak, strong–weak–weak, *etc.*)
- **quadruple** (very strong–weak–strong–weak, very strong–weak–strong–weak, *etc.*)

Beat division refers to the equal division of the beat into either two or three parts. **Simple meters** have beats divided into two parts, and **compound meters** have beats divided into three parts.

Composers indicate the number of beats in a measure, the rhythmic value that is assigned the beat, and the beat division in the **meter signature**. For simple meters, the top number of the meter signature indicates the number of beats in a measure, and the bottom number reflects the rhythmic value that equals one beat.

Top number = number of beats per measure	2, 3, or 4
Bottom number = rhythmic value that equals one beat	2 = ♩ 4 = ♩ 8 = ♪ 16 = ♪ *and so on*

Meter signatures do not have numbers that represent dotted note values. Since the beat in compound meters equals a dotted note, meter signatures cannot reflect the beats in a measure. Instead, meter signatures show information about the *beat divisions*: The top number indicates the number of *beat divisions* in one measure, and the bottom number represents the rhythmic value that equals one *beat division*.

Top number = number of beat divisions per measure	6 = 6 beat divisions, or 2 dotted beats per measure 9 = 9 beat divisions, or 3 dotted beats per measure 12 = 12 beat divisions, or 4 dotted beats per measure
Bottom number = rhythmic value that equals one beat division	2 = beat division is ♩, and ♩. equals one beat 4 = beat division is ♩, and ♩. equals one beat 8 = beat division is ♪, and ♩. equals one beat 16 = beat division is ♪, and ♪. equals one beat *and so on*

Accent in Music

We broadly define **musical accent** as a musical event that is marked for consciousness, such that a listener's attention is drawn to it. Thwarting a listener's expectations is a common way that composers mark events. This is accomplished by changing an established pattern. Accents can be produced in the domains of time, pitch, dynamics, register, and texture.

Temporal Accents

We saw that meter arises when pulses are grouped into recurring patterns of accented and unaccented beats. Accented beats are **metrical accents**, since they occur at important points in a metrical unit (e.g., a beat or a measure). Metrical accents are dependent on and arise from the intersection of a variety of other accents, as we will see later.

Rhythm refers to the ever-changing combinations of longer and shorter durations and silence that populate the surface of a piece of music. Rhythm is often patterned, and rhythmic groupings may divide the beat, align with the beat, or extend over several beats. **Rhythmic accents** take many forms; the most important form of rhythmic accent arises from duration—a long note tends to sound accented. Such **durational**, or **agogic, accents** usually coincide with metrical accents in order to support the prevailing meter.

Nontemporal Accents

Harmonic change creates a powerful accent. In the opening of Chopin's Waltz in A minor (Example 1.1), the metric accent on the downbeat of each measure is accompanied by a different chord. Composers usually balance the accent created by harmonic change with a consistent pattern in the rate of harmonic changes—called **harmonic rhythm**. Once the harmonic rhythm is established, the pattern usually continues. The harmonic rhythm generally aligns with metric accents, as in Chopin's waltz.

EXAMPLE 1.1   Chopin, Waltz in A minor, BI 150

A strong left-hand accent occurs on the downbeat of every measure—this **registral accent** occurs because the low notes on the downbeats are in a lower register, setting it in bold relief from the rest of the notes. Such accents may occur in any register and are often intensified by **articulative** (or **phenomenal**) **accents**, which include changes in dynamics, articulations, and ornamentations.

Most often the mood, the range, the accompanimental figures, and the number and density of voices remain consistent through long passages of music. We refer to the combination of these elements as **musical texture**. A **textural accent** involves a change in the overall patterning of a piece; this can be quite striking. For example, Bach's C minor Prelude (Example 1.2A) is a study in fast sixteenth notes that are relegated to the same register and melodic patterning. When the texture suddenly changes to a more improvisatory single line, the accent that is created certainly draws the listener's attention (Example 1.2B).

EXAMPLE 1.2   Bach, Prelude in C minor, *Well-Tempered Clavier*, Book 1

A.

B.

textural accent

Textural changes—and the accents they create—can be very subtle, as in the opening of Mozart's Piano Sonata in F (Example 1.3). The gentle, rocking accompaniment supports a rising melody; then, in m. 5, the melody falls, without any aid from the accompaniment. This textural change is intensified by the left hand abandoning its accompanimental role and imitating the right hand in the falling gesture in m. 7. In m. 9, the hands are reunited, and a new texture appears in m. 12 as all of the voices participate in the same rhythmic gestures. These textural changes are not capricious but are carefully planned, occurring every four measures.

EXAMPLE 1.3   Mozart, Piano Sonata in F major, K. 332, *Allegro*

There are other types of nontemporal accents in the Mozart excerpt. The first type involves the shape of the melody, created by changes in melodic direction. These shapes are part of the melody's contour, and changes in contour create **contour accents**. They can be obvious (as in the overall rising line of mm. 1–4, followed by the descending line in mm. 5–8) or subtle (as in the falling scalar line in m. 10 that changes direction on the downbeat of m. 11). Like most accents, contour accents usually align with metric accents.

When listening to Example 1.3, one's attention is surely drawn to the E♭ in m. 2, even though it occurred on a weak beat, hidden inside the texture. Such an accent is referred to as a **pitch accent**. These accents arise when one or more pitches are perceived as unstable. Unstable pitches are accented because they are foreign to the immediately surrounding pitch environment.

WORKBOOK
1.1

Metrical Disturbance

We have seen thus far that musical accents tend to align with metric accents. We will now see metric accent challenged by new, conflicting accents. When a musical accent occurs on a metrically unaccented beat or part of a beat, it creates **syncopation**. Example 1.4 presents two examples where a series of syncopated accents occur off of the beat.

EXAMPLE 1.4

A.   Mozart, Symphony in G minor, K. 183, *Allegro con brio*

B.   Mozart, Piano Concerto in D minor, K. 466, *Allegro*

Another type of metrical disturbance, closely related to syncopation, is the **hemiola**. In a hemiola, the established meter is temporarily displaced by a competing meter. It occurs most often when a duple meter is imposed on a triple meter. To create this effect, accents are placed on every other beat rather than every third beat. In Example 1.5A, a hemiola is created by articulative accents: The regular placement on every other quarter note creates a duple accent pattern, effectively weakening the triple meter for two measures. In Example 1.5B, hemiola arises through durational accents: The tied notes obscure the written downbeats and induce a temporary change of meter (from triple to duple).

EXAMPLE 1.5

A.   Hemiola by Surface Elements

B.   Hemiola by Duple Durations

The Pitch Realm

We have just explored the roles that pitch plays in creating musical accents. We continue our discussion of pitch with some definitions.

Pitches and Pitch Classes

A **pitch** is a tone that sounds at a particular frequency. If a pitch's frequency is twice another pitch's frequency, then the two pitches are separated by a **perfect octave** (commonly abbreviated to "octave"). If the frequencies of two pitches are in the ratio 3:2, then the two pitches are separated by a **perfect fifth**. Perfect octaves and perfect fifths are fundamental to tonal music, as we will see below.

Since pitches that are separated by an octave sound highly similar, we give these pitches the same letter name (chosen from A through G) with an octave designation. Example 1.6 shows one common way to describe pitches: Each pitch is assigned an octave number, with new octave numbers beginning on the pitch C. The lowest C on the piano, for example, is "C1," the next is "C2" and so on, with each higher octave incremented by 1.

EXAMPLE 1.6   Pitch and Octave Designations

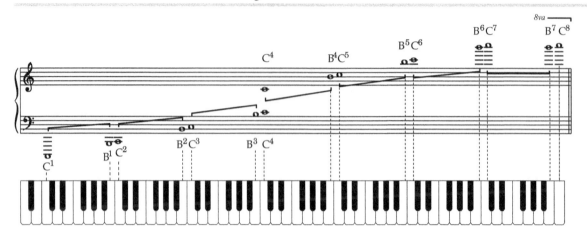

Pitch class refers to all pitches with the same letter name. Thus, the notes in Example 1.7 are in the pitch class "E," but they are the pitches E4, E5, and E6. In this text, we will generally refer to a pitch by its pitch-class designation, unless it is necessary to distinguish pitches by octave number.

EXAMPLE 1.7   Pitch versus Pitch Class

Pitches that sound the same but have different names are **enharmonically equivalent**. For example, in Example 1.8, we see that F♯ and G♭ are enharmonically equivalent. F♯ and G♭ are different notes—and, as we will see, they have different functions—but they sound the same.

EXAMPLE 1.8   Enharmonically Equivalent Pitches

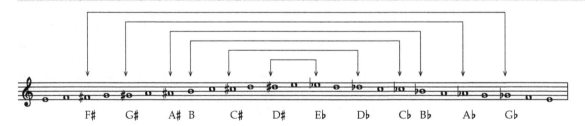

Scales

Listen to the opening of Mozart's well-known Piano Sonata in C major (Example 1.9). Taking an inventory of the pitch-class content of the passage, we see in m. 1 Cs, Es, and Gs. In m. 2, Ds, Fs, and Bs enter the picture; in m. 3, A is the single new pitch class. If we list this collection alphabetically, we get A, B, C, D, E, F, G. In fact, a review of the content of the rest of the example reveals that no new pitch classes occur. We refer to such a seven-note collection in which each letter name is used once as a **diatonic collection**. Diatonic, or "through the tones," also means that the all-important octave is divided rather evenly into seven steps (with the first step being repeated to form the octave). We refer to the stepwise ordering of the diatonic collection as a **scale**, from the Italian *scala*, or "ladder." Notice that ascending and descending scales begin in the right hand of m. 5.

EXAMPLE 1.9   Mozart, Piano Sonata in C major, K. 545, *Allegro*

Even though these seven pitches freely circulate throughout the example, Mozart has organized his music in such a way that certain pitches seem more stable than others. The excerpt begins on C, and there are points of repose where C is conspicuously present: at the end of mm. 2 and 4 and in m. 8. It also seems that other pitches are strongly attracted to C, such as the B in m. 2. Finally, there are still other pitches that seem to partner with C, and they too have their own power to attract pitches, such as the Gs and Es in m. 1: A in m. 3 is strongly attracted to the following G, while the F in m. 4 is pulled toward E (see arrows in Example 1.9). When pitches are hierarchically arranged in a diatonic scale and one pitch is stronger and more stable than all the others, this effect is referred to as **tonality**. Since C is the most important pitch in Example 1.9, we privilege it by beginning the scale with C and saying that C is the **tonic** of the excerpt.

The seven members of a scale can be numbered in ascending order as **scale degrees** (Example 1.10). Scale degree numbers—distinguished by a caret placed above the number—are also identified by names that reflect their relationship to the central tone of the scale, the tonic. The next most important scale members are the **dominant** (four steps, or a perfect fifth, above the tonic) and the **mediant** (halfway between the tonic and the dominant). The **subdominant** (four steps below the tonic) derives its name from the fact that it is as far below the tonic as the dominant is above the tonic. The **submediant**, two steps below the tonic, is halfway between the tonic and the subdominant. The **supertonic** is one step above the tonic, and the **leading tone** is one step below the tonic.

EXAMPLE 1.10   The Major Scale

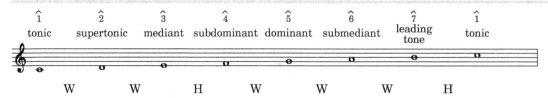

We will focus on two specific types of scales, the **major scale** and the **minor scale**, each of which is distinguished by the way its seven different pitches are distributed within the octave. Major scales contain the same pattern of **half steps** (or "semitones," which are adjacent keys on a piano keyboard) and **whole steps** (or "tones," which consist of two half steps or semitones). The pattern for major scales is W–W–H–W–W–W–H. Example 1.10 is an example of a C major scale.

   Minor scales are differentiated from major scales primarily by scale degree 3, which is one half step lower than in the major scale.

EXAMPLE 1.11   Mozart, Piano Sonata in A minor, K. 310, *Allegro maestoso*

The diatonic collection in Example 1.11 contains the following pitch classes: A, B, C, D, E, F, and G♯. Clearly, A is the tonic, accomplished by the leading tone (G♯), the prominence of A in the texture, and—as in major—the dominant (E) and the median (C) as important assistants to A. The difference in sound color in this scale versus the major scale can be attributed in large measure to the ordering of half and whole steps from tonic to dominant: The major scale has the pattern W–W–H–W, while the minor scale has the pattern W–H–W–W (Example 1.12).

EXAMPLE 1.12   The Minor Scale

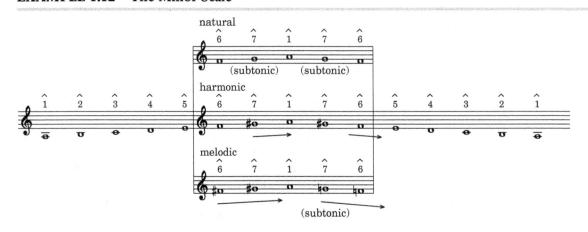

The other distinguishing characteristic between major and minor scales is the upper portion of the minor scale, namely, scale degrees 6 and 7, which are variable, with three common possibilities (Example 1.12). In its **natural** form, a minor scale lowers its scale degrees 6 and 7; the lowered scale degree 7 is called the **subtonic**, since it no longer acts as a tone that leads to the tonic. Two other common forms of the minor scale raise scale degrees 6 and/or 7 to produce an ascending line that pulls toward the tonic; however, there is no distinction among the variations in practice—they are all forms of the same minor scale.

In the **harmonic** minor form, scale degree 7 is raised to create a leading tone that is one half step below tonic. Recall Example 1.12, which uses harmonic minor: Arrows show how the leading tone G♯ pulls toward the tonic and the submediant F is not raised, so it leads down to E.

In the **melodic** minor form, scale degrees 6 and 7 are raised in an ascending line to pull toward the tonic; the same scale degrees are not raised in a descending line, in order to pull down toward the dominant.

Keys

Key signatures convey the pitch classes of major and natural minor scales. Example 1.13 summarizes the number and names of the sharps and flats for major and minor keys. Adjacent keys (e.g., G major and D major) are separated by a perfect fifth.

EXAMPLE 1.13   Sharps and Flats in Major and Minor Keys

MAJOR KEY	MINOR KEY	NUMBER OF ACCIDENTALS	ACCIDENTALS IN KEY
C♯	a♯	7 sharps	F♯ C♯ G♯ D♯ A♯ E♯ B♯
F♯	d♯	6 sharps	F♯ C♯ G♯ D♯ A♯ E♯
B	g♯	5 sharps	F♯ C♯ G♯ D♯ A♯
E	c♯	4 sharps	F♯ C♯ G♯ D♯
A	f♯	3 sharps	F♯ C♯ G♯
D	b	2 sharps	F♯ C♯
G	e	1 sharp	F♯
→ C	a	0	
F	d	1 flat	B♭
B♭	g	2 flats	B♭ E♭
E♭	c	3 flats	B♭ E♭ A♭
A♭	f	4 flats	B♭ E♭ A♭ D♭
D♭	b♭	5 flats	B♭ E♭ A♭ D♭ G♭
G♭	e♭	6 flats	B♭ E♭ A♭ D♭ G♭ C♭
C♭	a♭	7 flats	B♭ E♭ A♭ D♭ G♭ C♭ F♭

Major and minor keys with the same tonic (e.g., C major and C minor) are **parallel**. Major and minor keys with the same key signatures are **relative**. Example 1.14 illustrates the pairing of relative major and minor keys around the circle of fifths.

EXAMPLE 1.14   Relative Major and Minor Keys

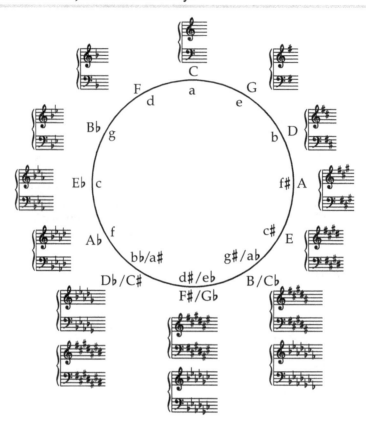

WORKBOOK
1.2

Intervals

The distance between two pitches is an **interval**. We have already encountered four intervals: the octave, the perfect fifth, the whole step, and the half step. Intervals are typically labeled with an ordinal number that represents the number of pitch letter names that span the two notes. For example, the distance from C up to F is a *fourth*, since there are four letter names that span C to F (C, D, E, F). The distance from E down to G is a *sixth* (E, D, C, B, A, G). (Note that another way to compute intervals is by counting half steps: C up to F is five half steps, and E down to G is nine half steps.)

Intervals up to an octave are **simple** (see Example 1.15). Intervals larger than an octave are **compound**. Compound intervals are often abbreviated to their simple counterparts. Although C3 to G5 is a nineteenth, we will refer to the interval between their pitch classes: C to G is a fifth.

EXAMPLE 1.15   Simple Intervals

unison   2nd   3rd   4th   5th   6th   7th   octave

Intervals thus far are **generic**, since they only label the distance spanned by pitch letters. C to E is a third, but so are C–E♭, C♯–E, C♭–E♯, C♯–E♯, C♭♭–E♯, and so on. In order to distinguish the **quality** of an interval, we use a **specific size**. We group intervals into two basic categories: the unison, fourth, fifth, and octave are **perfect** (P) intervals, and the rest are **major** (M)/**minor** (m) intervals. Each note in a major scale, when measured above the tonic, creates a perfect or major interval (Example 1.16).

EXAMPLE 1.16   Specific Intervals Above the Tonic in the Major Scale

P1   M2   M3   P4   P5   M6   M7   P8

Major intervals can be transformed into other interval qualities by increasing or decreasing the interval size. If we increase a major interval by one half step, an **augmented** (A) interval results. If we decrease a major interval by one half step, we get a minor interval; if we further decrease the interval by another half step, a **diminished** (d) interval results (Example 1.17A). Perfect intervals can also be transformed into augmented and diminished intervals by increasing or decreasing the interval size by one half step, respectively (Example 1.17B). Thus, major, minor, and perfect intervals can all become augmented or diminished (except for the unison, which can only be augmented). However, major and minor intervals can never become perfect, and perfect intervals can never become major or minor.

EXAMPLE 1.17

A.   Transforming Major and Minor Intervals (2, 3, 6, 7)

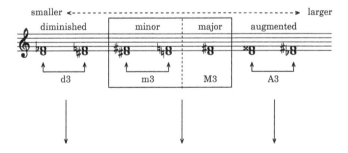

B.   Transforming Perfect Intervals (1, 4, 5, 8)

When we move the lower pitch of a simple interval above the higher pitch—or we move the higher pitch below the lower pitch—we have **inverted** the interval. Example 1.18A shows what happens when we invert generic intervals; Example 1.18B does the same for an interval's quality. Arrows represent the inversion process. Notice the following:

- The inversion process can move in either direction.
- The inversion of *generic* intervals always sums to 9.
- Perfect intervals retain their quality when inverted. However, quality is swapped for augmented/diminished and major/minor intervals.
- The number of *half steps* between inversionally related intervals always sums to 12. Example 1.18C shows the resulting pattern.

EXAMPLE 1.18   Interval Inversion

A.

Generic Interval Inversion
unison ←→ octave (1 + 8 = 9)
second ←→ seventh (2 + 7 = 9)
third ←→ sixth (3 + 6 = 9)
fourth ←→ fifth (4 + 5 = 9)

B.

Quality
Perfect ←→ Perfect
Augmented ←→ diminished
Major ←→ minor

C.

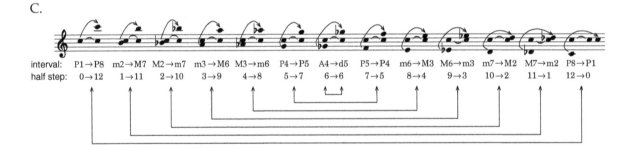

interval:	P1→P8	m2→M7	M2→m7	m3→M6	M3→m6	P4→P5	A4→d5	P5→P4	m6→M3	M6→m3	m7→M2	M7→m2	P8→P1
half step:	0→12	1→11	2→10	3→9	4→8	5→7	6→6	7→5	8→4	9→3	10→2	11→1	12→0

Consonance and Dissonance

When we compare the sound of an octave with that of a seventh, the octave seems stable and firmly planted, with no need to move to some other, more stable interval. On the other hand, the seventh is active, unstable, and even tense. At least as early as the ancient Greeks, Western musicians have felt that different-sized intervals provoked certain feelings, ranging from a pleasant stability to a restless yearning. We consider intervallic stability and instability on a continuum, from stable, **consonant** intervals to unstable, **dissonant** intervals. Stable intervals include the **perfect consonances** (P1, P5, P8) and **imperfect consonances** (M3, m3, M6, m6). Dissonant intervals include seconds, sevenths, and all diminished and augmented intervals. The P4 is usually viewed as a dissonant interval.

Melody: Characteristics and Writing

Intervals do not exist in isolation, but rather function as part of larger musical constructs, such as melody. We end this chapter with a brief study of attributes shared by many tonal melodies. These are the general guidelines we will apply to our melody writing for now.

- Melodies often begin on $\hat{1}$, $\hat{3}$, or $\hat{5}$.
- Melodies approach their final pitch—often $\hat{1}$—by step in a melodic **cadence**.
- The range of a melody should be limited to a tenth, and the **tessitura** (the comfortable, most used span of pitches) should be limited to about a sixth.
- Melodies move primarily by steps, or **conjunct motion**.
- Melodies can also move with occasional leaps to add interest. It is fine to use melodic leaps, or **disjunct motion**, if they:
  - are generally confined to small intervals, although one or two larger leaps may be used;
  - traverse consonant melodic intervals and avoid dissonant melodic intervals;
  - lead to a change of direction in order to fill some of the space created by the leap;
  - don't occur one after another (unless they arpeggiate a triad, which is discussed in the next chapter).
- Some scale members have strong melodic pulls toward other members. Such **tendency tones** create an important tension and should be resolved. For example, the leading tone is a tendency tone, because it tends to move toward $\hat{1}$.
- Melodies tend not to have repeated notes.
- Melodies have a logical shape. An arch is a very common melodic shape: A melody slowly rises to a peak and then returns to the starting point. There is usually one peak in a melodic shape, and it often occurs about midway through the melody.

Example 1.19 illustrates the basic tenets of a good melody. The melody begins with a stepwise descent from $\hat{3}$, past $\hat{1}$ to the leading tone, followed by a change of direction—this satisfies the need for the leading tone to resolve to the tonic and to balance the falling motion with rising motion. The ascent back to $\hat{3}$ (in m. 4) is not an arrival, since the line falls back to $\hat{2}$, in the same way that the line turned on the leading tone in m. 2. The melody then pushes higher, first to D, then to the peak on F. Note that after the leap to D, there is a change of direction and a fall to C, which balances the leap with a contour change. Further, the peak on F is followed by a stepwise descent to the cadence on B in m. 8; this leaves the listener hanging, waiting for a resolution to $\hat{1}$. The melody from mm. 1–4 repeats in mm. 9–12, but then there is a dramatic leap to F in m. 13. After the peak of the second phrase (in m. 13), there is a stepwise descent that fills in the space created by the leap. The descent leads to a cadence that closes strongly on the long-anticipated A ($\hat{1}$).

EXAMPLE 1.19   Mozart, Piano Sonata in A minor, K. 310, *Presto*

WORKBOOK
1.4

CHAPTER 2

Harnessing Musical Time and Space

The study of tonal harmony concerns how chords connect to one another—and individual melodies, or "voices," combine with one another—and move through time. The highest and lowest voices provide the structural skeleton in tonal music, and harmony is most easily viewed as filling in the musical space with additional voices. The movement and relationship among two or more voices is called **counterpoint**. Counterpoint has been the focus of Western music study since the tenth century, and it continues to serve musicians to this day. Contrapuntal relationships depend on the following two elements:

* The behavior of consonant and dissonant intervals
* The harmonies implied by melodic interaction

In this brief introduction to two-voice counterpoint, we will focus primarily on how consonance and dissonance among voices create musical motion in time. Such harnessing of the horizontal plane (i.e., the linear, temporal domain) and the vertical plane (i.e., the spatial, harmonic domain) is the goal of our studies in tonal music.

Species Counterpoint

By the early eighteenth century, musicians had developed user-friendly ways to teach counterpoint, and Johann Fux is credited today with a particularly succinct pedagogy in his book *Gradus ad Parnassum* (1725). Fux uses melodies—called **cantus firmi** ["fixed songs"; singular: **cantus firmus (CF)**]—as the structural pillars against which he teaches how to add first one voice, later two, and still later three, creating a total of four parts. In order to make these studies as pedagogical as possible, Fux presents a series of five steps—or **species**—each of which isolates the way that an added voice (called the **contrapuntal voice**, or **counterpoint**) moves against a CF. These five species begin with the addition of a single pitch above or below each pitch of a CF, resulting in **note-against-note (1:1) counterpoint**, or **first-species counterpoint**. In **second-species counterpoint**, or **2:1 counterpoint**, two pitches are written against a single pitch of a CF. Subsequent species add more pitches to the contrapuntal voice as well as new rhythmic procedures and dissonance treatment. Fifth-species counterpoint combines all of the techniques of the previous four species. Our counterpoint studies will focus on first and second species in two voices and will provide the springboard for our upcoming harmony studies, which draw heavily on principles of melody and intervals.

First-Species (1:1) Counterpoint

A melodic tone most often moves to another in the smoothest manner, by step or by third. When we combine two voices, we must consider not only the intervallic movement *within* an individual voice, but we must also consider the intervals formed *between* the two voices. Look at the note-against-note counterpoint in Example 2.1. The horizontal (melodic) intervals formed within each line are marked above the upper voice and below the lower voice. The vertical (harmonic) intervals formed between the voices are also labeled.

EXAMPLE 2.1

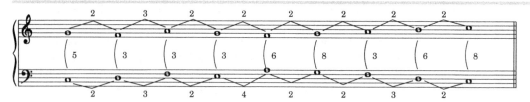

Note the following from the example:

1. Each voice moves primarily by step. Leaps are restricted to small intervals (mostly thirds, with one fourth).
2. Each voice's contour is varied. Initially, the voices change direction after every 1–2 pitches.
3. There are only consonant harmonic intervals, most of which are imperfect consonances (thirds and sixths). The beginning and ending are perfect consonances, and there is only one perfect consonance (an octave) within the example. There are no fourths in two-voice counterpoint, since fourths are unstable and considered dissonant.
4. The voices often move in different directions. Each melody maintains its own independence.

In first-species counterpoint, only consonant harmonic intervals are permitted (P8, P5, P1, M3, m3, M6, m6). Melodic lines must be independent from one another, yet they must work together to create only consonant intervals. The source of successful counterpoint is the contrapuntal motion that results from the interaction of the melodies.

Contrapuntal Motions

Contrapuntal motion refers to the contours produced between two voices. Note-against-note counterpoint has three allowable motions.

EXAMPLE 2.2

A.   B.

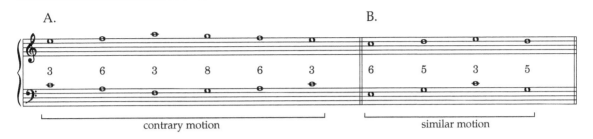

contrary motion   similar motion

C.

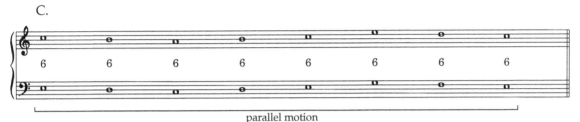

parallel motion

1. When voices move in the opposite direction from one another, they create **contrary motion** (Example 2.2A). Contrary motion creates the most independence between voices and should be used as much as possible.
2. When voices move in the same direction, they create **similar motion** (Example 2.2B). Similar motion can provide more drama to the counterpoint, because both voices ascend or descend, but they move by different-sized intervals. Similar motion is most effective with imperfect consonances.
3. When voices move in similar motion *and* maintain the same generic interval, they create **parallel motion** (Example 2.2C). Parallel motion can be beautiful, but the motion reduces voice independence substantially, given that the voices are heard as shadowing one another.

In order to maintain as much independence and momentum as is possible, there are restrictions on parallel and similar motion.

- For parallel motion, use imperfect consonances. In order to avoid monotony, limit the number of consecutive uses of thirds or sixths to three (6–6–6 or 3–3–3). **Parallel perfect intervals** are forbidden, since they ruin the independence of the voices.
- Do not approach perfect consonances by similar motion with a leap in the upper voice. These create **direct** fifths and octaves, which sound thin, due to the ear being drawn to the exposed perfect consonance (Example 2.3A). There is one situation in which we may move to an octave or a fifth in similar motion: when an upper voice moves by step (Examples 2.3B and C).

EXAMPLE 2.3

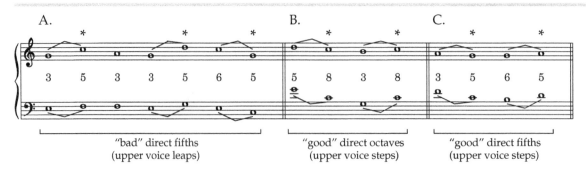

"bad" direct fifths
(upper voice leaps)

"good" direct octaves
(upper voice steps)

"good" direct fifths
(upper voice steps)

Rules and Guidelines for First-Species Counterpoint

The following rules for 1:1 counterpoint create a structural foundation, while the guidelines are suggestions for creating a more aesthetically pleasing musical surface.

RULE 1 All harmonic intervals must be consonances.

RULE 2 Parallel perfect intervals are forbidden.

RULE 3 Direct fifths and octaves are forbidden, except when the soprano moves by step.

RULE 4 The lower voice must begin on $\hat{1}$; the upper voice can begin on $\hat{1}$, $\hat{3}$, or $\hat{5}$. Both voices end on $\hat{1}$.

RULE 5 Unisons are allowed only at the beginning and end of a counterpoint.

RULE 6 In minor keys, raise $\hat{6}$ and $\hat{7}$ only if they immediately precede the cadence.

GUIDELINE 1 Label every harmonic interval, and mark perfect consonances (P1, P5, P8) with an asterisk.

GUIDELINE 2 Use stepwise motion as much as possible, with occasional leaps to add interest. After a leap of a fourth or larger, change direction and move by step.

GUIDELINE 3 Use contrary motion as much as possible. Limit parallel motion to three consecutive uses of an interval (e.g., 6–6–6 or 3–3–3).

GUIDELINE 4 Use imperfect consonances for harmonic intervals when possible. Restrict the use of octaves and fifths.

WORKBOOK
2.1

GUIDELINE 5 Avoid two perfect consonances in a row for harmonic intervals (e.g., 5–8 or 8–5), since they create a hollow sound.

Second-Species (2:1) Counterpoint

In 2:1 counterpoint, one melody uses rhythmic values that are twice as fast as the other. In addition to parallel, similar, and contrary motions, 2:1 counterpoint allows for one more motion that will complete our list: When one voice moves while another remains stationary, the voices create **oblique motion** (Example 2.4).

EXAMPLE 2.4

Given that there are now strong beats (on the downbeats of measures, where both voices move to new pitches) and weak beats (where only one melody moves to a new pitch), a metrical hierarchy arises. We observe the rules and guidelines from 1:1 counterpoint, but we also must attend to the added dimension of the metrical hierarchy.

Rules and Guidelines for Second-Species Counterpoint

RULE 1 Strong beats must be consonant.

RULE 2 Weak beats may be consonant or dissonant.

* Dissonance is the most important new feature of 2:1 counterpoint. Only one type of dissonance is allowed: the **unaccented passing tone** (P). Passing tones fill the space between the melodic interval of a third, creating a stepwise motion (Example 2.5).

EXAMPLE 2.5

RULE 3 No parallel perfect intervals are allowed between successive strong beats, and no parallel perfect intervals are allowed from weak beats to strong beats (Example 2.6). We might be tempted to think that an intervening weak-beat interval reduces the effects of strong-beat parallels, but this is not the case.

EXAMPLE 2.6

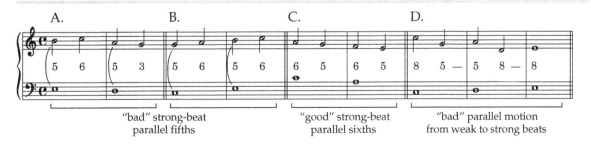

RULE 4 No "bad" direct fifths or octaves are allowed from weak beats to strong beats (Example 2.7).

EXAMPLE 2.7

"bad" direct fifth
from weak to strong beats

RULE 5 The lower voice must begin on $\hat{1}$; the upper voice can begin on $\hat{1}$, $\hat{3}$, or $\hat{5}$. Both voices end on $\hat{1}$.

- The final measure must contain whole notes in both melodies.

RULE 6 In minor keys, raise $\hat{6}$ and $\hat{7}$ only if they immediately precede the cadence.

WORKBOOK
2.2

GUIDELINE 1 Label every harmonic interval. Mark perfect consonances (P1, P5, P8) with an asterisk, and mark dissonant intervals with a circle.

GUIDELINE 2 Incorporate as many dissonant passing tones as possible.

GUIDELINE 3 Use leaps to balance the dissonant passing tones. It is best to leap *within* measures rather than *between* measures.

Adding Voices: Triads and Seventh Chords

So far, our studies have led us through melody and two-voice counterpoint. We now move into the third and final building block of tonal music: harmony. As stated earlier, harmony is most easily viewed as filling in the musical space provided by the counterpoint of two outer voices. The usual format for discussing harmony is the chorale texture: soprano, alto, tenor, and bass. Thus, the soprano and bass provide the **outer-voice counterpoint**, and the alto and tenor fill in the space between the soprano and bass, creating **chords**.

Triads

Chords that comprise three distinct pitches stacked in thirds are called **triads**. The lowest pitch is the **root**, the note that is a third above the root is the **third**, and the note that is a fifth above the root is the **fifth**. There are four **qualities** of triads above a given root (Example 2.8). **Major** and **minor** triads are *consonant* triads, since they span a consonant interval (P5). **Augmented** and **diminished** triads are *dissonant* triads: The augmented triad spans an A5, and a diminished triad spans a d5. Only major, minor, and diminished triads are used as harmonic units in common-practice music.

EXAMPLE 2.8

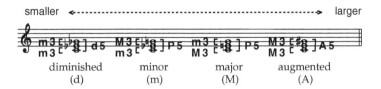

| | diminished (d) | minor (m) | major (M) | augmented (A) |

A triad is in **root position** if the root is the lowest-sounding pitch—that is, the root is in the bass. If the third or the fifth of a triad appears in the bass, the triad is in **first inversion** or **second inversion**, respectively (Example 2.9). It doesn't matter how the pitches above the bass are distributed. It is only the pitch in the bass that determines root position or an inversion. Root-position major and minor triads are stable by virtue of the perfect fifths, while inverted triads are less stable because they are bound by sixths.

EXAMPLE 2.9

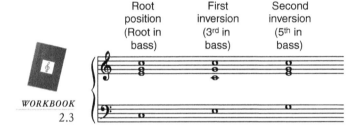

WORKBOOK
2.3

Figured Bass

Many composers who were active between 1600 and 1800 used a shorthand notation to describe the intervals created by notes sounding above the bass. This type of shorthand, **figured bass**, is a handy way of understanding chord construction as well as melodic movement between chords. (Today's lead sheet symbols of jazz and popular music serve a similar purpose.) Figured bass is predicated on the fact that the bass is harmonically the most important voice of any texture. A figured bass has two components:

1. A bass note.
2. Numbers, or "figures"—listed under the bass—that indicate the generic intervals formed by the bass and each of the other voices. The numbers are typically listed one below another, from largest to smallest.

Figured bass does not show which voices have which notes above the bass; it is a catalog of the intervals that occur above the bass, regardless of spacing or doubling. Example 2.10 shows how to represent chords using figured bass. Note that the figures tend to have simple intervals, and the figure "8" is not necessary, since a note one octave above the bass simply doubles the given bass note. Root-position triads yield the figure "$\frac{5}{3}$," first inversion "$\frac{6}{3}$," and second inversion "$\frac{6}{4}$."

EXAMPLE 2.10

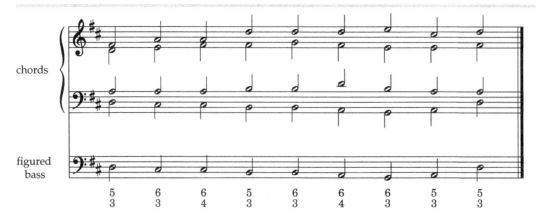

Example 2.11 shows how to fill out, or **realize**, a figured bass to create chords. There is a remarkable amount of freedom in the realization of figured bass. It is up to the performer to decide the arrangement of the upper voices, as long as the given intervals are sounded with the bass note. For this reason, figured bass works well with improvisatory music. For our work, we will analyze and realize chords in four-part harmony. Example 2.11 shows two realizations of the same figured bass that results in successions of four-voice chords.

EXAMPLE 2.11

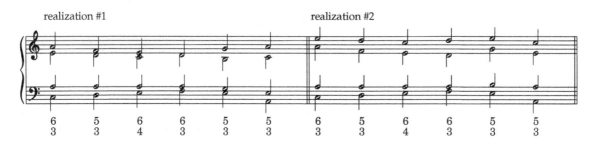

Root-position and first-inversion triads are common, so their figured bass notation is often abbreviated (Example 2.12). Normally, the figure "$\frac{5}{3}$" is omitted entirely; thus, the absence of a figure under a bass note usually indicates a root-position triad. Similarly, "6" by itself is used instead of "$\frac{6}{3}$" for first-inversion triads. The figure for a second-inversion triad is not abbreviated and remains "$\frac{6}{4}$."

EXAMPLE 2.12

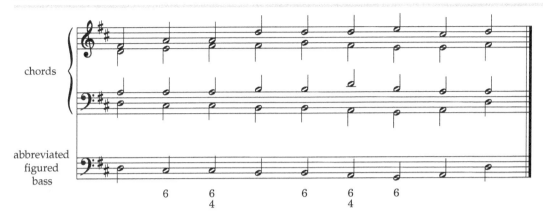

chords

abbreviated
figured
bass

Figured bass follows the given key signature—that is, the notes above the bass follow the given key signature unless the figure is altered. There are a few common ways to indicate chromatic alterations to notes above the bass:

- If there is an accidental on a pitch above the bass, the same accidental is attached to the corresponding interval in the figured bass (Example 2.13A).
- If an accidental occurs on the pitch that is a third above the bass, the number 3 is omitted and only the accidental is written (Example 2.13B).
- A plus sign or a slash through a number raises the pitch by one half step (Example 2.13C).
- If the bass note is chromatically altered, nothing changes in the figure, since the figure indicates only intervals above the bass (Example 2.13D).

EXAMPLE 2.13

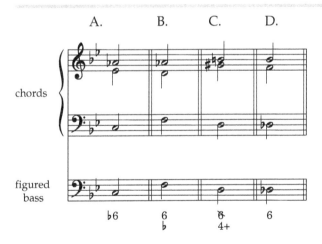

chords

figured
bass

Figured bass can also show the melodic motion of individual voices, especially voices that move by step (Example 2.14). A dash between numbers shows motion in the same voice, as viewed from the bass.

EXAMPLE 2.14

WORKBOOK
2.4   D: 5—6   5—6   5—6   4—3

Triads and the Scale: Harmonic Analysis

Each scale degree of a major or minor scale can support a triad constructed of pitches from that scale. We use roman numerals to represent triads: The numeral indicates the scale degree on which a triad is built, and the size of the roman numeral reflects a triad's quality. Uppercase roman numerals are used for major triads, lowercase numerals for minor triads, and diminished triads are represented by lowercase roman numerals with the addition of a degree sign. Example 2.15 illustrates which quality of triad occurs on each scale degree in the major mode and shows the corresponding roman numerals.

EXAMPLE 2.15

Since $\hat{6}$ and $\hat{7}$ can exist in "natural" or "raised" forms in minor scales, chords that contain these scale degrees can have different qualities. Example 2.16 summarizes the most common triads that occur in minor scales, along with their roman numerals.

EXAMPLE 2.16

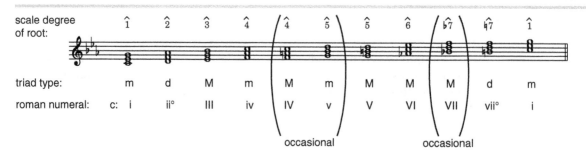

A complete harmonic analysis combines roman numerals and figured bass. The roman numeral identifies the root (by scale degree) and quality of a triad, and a figure identifies root position or inversion (Example 2.17). Finally, figured bass can also identify melodic motion by individual voices above the bass (such as "5—6" or "4—3").

EXAMPLE 2.17

WORKBOOK
2.5

Bb: I V$^6_4$ I^6 V$^{4—3}$ I

Seventh Chords

Sonorities with four notes that can be stacked in thirds are called **seventh chords**. We identify seventh chords by their two most audible features: the type of triad formed by the root, third, and fifth of the chord; and the type of seventh above the root of the chord. There are five important types of seventh chords—though, like the triad types, they are not used with equal frequency. Example 2.18 shows the following qualities of chords, built on the root C.

- major seventh chord (MM7)
- dominant seventh chord (Mm7)
- minor seventh chord (mm7)
- half-diminished seventh chord (dm7)
- diminished, or fully diminished, seventh chord (dd7)

EXAMPLE 2.18

major 7th (MM 7th) · major minor 7th (Mm 7th) · minor 7th (mm 7th) · half–diminished 7th (dm 7th) · diminished 7th (dd 7th)

Seventh chords appear in root position or inversion. Example 2.19 shows the inversions of a Mm7 chord with the root G, along with abbreviated figured bass symbols.

EXAMPLE 2.19

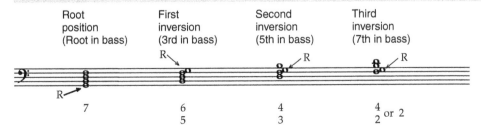

Root position (Root in bass) · First inversion (3rd in bass) · Second inversion (5th in bass) · Third inversion (7th in bass)

7   6/5   4/3   4/2 or 2

The abbreviated figures from Example 2.19 are combined with roman numerals for a complete harmonic analysis of seventh chords. When we analyze seventh chords with roman numerals, we use the following to show the chord qualities:

- MM7 and Mm7 chords use uppercase roman numerals.
- mm7 chords use lowercase roman numerals.
- dm7 chords use lowercase roman numerals, plus a slashed degree sign ($^\emptyset$).
- dd7 chords use lowercase roman numerals, plus a degree sign ($^\circ$).

Example 2.20 shows the most common qualities of seventh chords that occur in major and minor keys, with their corresponding roman numerals. Example 2.21 demonstrates the harmonic analysis of seventh chords in root position and inversion.

EXAMPLE 2.20

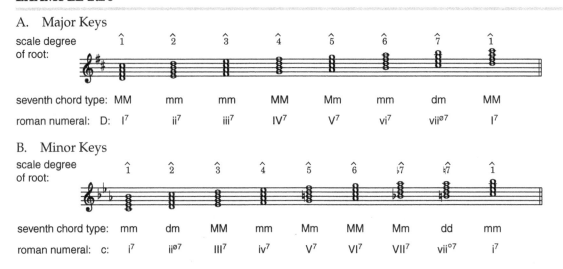

A. Major Keys

scale degree of root: $\hat1$ $\hat2$ $\hat3$ $\hat4$ $\hat5$ $\hat6$ $\hat7$ $\hat1$

seventh chord type: MM   mm   mm   MM   Mm   mm   dm   MM

roman numeral: D: I^7 ii^7 iii^7 IV^7 V^7 vi^7 $vii^{\emptyset7}$ I^7

B. Minor Keys

scale degree of root: $\hat1$ $\hat2$ $\hat3$ $\hat4$ $\hat5$ $\hat6$ $\flat\hat7$ $\natural\hat7$ $\hat1$

seventh chord type: mm   dm   MM   mm   Mm   MM   Mm   dd   mm

roman numeral: c: i^7 $ii^{\emptyset7}$ III^7 iv^7 V^7 VI^7 VII^7 $vii^{\circ7}$ i^7

EXAMPLE 2.21

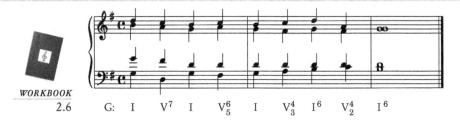

WORKBOOK
2.6   G: I V^7 I V^6_5 I V^4_3 I^6 V^4_2 I^6

Musical Texture

So far, we have explored triads and seventh chords in their simplest form, as simultaneously sounding vertical sonorities. Vertical alignment is just one of many ways that composers distribute the members of a chord. **Texture** refers to many elements of music, but, in particular, it refers to music's density (e.g., the number of voices and their spacing). Each of the following categories of texture is distinguished by the way the melody is projected.

- **Monophonic** texture has a single-voice melody with no accompanying voices.

- **Polyphonic,** or **contrapuntal**, texture has a combination of two or more voices with melodies, such that there is no clear distinction between melody and accompaniment.
- **Homophonic** texture is a cross between monophonic and polyphonic, since there is usually a clear melody with additional, accompanying voices.

The accompaniments in homophonic texture are highly varied. It is because of the richness of possibilities that homophonic texture is the most widespread of the three texture types in common-practice music. Accompaniments include:

- **Chorale texture**, with a vertical, block-chord format. This is one of the simplest homophonic textures, given that the accompanying voices are rhythmically aligned with the melody, which usually appears in the highest register (see Example 2.22A).
- In most homophonic textures, single harmonies are spread out over time, with their chordal members distributed over one or more beats—or even measures—as shown in Example 2.22B, where the pulsing F major triad holds forth for three measures.
- The broken-chord accompanimental pattern in Example 2.22C is an **Alberti bass**. The Alberti bass and other similar accompanimental patterns are effective because our ears collect the individual pitches of the broken-chord figure into a single harmony.
- Often, the members of a chord in a homophonic texture are distributed among various registers and different instruments, as in Example 2.22D. The piano moves in a basic 2:1 contrapuntal motion and contains most, but not all, of the chord tones for each harmony. The violin presents pitches that complete the chords. For this example, Beethoven must consider voicing, doubling, register, and instrumentation in order to distribute most effectively this opening tonic triad in homophonic texture.

Harmonic analysis of homophonic textures requires that we group members of harmony quickly. In order to do so, we must read pitches fluently in bass and treble clefs. The ability to scan music quickly and identify patterns and repetitions is a crucial skill that we will develop in the following chapters.

EXAMPLE 2.22

A.   Hassler, "O Haupt voll Blut und Wunden"

B.   Mozart, Piano Concerto in C major, K. 467, ii

C.   Mozart, Piano Sonata in C major, K. 545, *Allegro*

D.   Beethoven, Piano Trio in C minor, op. 1, no. 3, ii

WORKBOOK
2.7

CHAPTER 3

When Harmony, Melody, and Rhythm Converge

This chapter provides a bridge that leads from our study of fundamentals to our exploration of harmony and form. Fundamentals included the terminology and concepts for the basic building blocks of tonal music. In our studies of two-voice counterpoint, triads, and seventh chords, we learned the importance of intervallic consonance and dissonance. In this chapter we begin to extend these concepts so that we will comprehend not only the note-to-note behavior of pitches, but also how certain pitches connect to others despite the fact that there are intervening pitches. We will accomplish this by a brief look at a few of the underlying and consistent principles of cognition and perception that humans instinctually (and unconsciously) invoke in order to deal with the myriad stimuli presented in the world around them. This procedure is crucial, because when we understand how our hardwired instincts allow us to perceive musical structures, we are able to craft a more informed approach to the music we play and sing.

Tonal Hierarchy in Music

Musicians spend a great deal of their practice time weighing the relative importance of individual musical events and how these events interact with one another. Given that music unfolds in time and that we must fill that time with the most effective and dramatic rendering of a piece, we ask questions like "Is this cadence as important as the next one?" and "Which pitches in this melody carry more structural weight?" In addition to considering general issues such as musical accent (which was discussed in Chapter 1), we are particularly attuned to whether a musical event participates in a motion toward or away from a climactic event. One of the most helpful criteria we use is whether an event is dissonant (unstable, initiates motion toward consonance) or consonant (dissipates the dissonance's instability). Of course, the distinction between consonance and dissonance is not ironclad but depends on the immediate musical context. For example, the minor sixth C–A♭ in Example 3.1A is consonant if either F or A♭ appears below it (creating an F-minor triad or an A♭-major triad, as in Example 3.1B) but is unstable if C or E♭ appears in the bass (Example 3.1C–D).

EXAMPLE 3.1

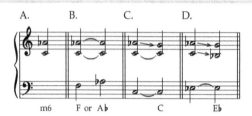

Dissonant intervals—with their harmonic and melodic instability—provide musical tension and energy. Only through resolution can this energy be discharged. Example 3.2 illustrates where perfect consonances (labeled *PC*), imperfect consonances (labeled *IC*), and dissonances (labeled *D*) occur within a descending major scale over a sustained bass note. The label *P* indicates which pitches are passing between, and therefore subordinate to, more important notes.

EXAMPLE 3.2

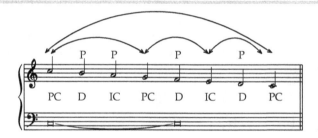

The octave is stable, but the dissonant major seventh (B over C) requires resolution. Depending on the direction of the line, $\hat{7}$ will either ascend to $\hat{1}$ or descend to $\hat{6}$, where, in the latter case, it forms a consonant sixth with the bass. And while the sixth is more stable than the seventh, it is less stable than the following perfect fifth, to which the sixth resolves. We can see that the dependence between various intervals establishes a hierarchical relationship between consonance and dissonance. If we view this scale as a crude melody, we now see that the passing tones B, A, F, and D ($\hat{7}$, $\hat{6}$, $\hat{4}$, and $\hat{2}$) appear between and therefore connect the stable pitches C, E, G, whose combination results in a triad. Since these passing tones are not members of the underlying C-major triad, which is implied by the sustained C in the bass, we call them **nonchord tones** (also called *nonharmonic tones*). Thus passing tones (P) tend to create tension that requires resolution by chord tones.

Tones of Figuration

If we turn the C-major scale into a melody with a more interesting contour as in Example 3.3, another type of nonchord tone is created: the **neighbor tone** (N), also called **auxiliary tone**. Neighbors that lie above a stable pitch are called **upper neighbors**, whereas those that lie below are called **lower neighbors**.

EXAMPLE 3.3   Consonances and Dissonances

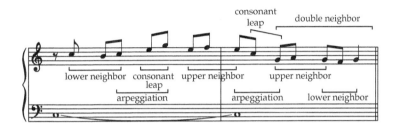

Neighbor tones can be dissonant or consonant. Dissonant neighbors form intervals of a second, fourth, or seventh above the bass. The sixth and the fifth are the only adjacent intervals that are consonant above a bass. An example of a dissonant neighbor occurs between mm. 1 and 2 of Example 3.3: F, which is a fourth above the bass, resolves down to E, a third. A consonant neighbor occurs on beats 2 and 3 of m. 2: A, which is a sixth above the bass, resolves down to G, a fifth. Finally, a **double neighbor** results from the combination of the upper neighbor and lower neighbor in m. 2.

The melody in Example 3.3 also contains leaps that are consonant with the bass note, C. We already learned in our counterpoint studies that leaps are permitted only if they are consonant with the cantus. Similarly, triadic leaps are possible as long as they are members of the underlying harmony. We refer to leaps that are members of the underlying harmony as **consonant leaps** or **chordal leaps** (CL). If three or more tones from the same harmony appear in succession they form an **arpeggiation** (ARP).

Because we have encountered both consonant embellishments (chordal leap, arpeggiation, consonant neighbor tones) and dissonant embellishments (passing tones, dissonant neighbor tones), we will refer to all melodic embellishments as **tones of figuration** rather than nonharmonic tones.

Melodic Fluency

We have seen that melodies share particular attributes. For example, they often rise from a stable initiating point (usually $\hat{1}$), ascend to a climax, and descend to a point of repose. Melodies move primarily by step, and large leaps are balanced by stepwise changes of direction. One such melody is heard in Example 3.4, where a rapid ascent to $\hat{5}$ is followed by a long neighbor note on $\hat{6}$ that returns to $\hat{5}$. The following leisurely stepwise descent convincingly closes on $\hat{1}$.

EXAMPLE 3.4   Smetana, "Moldau," from *My Country*

A given melody (e.g., a cantus firmus) or harmony provides a standard against which we can measure dissonance and consonance. Such a structural foundation allows us to **embellish** the melody or harmony with both consonant and dissonant tones of figuration. Conversely, by pruning away, or **reducing**, these embellishing pitches we discover structural lines, and these nonadjacent stepwise pitches provide an underlying skeleton for the piece. Step motions occurring below the embellished surface of a melody are central to tonal music; such embellishments reflect a larger human preoccupation to elaborate and dramatize forms of discourse and communication.

Further, humans possess the basic desire to make sense of the myriad stimuli presented them in their day-to-day activities and therefore subconsciously to group these stimuli into meaningful shapes. In order to accomplish this we necessarily ignore superfluous and confusing stimuli, give priority to the most logical, clear, and useful bits of information, and fill in incomplete yet necessary pieces, all in order to create an entity that makes the most sense. Composers and performers instinctively invoke these procedures, which include various types of balance, expectation and realization (e.g., the buildup toward a climax), the thwarting of expectations, surprise, ambiguity, and so forth. We have already invoked several of these principles in our discussion of musical accent in Chapter 1, and we now encounter a few additional types in the following discussion of below-the-surface step motions.

Melodic fluency refers to underlying scalar patterns that support the infinite variety of melodic embellishments that lie on the music's surface. We sense these lines intuitively and use them to guide our interpretations of phrases. Indeed, composers guide our ears by aurally "marking" these underlying melodic lines in a variety of ways. Powerful goal-oriented motions arise when accented musical events are coordinated with hierarchical pitch structures (such as the tonic triad). As you listen to Example 3.5, ask yourself whether or not the melody's register and general contour are static, or whether there is an ascent or descent over the course of the excerpt.

EXAMPLE 3.5   Donizetti, *Lucrezia Borgia*, Act I, no. 3

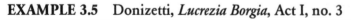

The melody begins on B and slowly descends during the phrase to close a fifth lower on E. That we heard this descent is noteworthy, given that many of the pitch-to-pitch melodic gestures actually *ascend* (e.g., the piece opens with a leap up to E, and ascending gestures occur in mm. 3, 5, and 7). By tracing metrically and durationally accented pitches in this phrase, we understand why we hear the underlying descent (see Example 3.6): B, which holds forth in mm. 1–2 falls first to A and then to G♯ (m. 4). G♯, like the preceding B, is a member of the tonic triad that is sustained in m. 5. G♯ then falls to F♯ (which is extended in mm. 6–7) and on to E.

EXAMPLE 3.6   Donizetti, *Lucrezia Borgia*, Act I, no. 3 (reduction)

Donizetti uses specific embellishments to elaborate the fifth descent. A chordal leap of a fourth in m. 1 (from B to E) is filled in as the fourth retraces itself by stepwise motion. We have learned that changing direction after a leap creates melodic balance. The specific procedure of filling in a leap is called **gap-fill**, another principle predicated on the listener's expectation that a melodic leap will eventually be filled in by stepwise motion in the opposite direction.

Composers, of course, can also create rising structural lines. Placed within the first half of phrases, such lines produce a subtle tension that is balanced and discharged by the later cadential falling. In Example 3.7A, a slow structural ascent from E to G♯ in the first phrase (mm. 1–4) is nicely balanced with the descending stepwise contour of the second phrase (mm. 4–9). This arch-like contour is also found in single phrases, as in Example 3.7B.

EXAMPLE 3.7

A.   Beethoven, Piano Trio in E♭ major, op. 1, no. 2, *Largo, con espressione*

B.   Mozart, Symphony No. 41 in C major ("Jupiter"), K. 551, *Andante cantabile*

In order to delay ascending and descending lines, composers may momentarily change a line's direction. This postpones—and even thwarts—what listeners assume will happen. The longer the postponement, the more dramatic its effect. This process, called **expectation/fulfillment**, is central to the unfolding of a musical work. Listen to Example 3.8. The stepwise fifth descent from A to D accelerates so that four of the five pitches of the descent occur in mm. 3–4. The descent is postponed, however, by the upper neighbor A–B♭–A that follows the initial descending arpeggiation in m. 1. Notice that the upper neighbor B♭ is consonant, given that it is supported by G.

EXAMPLE 3.8   Corelli, Sarabande in D minor, from Sonata no. 7, op. 5

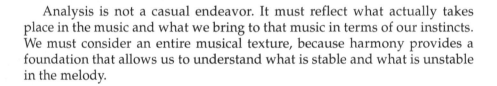

WORKBOOK
3.1–3.3

Analysis is not a casual endeavor. It must reflect what actually takes place in the music and what we bring to that music in terms of our instincts. We must consider an entire musical texture, because harmony provides a foundation that allows us to understand what is stable and what is unstable in the melody.

CHAPTER 4

Composition and Analysis: Using I, V, and V⁷

We now begin to develop new analytical techniques that represent the hierarchical nature of music and that will help you develop a basis for making critically informed interpretations about musical structure. We will also compose in the common-practice style. We'll continue to explore how melody, counterpoint, and harmony are interdependent to the degree that they are inseparable. Finally, we'll see that chords—like melodic pitches—are not created equal.

Tonic and Dominant as Tonal Pillars and Introduction to Voice Leading

Despite the large number of possible triads and seventh chords, composers of common-practice music tend to use some more than others. Indeed, the tonic and dominant triads (and dominant seventh chord) are the most important harmonies. These two chords form the harmonic axis of practically every phrase of tonal music. When used in conjunction with other chords, these two pillars create a sense of arrival and departure. The tonic that is stated at the opening of a phrase or piece is under no obligation to progress to any particular chord. The dominant, however, inevitably leads back to the tonic.

In the V chord, melodic and harmonic functions work together to create a powerful expectation of the tonic's return (see Example 4.1).

EXAMPLE 4.1   The V Chord: Harmonic and Melodic Functions

The V harmony comprises active scale degrees, called **tendency tones**, that are less stable than those of the tonic triad. $\hat{7}$ and $\hat{2}$ are melodic tendency tones: $\hat{7}$ wants to ascend to $\hat{1}$, and $\hat{2}$ can move to either $\hat{1}$ or $\hat{3}$. Although $\hat{5}$ is stable as a member of the tonic harmony, it is unstable as the root of the dominant harmony and has a tendency to return to $\hat{1}$. The V^7 chord contains a fourth tone, $\hat{4}$, which forms the dissonant seventh of the chord.

The Cadence

A **cadence** is a point of arrival (on I or V) that usually occurs at the end of a phrase. When a phrase ends on I or V, there is a sense of closure—often from rhythmic acceleration that leads to a stop in the forward motion of the music, along with the completion of larger metrical patterns. Further, specific soprano scale degrees are often coordinated with these harmonic arrivals such that the entire musical fabric of melody, harmony, counterpoint, rhythm, and meter participate in this phrase-defining moment.

Mozart's Rondo contains examples of the two structural cadences used in tonal music (see Example 4.2). It can be divided into two parallel four-measure phrases. Harmonic as well as melodic motion is necessary to create a phrase. The first phrase closes on the dominant of C major (m. 4), and the second phrase closes on the tonic (m. 8).

EXAMPLE 4.2   Mozart, Rondo in C major, K. 144

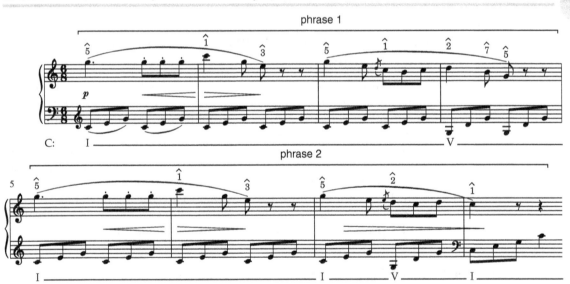

Cadences that close V–I (dominant to tonic in root position) are called **authentic cadences** and are labeled *AC*. Those that close on a root-position dominant are called **half cadences** and are labeled *HC*.

Authentic cadences are graded in strength based on the outer voices. If the soprano moves $\hat{2}$–$\hat{1}$ or $\hat{7}$–$\hat{1}$ while the bass moves $\hat{5}$–$\hat{1}$, the cadence is called a **perfect authentic cadence** and is labeled *PAC* (Example 4.3A–B). If the soprano closes on $\hat{5}$ or $\hat{3}$, it is part of an **imperfect authentic cadence** and is labeled *IAC* (Example 4.3C–D). Any bass motion other than $\hat{5}$–$\hat{1}$ (such as $\hat{7}$–$\hat{1}$ or $\hat{2}$–$\hat{1}$) also creates a special type of IAC called a **contrapuntal cadence** (Example 4.3E–F). Contrapuntal cadences are so named because of their relation to the cadences we used in our contrapuntal studies, which are harmonically weaker than the more common leaping bass motion from $\hat{5}$ to $\hat{1}$. Example 4.3G–I shows common half cadences. In minor, two chromatic alterations occur. First, the dominant will be a major triad, so $\hat{7}$ must be raised to create a leading tone (Example 4.3J). Second, the tonic harmony that closes a piece will sometimes contain a raised third to form a major triad and is called a **Picardy third** (Example 4.3K).

EXAMPLE 4.3

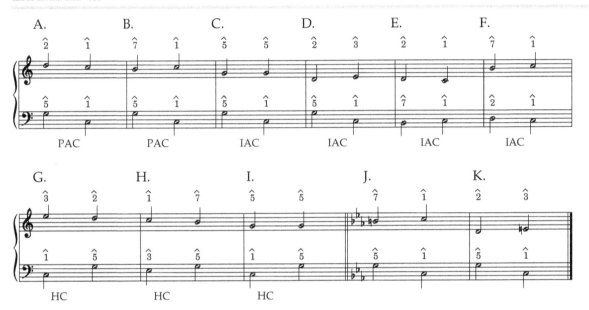

Introduction to Voice Leading

Although we have at our disposal only two harmonies, I and V, they are crucial ones, and we will have plenty of opportunities to incorporate the remaining harmonies once they too are introduced. The idea of an underlying harmonic foundation includes both the permissible chords (harmonic vocabulary) and the order in which chords appear (harmonic progression). The connection between chords must be smooth; therefore, we will focus on how members of one chord connect to members of the following chord. **Voice leading** refers to the way individual voices move. Voice-leading rules are derived from the principles we learned in Chapter 3 concerning two-voice counterpoint.

Texture and Register

Tonal music of the common-practice era was generally conceived in four voices. Such a four-voice framework underlies compositions that may have many more than four voices, such as works for large forces, including the symphony and concerto, or those that may have fewer than four voices, such as solos, duets, and trios in which the framework is implicit (though no less audible). The four-voice texture represents a happy medium because it nicely accommodates the triads and seventh chords.

We order voices from highest to lowest: soprano, alto, tenor, and bass (SATB). Composers notate these four voices in one of the following ways: In **chorale style**, each voice appears on its own staff, or women's voices (SA) and men's voices (TB) have their own staves. In **keyboard style**, the bass is alone in the bass clef; the three upper voices are placed in the treble clef and fit within an octave in order to fit comfortably within the range of one hand at the piano.

Voices, like most instruments, are limited to particular registers, with ranges that roughly cover the interval of a twelfth. Often, a voice will spend most of its time in a more comfortable register, which is referred to as its **tessitura**. Example 4.4 shows both the range and the tessitura for each of the four vocal parts.

EXAMPLE 4.4   Vocal Ranges and Tessituras

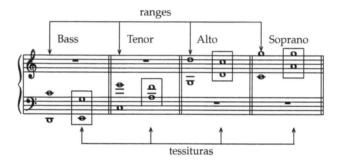

Spacing

In general, keep adjacent upper voices (i.e., soprano, alto, and tenor) within one octave of one another. **Close position** (in which the three upper voices are packed as close to one another as possible) ensures correct spacing, easier voice leading with fewer chances for parallels and other forbidden motions, and an excellent sound. When the total spacing of the upper voices is an octave or more, we call this **open position**. It is a good idea to begin an exercise in close position; to accomplish this, keep the inner voices relatively high. Then, as you continue, it is perfectly acceptable to move the upper voices to open position, which results in a fuller, nicely contrasting sound.

Summary of Voice-Leading Rules and Guidelines

The following voice-leading rules and guidelines will remain in effect for our entire study of harmony. Voice-leading rules cannot be broken; guidelines are suggestions, based on style and aesthetics. Many of these rules were first introduced in the counterpoint studies in Chapter 2.

Move the Voices as Little as Possible When Changing Chords

> RULE 1 Resolve tendency tones ($\hat{7}$, chordal dissonances, or chromatically altered tones) by step. *Exception:* The leading tone, $\hat{7}$, does not need to resolve up to $\hat{1}$ when it is in an inner voice.

> GUIDELINE 1 Retain common tones, and move upper voices mostly by step.

> GUIDELINE 2 Avoid melodic leaps involving dissonant intervals.

Maintain the Independence and Musical Territory for Each Voice

> RULE 2 A pair of voices cannot move from one unison, octave, or perfect fifth to another interval of the same size in parallel or contrary motion.

> RULE 3 Tendency tones cannot be doubled. They are aurally marked and often require special treatment.

> RULE 4 Keep adjacent upper voices (S-A and A-T) within an octave of each other.

> GUIDELINE 3 Avoid voice crossings and voice overlappings. A *voice overlap* occurs when a part leaps above (or below) a higher (or lower) part's previous pitch, infringing on that part's territory, so to speak. A *voice crossing*, on the other hand, occurs when a part is above (or below) a higher (or lower) part's current pitch, swapping places with the adjacent part.

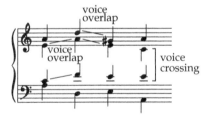

> GUIDELINE 4 Avoid direct octaves and fifths between the soprano and bass (unless the soprano moves by step).

Construct Chords Logically

> GUIDELINE 5 In general, write complete chords. If you must write an incomplete chord for the sake of smooth voice leading or the requirements of dissonance treatment, you may omit only the fifth; all chords must contain a root and a third.

> GUIDELINE 6 In general, double the root of a chord. However, you may double the fifth (and, as a last resort, the third) if it makes the voice leading smoother.

Tips for Avoiding Problems

WORKBOOK
4.1–4.2

GUIDELINE 7 Write the outer voices first. Their counterpoint controls everything.

GUIDELINE 8 Move the upper voices in contrary motion (and, if possible, by step) to the bass.

GUIDELINE 9 Begin part-writing exercises with a complete chord in close position, and try to maintain close position as much as possible.

GUIDELINE 10 If any pair of upper voices leaps simultaneously by more than a third, try revoicing a chord to smooth things out.

The Dominant Seventh and Chordal Dissonance

The seventh is a dissonant interval, and chords that contain the seventh are dissonant. And, just as dissonant intervals resolve to consonant ones, dissonant chords seek resolution to consonant chords. Dissonant chords create tension and heighten expectation in tonal music.

EXAMPLE 4.5

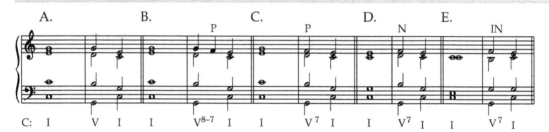

Chordal sevenths can participate in passing motions, as in Example 4.5: A soprano skip from G to E (Example 4.5A) is filled in by a passing F (Example 4.5B). Notice how the "8–7" in the figured bass acknowledges the voice leading of the soprano voice over the bass G: The octave G moves to a passing seventh. In Example 4.5C, the F becomes the seventh of a V^7 chord; however, melodic motion remains intact as the F passes between G and E.

Chordal sevenths also participate in neighboring motions. In Example 4.5D, the note F—the seventh of the V^7 chord—functions as a neighbor to the surrounding Es. The treatment of the chordal seventh in Example 4.5E differs significantly from the preceding examples, since F is not preceded by step. How the seventh of a V^7 chord is approached (its **preparation**) can occur in different ways, but there is only one way to leave the dissonant seventh (its **resolution**): by descending step. Preparation by step from above (as in Example 4.5A–D) is the preferred method.

With the addition of the V^7 chord to our harmonic palette, we can add $\hat{4}$ to the soprano scale degrees that can be harmonized by the chords discussed thus far: $\hat{1}, \hat{2}, \hat{3}, \hat{4}, \hat{5}, \hat{7}$. Using $\hat{4}$ opens up the possibility of harmonizing a complete descending-fifth soprano melody from $\hat{5}$ to $\hat{1}$ (Example 4.6). The passing motion from $\hat{5}$ to $\hat{3}$ in the soprano is imitated in the tenor over the last three beats.

EXAMPLE 4.6   Harmonizing the Falling Fifth: $\hat{5}$–$\hat{1}$

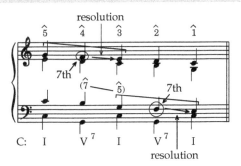

Adding the seventh to a dominant triad results in two tendency tones—the leading tone ($\hat{7}$) and the chordal seventh ($\hat{4}$). These two members of the V⁷ chord create a *tritone* (either an augmented fourth or a diminished fifth) that seeks resolution to notes in the tonic triad. Note that we can add the seventh to V and create a V⁷ chord, but we can't go from V⁷ to V; to do so would contradict the natural drive to the tonic chord when the tritone is created.

Part Writing with the Dominant Seventh Chord

When writing the V⁷ chord, resolve the following tendency tones: The chordal seventh ($\hat{4}$) *always descends* in any voice (as a *dissonant* tendency tone there are no other options), and the leading tone ($\hat{7}$) *always ascends* when it occurs in the soprano.

Incomplete chords occur frequently in V⁷–I progressions, often due to the resolution of tendency tones. The only member of a triad or a seventh chord that we may omit is the fifth. In Example 4.7A, the V⁷ chord is complete, and the tonic triad is incomplete. The tendency tones in the soprano and alto resolve as expected, and the bass moves from $\hat{5}$ to $\hat{1}$. The tenor cannot create a complete C-major triad; to do so would require a jump to G, which would cause consecutive perfect fifths in the bass and tenor. Instead, the tenor moves by step and triples the root, omitting the fifth of the C-major triad.

In Example 4.7B, it is the I chord that is complete. The soprano and alto again have the two tendency tones of the V⁷ chord, and the tenor cannot complete the V⁷ chord with a D. If the tenor were to take the D in the first chord, parallel fifths would occur between the bass and tenor. Instead, the tenor doubles the root of the V⁷ chord and omits the fifth. Generally, a complete V⁷ resolves to an incomplete tonic, and an incomplete V⁷ resolves to a complete tonic.

EXAMPLE 4.7   Resolving the V⁷ Chord

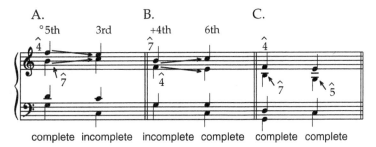

There is one way to have both the V⁷ and I chords complete. When the leading tone is in an inner voice, it can move down to $\hat{5}$ instead of resolving to $\hat{1}$ (Example 4.7C). This exception to the rule that the leading tone must ascend by step to $\hat{1}$ is permissible because the leading tone occurs in an inner voice, where its skip to $\hat{5}$ is less audible than it would be had it occurred in an outer voice.

The final part-writing issue concerns I moving to V⁷, where the perfect fifth in I moves to the diminished fifth in V⁷ (see Example 4.8). These fifths are not parallel perfect fifths, but rather **unequal fifths**, and they are permissible as long as the diminished fifth resolves to a third. Note that the reverse—a diminished fifth moving to a perfect fifth—is generally not permitted, since it contradicts the natural tendency of the diminished fifth to resolve to a third.

EXAMPLE 4.8   Approaching the V⁷ Chord

WORKBOOK
4.3

Analytical Extension: The Interaction of Harmony, Melody, Meter, and Rhythm

Tonal music—a composite of harmony, melody, rhythm, meter, dynamics, and register—is crafted through a series of checks and balances. For example, the bass (or harmonic foundation) often contains large leaps that are a result of the alternation of root-position tonic and dominant harmonies. These leaps are, in a sense, compensated for and balanced by a soprano line that moves primarily by step. Meter and rhythm help to coordinate all this activity. For example, not only is harmony governed by the ebb and flow of weak (unaccented) and strong (accented) beats, but the counterpoint between bass and soprano is also dependent on meter and rhythm. We have already encountered the importance of this contrapuntal relationship: For every change of harmony (bass note) there is a single, primary soprano note. We now place the outer-voice framework in a rhythmical-metrical context, one that is fleshed out with complete chords and textural embellishments. Such embellishments are much like the leaves on a tree, which can decorate but not obscure the structural branches on which their existence depends.

Embellishment

In order to see how we might **embellish** a basic outer-voice structure, we begin with a single implied harmony, the tonic, which supports $\hat{1}$ (Example 4.9A). We can elaborate this soprano pitch with tones of figuration to create a melody of sorts (Example 4.9B). The hierarchy is clear, since not only are the tones of figuration dissonant, but they fall on unaccented beats or parts of beats. We can also stabilize these tones of figuration by harmonizing them with chords that render them consonant. Since the neighbor (B) and passing tone (D) are members of the dominant harmony, we simply place the root of the dominant, G, in the bass (Example 4.9C).

While it's true that each soprano pitch is now consonantly harmonized, we can still distinguish aurally between the more important melody notes that are members of the tonic triad (the soprano C and E) and the subordinate tones of figuration (the soprano B and D). This is because both the contour of the soprano line and the weak metric and rhythmic placement of the dominant harmony strongly prioritize the tonic. Indeed, these less important melodic and harmonic events allow us to hear the underlying tonic harmony. Specifically, the neighbor B is there to extend the flanking C, and the passing Ds provide a bridge that connects the C and the E. One might even go so far as to say that the D in m. 1 is less important than the D in m. 2 because the second D is a member of the perfect authentic cadence. It is possible to illustrate this hierarchy in our harmonic analysis. After labeling every chord and standing back to consider their function within the context, we add a **second-level analysis**, with roman numerals, that reveals our interpretation of the underlying harmonic progression: The first five chords embellish tonic, and the last two chords are part of a PAC (Example 4.9D). Notice the absence of the *P* over the final soprano D, which indicates that this pitch and the accompanying harmony are interpreted as very important, since the V chord is part of the structural authentic cadence and the soprano D is not just another harmonized tone of figuration.

EXAMPLE 4.9

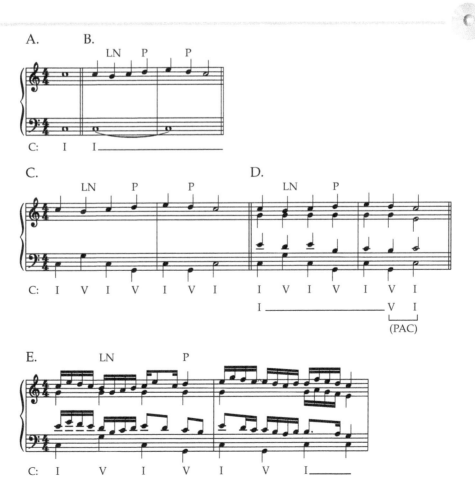

F.

It is possible to repeat the procedure of adding tones of figuration and then harmonizing them; done enough times, we could generate an actual piece of music. However, we shall merely embellish Example 4.9D twice more with tones of figuration to show that neighbors, passing tones, and chordal leaps can be used to create examples in contrasting styles. Although the harmony and outer-voice counterpoint are preserved in Example 4.9E and F, the musical surfaces are quite different. Cast in the parallel mode of C minor with each chord change occupying an entire measure rather than a single beat, Exercise 4.9F is in a freer texture; the arpeggiated figuration creates a seamless flurry of sixteenth notes that is punctuated by the sparse upper-neighbor figure on the fourth beat of each of mm. 1–3.

Reduction

Example 4.9 has demonstrated how a soprano voice can help distinguish structural from ornamental harmonies and how a basic two-voice structure might be ornamented, a process called **embellishment**. Let us now reverse the process by using the harmony as a means of distinguishing structural tones from embellishing tones. This process, called **reduction**, reveals the underlying two-voice contrapuntal framework of a musical passage (Example 4.10).

EXAMPLE 4.10   Beethoven, Piano Sonata in D minor ("Tempest"), op. 31, no. 2,
                  Allegretto

On the downbeat of m. 8, the musical unit sounds relatively complete, as if closure has been achieved. There are two reasons why we hear a strong arrival in m. 8, in spite of the fact that there are no obvious visual clues. First, the eight measures can be subdivided into two symmetrical harmonic and metrical units of four measures each; given the change to dominant harmony in m. 4 (following three measures of tonic), we expect a similar change to occur in the corresponding spot four measures later, which indeed does occur. At the end of m. 4, the addition of the high G in the melody creates a V^7 chord that destabilizes the dominant and sends it forward into the next musical unit, which reverses the harmonic process of mm. 1–4: Three measures of dominant seventh harmony lead to one measure of tonic. The return to tonic in m. 8 is what creates the sense of resolution.

Second, the relationship between the melody and the harmony enhances the effect of closure. The opening D ($\hat{1}$) over tonic harmony repeats on the downbeats of mm. 2 and 3, after which E ($\hat{2}$) arrives over the dominant on the downbeat of m. 4. Thereafter, E is similarly emphasized over a repeated V^7 chord until it ascends to F ($\hat{3}$), coinciding with the return of tonic harmony in m. 8. Thus, a sense of harmonic arrival is balanced by the forward motion of the melody: Tonic harmony returns at the moment the melody dramatically attains $\hat{3}$.

Example 4.11 is a reduction of Example 4.10. Literal repetitions of patterns are not shown. Ties illustrate restatements of important pitches, such as the two Ds and the three Es. Slurs convey the dependency of less important melodic pitches on the important ones; slurred notes arise from tones of figuration, such as neighbor tones, passing tones, and chordal leaps. Notice that the pitches aligned with a slur's beginning and ending points are members of the underlying harmony: The notes D, F, and A begin and end slurs over the tonic harmony, and the notes A, E, and G begin and end slurs over the V^7 harmony.

EXAMPLE 4.11   Structural Analysis of Beethoven, *Allegretto*

In Example 4.11, we can view the E in mm. 4–7—at a deeper melodic level—as a large-scale passing tone that connects D and F. This motion is represented by the beamed pitches, which are supported by the bass voice as in previous chapters. This large-scale melodic ascent ($\hat{1}$–$\hat{2}$–$\hat{3}$) is reflected in reverse order within the right hand's sixteenth-note figuration in Example 4.10.

Second-Level Analysis

With an understanding of the important roles played by meter, rhythm, melody, harmony, and their contrapuntal combinations, we have a standard by which to measure the relative strength and weakness of certain chords. Even when they appear in root position, as we saw in previous examples, we can distinguish between structural and ornamental harmonies.

EXAMPLE 4.12   Two Levels of I–V Harmonies

In Example 4.12, tonic controls m. 1, since the dominant appears on a weak beat and is outnumbered by the tonic harmonies that flank it on the stronger beats (1 and 3). The D, as a result, is a harmonized passing tone that connects E and C. V acts as a "passing chord" that extends (or prolongs) the underlying tonic chord for the first measure. The relationship between tonic and dominant is reversed in m. 2: Tonic harmony helps to extend the dominant, with C as a harmonized passing tone between B and D. Tonic controls m. 3, postponing the arrival on the cadential V chord until the downbeat of m. 4. Example 4.13 summarizes our analysis so far.

EXAMPLE 4.13   Second-Level Analysis of Example 4.12

The soprano pitches in each measure that we interpreted as being subordinate to more structural pitches are circled and labeled as passing or neighboring tones. Also, each chord is labeled with a roman numeral, and the bracketed groups indicate larger harmonic units, with the controlling harmonies labeled beneath the brackets.

This multileveled analysis, a reduction that uses counterpoint and harmony to distinguish structural harmonies and melodies from embellishments, is called a **second-level analysis**. Depending on the number of musical events, there may be more than one level of reduction required; for example, in m. 3 of Example 4.13, the I–V–I harmonies that occur on beats 1 and 2 require their own interpretation before it is possible to analyze the entire measure.

If we consider the possibility of a melodically fluent large-scale soprano controlling the entire passage, we can view the E in m. 1 moving to the C in m. 3 through a large-scale passing tone in m. 2 (shown with beams in Example 4.14). Finally, since our attention will be naturally drawn to the opening E, and, given the extension of the tonic over mm. 1–3 and the accent created by the change to the dominant harmony on the half cadence in m. 4, our ears might connect the opening E to the final D in the melody. Such deep-level melodic fluency is a feature of musical unity, one that composers were well aware of.

EXAMPLE 4.14   Structural Analysis of Example 4.12

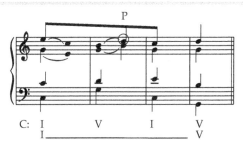

As we have just seen, the harmonies in a progression are not always of equal structural value. Indeed, there are many musical contexts in which I and V, chords that are usually viewed as structural, may become subordinate to each other and to other harmonies. The key to hearing and analyzing music is being sensitive to the musical context, especially the meter, the rhythm, and the counterpoint between bass and soprano.

CHAPTER 5

Contrapuntal Expansions of Tonic and Dominant

In this chapter we will explore how inversions of specific triads and seventh chords enrich musical structure by elaborating the tonic–dominant axis within a phrase. Because inverted triads are less stable than their root-position counterparts, they allow for greater harmonic nuance. And by using inversions, composers turn the bass line into a melody.

Contrapuntal Expansions with First-Inversion Triads

Chordal Leaps in the Bass: I^6 and V^6

The first tonic chord in the progression I–V–I (Example 5.1A) can be expanded by changing the voicing of the upper parts for added interest (Example 5.1B). But a more dramatic and contrapuntally interesting way to expand tonic is to use the first-inversion I^6 chord: I–I^6–V–I (Example 5.1C). Instead of the leap of a fifth, the bass first moves by a chordal leap to another note in the tonic chord. The I^6 chord is less stable than the root-position I chord; this instability helps to push the music forward.

EXAMPLE 5.1

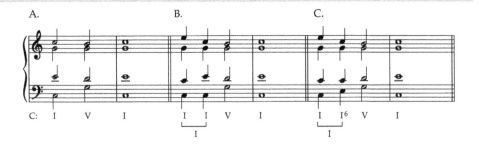

Whereas root-position and first-inversion triads can often be interchanged, second-inversion triads are not an effective substitute for either root-position or first-inversion given their dissonant fourth above the bass. As we shall see later, triads in second inversion function quite differently from those in root position and first inversion. For the time being, we will use only root-position and first-inversion chords.

First-inversion chords energize phrases because they render the bass more melodic; a brief look at the lowest voice in Brahms' folk song setting (Example 5.2A) reveals a melodic arch created by the descent of a sixth from C to E and ascent of an octave to the half cadence. Thus, the bass plays multiple roles, fusing harmonic function with melodic interest. The relationship between bass and soprano is intensified by the fact that the intervals in mm. 1 and 3 are inverted, as are the pitches swapped, creating voice exchanges (Example 5.2B).

EXAMPLE 5.2

A. "Vom Verwundeten Knaben," Setting by Brahms, op. 14, no. 2

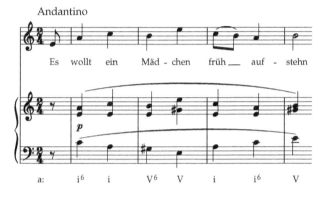

B. With Voice Exchanges

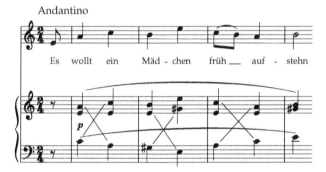

Moving between a chord's root position and first inversion is analogous to revoicing the upper voices of a harmony; that is, there is no harmonic change but rather the extension or prolongation of a single harmony. That this can occur in the bass simply makes the change more dramatic. As a rule, it is much more common to extend the tonic harmony using its first inversion than it is to extend the dominant with its first inversion. Example 5.3 presents common bass and soprano settings for motions between I and I⁶: Example 5.3A shows a voice exchange, Example 5.3B shows similar motion in the outer voices, and Example 5.3C shows parallel motion in the outer voices. Note that all of these are applicable to expanding V with V⁶ (as shown in Example 5.3D–F). Using I⁶ between I and V breaks up the large leap of a fifth into two smaller leaps of a third.

EXAMPLE 5.3

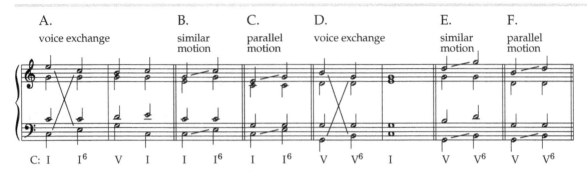

A. voice exchange   B. similar motion   C. parallel motion   D. voice exchange   E. similar motion   F. parallel motion

C: I   I⁶   V   I   I   I⁶   I   I⁶   V   V⁶   I   V   V⁶   V   V⁶

Neighboring Tones in the Bass: V⁶

We have seen that a harmony can be ornamented with a neighboring tone; in Example 5.4A, the B in the bass is a neighboring tone that ties together the surrounding root-position tonic chords. However, the B is dissonant because it is not a part of the tonic harmony. We can change the upper voices to pitches that are consonant with the bass note B, thus **harmonizing** the bass note. The result is a V⁶ chord (see Example 5.4B). Although we have created a new chord, it is still ornamental and subordinate to the surrounding chords. We refer to the V⁶ harmony as a **neighboring chord**.

EXAMPLE 5.4

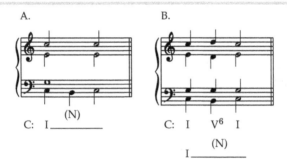

A.   B.

C: I_____   C: I   V⁶   I
        (N)   (N)
                                   I_____

The V⁶ can also be used as an **incomplete neighboring chord**. The most common type of incomplete neighbor occurs when I⁶ is followed by V⁶, which then returns to I (Example 5.5A). In minor, the bass leap from 3̂ to 7̂ forms a diminished fourth, which, given its extreme pathos and that the leading tone is immediately resolved, is permitted. In Example 5.5B, Corelli presents a dramatic diminished-fourth leap from E♭ (the bass of i⁶) to B natural (bass of V⁶).

EXAMPLE 5.5

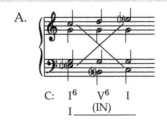

A.

C: I⁶   V⁶   I
        I_____(IN)

B.   Corelli, Concerto Grosso No. 8 in F major, *Allegro* no. 2

c: i⁶_____ V⁶_____ i _____

(IN)

i _____

Structural and Subordinate Harmonies

Harmonic analysis is a two-stage process: The first stage (or **first-level analysis**) identifies each sonority with roman numerals; such labeling represents the descriptive analysis of the progression. The second stage (or **second-level analysis**) reflects the functions of the sonorities: Some harmonies are structural, and other harmonies are subordinate. Structural harmonies are **progressional**, because they indicate movement from one harmonic function (such as tonic) to another (such as dominant); structural harmonies keep their roman numerals in second-level analysis. Subordinate harmonies—such as the neighboring V⁶ chord in the Example 5.5—are **prolongational**, since they help to extend or prolong a single structural harmony. In second-level analysis, prolongational chords are labeled by melodic function.

Structural harmonies . . .
- are progressional
- have harmonic function
  (tonic, dominant)
- are usually on strong beats
- are usually in root position
- are part of a harmonic progression
- keep their roman numerals
  in second-level analysis

Subordinate harmonies . . .
- are prolongational
- have melodic function
  (chordal leap, neighboring tone)
- are usually on weak beats
- are usually in inversion
- are part of a contrapuntal progression
- are labeled as ornaments ("N," "CL")
  in second-level analysis

> *Voice Leading and Doubling Rules for I⁶ and V⁶*
> • Keep common tones (unless you use a voice exchange, which often requires movement in multiple voices).
> • When possible, double the root (you can double the third or fifth if it smoothes the voice leading).
> • Never double the leading tone, $\hat{7}$ (the third of a dominant chord).
> • If the bass is not doubled, choose one of the following spacings for first-inversion triads:
>   • *Doubled unison:* Two voices share the same pitch at the unison (Example 5.6A–B).
>   • *Neutral position:* Two voices share the same pitch at the octave (Example 5.6C).
> • Subordinate harmonies, especially those that neighbor, usually appear on metrically weak beats or parts of beats.

EXAMPLE 5.6

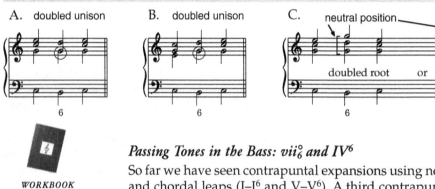

WORKBOOK
5.1

Passing Tones in the Bass: vii°₆ and IV⁶

So far we have seen contrapuntal expansions using neighboring tones (I–V⁶–I) and chordal leaps (I–I⁶ and V–V⁶). A third contrapuntal motion, **passing**, expands the tonic by inserting a bass passing tone between I and I⁶ chords.

Example 5.7 illustrates how each of the tonic's bass tones ($\hat{1}$ and $\hat{3}$ in m. 1 and the reverse in m. 2) is harmonized by root-position and first-inversion triads; in m. 1 a voice exchange is created between the bass and flute Bs and Ds.

EXAMPLE 5.7   Handel, Flute Sonata in B minor, HWV 367b

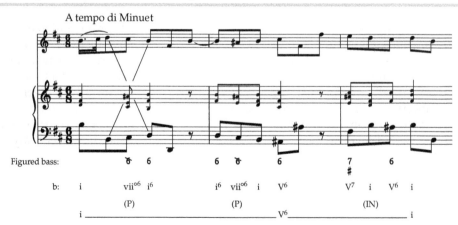

Notice, in addition, that Handel has harmonized the bass and soprano passing tones C♯ (2̂) with first-inversion chords built on the vii° triad. Given that vii°⁶ harmonizes the passing tone C♯, it is called a **passing chord**, as shown below the example in the second-level analysis. Just as we learned for neighboring embellishing chords, passing chords usually fall on metrically weak beats or parts of beats. Before we leave the Handel example, notice in m. 3 that the tonic harmony first appears on a weak part of the beat; sandwiched between two dominant harmonies and harmonizing D, a weak-beat passing tone in the flute (we interpret the tonic chord as an incomplete neighbor that helps to extend the dominant that began its control on the second beat of m. 2 and that remains in force until the strong-beat arrival of tonic at the end of the excerpt). Standing back even further, we might assign the extended V⁶ chord a neighboring function given that it is flanked by the opening and closing tonic chords in root position.

Example 5.8 shows common settings of vii°⁶, with both first- and second-level analysis. Again, each of the contrapuntal chords occurs on a metrically unaccented beat, while the underlying harmony that is expanded usually occurs in a metrically accented position.

EXAMPLE 5.8

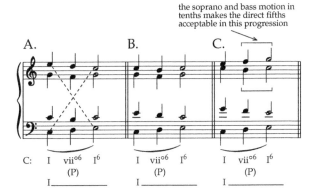

Voice Leading for vii°⁶
- **Never** double the leading tone, 7̂.
- Try to double the third of the chord (2̂), which may move to either 1̂ or 3̂ (you may double 4̂, but only to make the voice leading smoother).
- If possible, resolve the tritone (as with V⁷).

Just as tonic may be expanded with a passing vii°⁶ chord, so too may the dominant be expanded by a first-inversion IV⁶ chord. Observe in Example 5.9 how V–IV⁶–V⁶ is used in major and minor keys.

EXAMPLE 5.9

C: I⁶   V   IV⁶ V⁶   I   c: i⁶   V   IV⁶ V⁶   i
         (P)   (P)
    I⁶   V_____ I   i⁶   V_____ i

> *Voice Leading for V–IV⁶–V⁶*
> - In minor keys, 6̂ must be raised to avoid an augmented second be-
>   tween 6̂ and 7̂—this results in a major IV⁶ chord.
> - Avoid parallel fifths and octaves in IV⁶–V⁶ by moving the upper
>   voices in contrary motion to the bass.

Tonic Expansion with an Arpeggiating Bass: IV⁶

We know that I⁶ expands I, with the bass *ascending* by a *third* (from 1̂ up
to 3̂). Sometimes, for reasons of drama or range, the bass moves from I to I⁶
by *falling* a *sixth*, from 1̂ down to 3̂. The large leap of a sixth is often split into
the arpeggiation 1̂–6̂–3̂ by the addition of a IV⁶ chord (see Example 5.10).
Notice the stepwise ascent, 3̂–4̂–5̂, in the soprano; this ascent of 4̂ to 5̂ provides an important contrast to its more usual descent, as the dissonant seventh in dominant harmony. When we write IV⁶, it is common to double 1̂
(the third above the bass), but we are free to double any member of the
chord, since smooth voice leading must always take priority over doublings
in our writing.

EXAMPLE 5.10

WORKBOOK
5.2

C: I   IV⁶   I⁶
        (arp)
    I_____

Contrapuntal Expansions with Seventh Chords

V⁷ and Its Inversions

Root-position V⁷ generally does not expand the tonic; it is a progressional harmony that often signals a *cadence*; thus, it should be used sparingly. Inverted
chords are inherently unstable and give rise to the kind of motion that is

needed *within* a phrase. The inversions of V^7 are ideal embellishing chords. The voice leading for inverted V^7 chords is identical to root position (Example 5.11). The chordal third ($\hat{7}$) rises (to $\hat{1}$), and the chordal seventh ($\hat{4}$) resolves down by step (to $\hat{3}$).

EXAMPLE 5.11

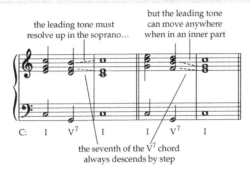

V$^6_5$ (first inversion) places the chordal third ($\hat{7}$) in the bass; like the V^6 triad, V$^6_5$ is usually a neighboring chord (Example 5.12A). The single difference between V^6 and V$^6_5$ is the presence of the chordal seventh ($\hat{4}$) in the latter, which often appears in the soprano. The seventh often appears within a *neighboring* configuration, where it mirrors the neighboring bass in contrary motion, as shown in Example 5.12B.

EXAMPLE 5.12

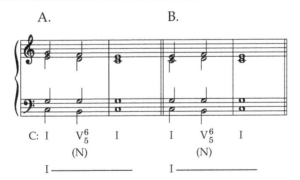

V$^4_3$ (second inversion) places the chordal fifth ($\hat{2}$) in the bass. Since $\hat{2}$ also appears in the bass of vii°^{6}, V$^4_3$ functions in much the same way—as a neighboring chord to I or, more often, as a passing chord between I and I^6. Example 5.13A shows this passing motion as V$^4_3$ connects I^6 and I. The soprano moves in parallel tenths with the bass. In Example 5.13B the contour is reversed: V$^4_3$ is part of an ascending line, connecting I and I^6. Notice that the chordal seventh (F) *ascends* to G instead of resolving normally to E. This exception to the rule that chordal dissonance must resolve by step *descent* is permitted because the strong parallel-tenth motion between bass and soprano overrides the normal resolution of the seventh.

6666

EXAMPLE 5.13

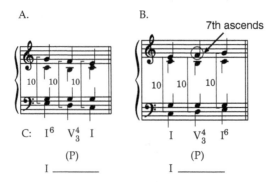

V_2^4 (third inversion) places the chordal seventh ($\hat{4}$) in the bass. Given the prominent placement of the seventh, V_2^4 is the least stable of the inverted dominants. Example 5.14A presents a setting of V_2^4 in which it participates in a tonic expansion from I to I^6 that includes a voice exchange. Composers often soften the effect of V_2^4 by preparing the seventh as a passing tone, as shown in Example 5.14B. Finally, placing the passing seventh in the bass at a cadence destabilizes the dominant and transforms it into part of a tonic prolongation. Example 5.14C shows a tonic expansion and typical PAC (with passing seventh in the alto). Example 5.14D presents the passing seventh in the bass, creating an **evaded cadence**.

EXAMPLE 5.14

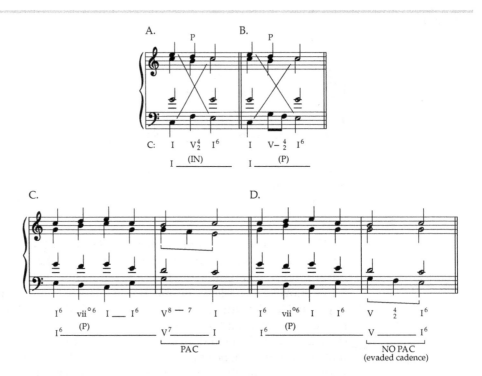

Voice-Leading Inversions of V⁷

There are no new voice-leading rules for the inversions of V⁷, but do not lose sight of the tenets of good part writing that have already been discussed:

1. Move most if not all of the voices by step or common tone when leading to and from inversions of V⁷.
2. Inversions of V⁷ should appear as complete chords.
3. Inversions of V⁷ tend to fall on metrically unaccented beats, connecting the more stable tonic triads, which tend to fall on strong beats.
4. Resolve tendency tones: $\hat{7}$ (the leading tone) *must* ascend when it occurs in an outer voice (but may fall to $\hat{5}$ when it occurs in an inner voice). $\hat{4}$ (the seventh of V⁷) *must* descend to $\hat{3}$ (except in the progression I–V$_3^4$–I⁶, harmonizing a $\hat{3}$–$\hat{4}$–$\hat{5}$ soprano).

Leading Tone Seventh Chords: vii°⁷

A glance at the bass line of Gluck's *Orfeo* in Example 5.15 reveals contrapuntal expansions of the tonic similar to inversions of V⁷. However, when we listen to the example, we will hear that each neighboring and passing sonority is a form of vii°⁷. vii°⁷ and its inversions are much more dissonant than V⁷ and its inversions. This is because vii°⁷ contains the interval of the diminished seventh as well as two tritones (in C minor, B–F and D–A♭). Further, V⁷ shares one common tone with tonic ($\hat{5}$), but vii°⁷ ($\hat{7}$, $\hat{2}$, $\hat{4}$, $\hat{6}$) does not share any common tones with tonic.

EXAMPLE 5.15   Gluck, *Orfeo*, Act I, no. 1

vii°⁷ and its inversions function the same way as V⁷ and its inversions because they share three pitches ($\hat{7}$, $\hat{2}$, and $\hat{4}$). vii°⁷ and V⁷ are interchangeable, as shown here:

- vii°⁷ behaves just like V$_5^6$—it is a neighboring chord to root-position tonic.
- vii°$_5^6$ behaves like V$_3^4$—it is a passing chord between i and i⁶.

- vii^{o4}_{3} behaves like V^{4}_{3}—it is a passing chord between V and i^{6}, or it is a neighboring chord to i^{6}.
- vii^{o4}_{2} is rare and usually is a neighboring chord to root-position V^{7}.

The diminished seventh chord appears more often in minor-mode compositions because the chord appears within the minor scale. In addition, the diminished seventh provides support of $\hat{6}$, a scale degree that we have not harmonized before and that is particularly expressive when it occurs in the soprano voice. Example 5.16A shows the contrapuntal functions of vii^{o7} and its inversions. Example 5.16B compares V^{7} with vii^{o7}; unfilled noteheads show common tones and filled noteheads show the pitch difference between V^{7} and vii^{o7}.

EXAMPLE 5.16

A.

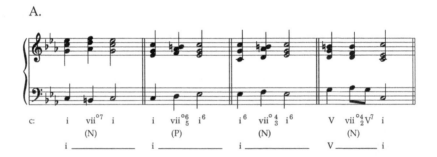

B.

The best way to approach writing vii^{o7} is first to think of the inversions of V^{7} and then to substitute $\hat{6}$ for $\hat{5}$. *Note:* Correct resolution of vii^{o7} and its inversions to tonic usually results in a doubled third. Since all notes in vii^{o7} are tendency tones, here is a guide to resolving the vii^{o7} chord to tonic (see Example 5.17):

EXAMPLE 5.17

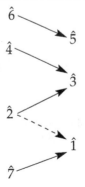

WORKBOOK

5.3–5.4

- Prepare $\hat{6}$—approach by step or with a common tone.
- $\hat{6}$ moves down to $\hat{5}$.
- $\hat{4}$ moves down to $\hat{3}$.
- $\hat{2}$ usually moves to $\hat{3}$, or it can move down to $\hat{1}$.
- $\hat{7}$ moves up to $\hat{1}$.

Analytical Extension: Invertible Counterpoint

The intimate contrapuntal relationship between the bass and the soprano is the foundation of the standard four-voice harmonic texture. Composers take advantage of an important aspect of this contrapuntal relationship that allows them to spin out their musical material. Listen to Example 5.18.

EXAMPLE 5.18   Mozart, Piano Sonata in G major, K. 283, *Allegro*

The sections marked 1 and 2 have similar sounds, and, in fact, there is a very strong relationship between them. If you compare the outer-voice counterpoint in section 1 with that of section 2, you will discover that the soprano and bass melodies swap places: What was on top is now on the bottom, and vice versa. Thus, even though the lines trade places, they retain their original contour. This swapping of parts between voices is called **invertible counterpoint** or **double counterpoint**, and it is an important compositional procedure, for two reasons. First, economically, it allows composers to reap twice as much musical value from a single idea. Second, it allows the music to remain clearly unified because the listener is repeatedly exposed to the same material, presented in different ways. The registral exchange of figures in invertible counterpoint creates sections of music that, although strongly related, have their own distinctive sound. The result is a perfect mix that satisfies the listener's desire for variety and contrast.

In the music of Example 5.18, Mozart has inverted his tunes at the octave (or its compound, the double or triple octave); that is, the rearrangement of upper and lower material is accomplished solely by octave leaps in one or both voices. This octave switching is called **invertible counterpoint at the octave**. It is also possible to invert two-voice counterpoint at other intervals, most commonly the twelfth, but we will restrict the following discussion to the octave.

EXAMPLE 5.19

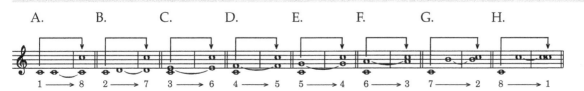

When intervals are inverted *at the octave*, they maintain their consonant or dissonant characters (Example 5.19). This retention of consonance and dissonance is what allows for invertible counterpoint. For example, any dissonant seventh in an upper voice that properly resolves downward to a sixth will resolve in the same way in inversion; thus a second will resolve to a third because the moving voice is now in the bass. Dissonances can be treated correctly in inversion if they were treated correctly in the original version. The only potential danger is the interval of a fifth, which turns into a dissonant fourth when inverted. Thus, composers writing invertible counterpoint must be careful to treat all perfect fifths as potential dissonant intervals (by preparing and resolving them and by generally placing them on the weak beats). Example 5.20 presents two instances of invertible counterpoint. Example 5.20A is written in one-to-one counterpoint that includes a few examples of two-to-one counterpoint. Example 5.20B is written in two-to-one counterpoint, but the faster-moving notes are distributed across both voices.

EXAMPLE 5.20

A.

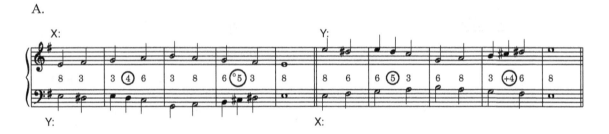

B.

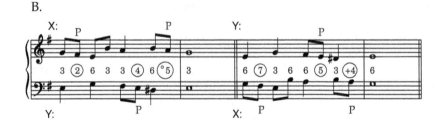

Invertible Counterpoint Below the Music's Surface

Occurrences of invertible counterpoint are often far subtler than the literal contrapuntal switch seen in the previous examples. Through various embellishing processes, composers camouflage their use of invertible counterpoint as a structural agent, where it becomes the backbone of the harmonic progression itself. In Example 5.21, Schubert uses a full, homophonic texture that disguises the invertible relationship between the soprano and the bass.

The first six measures serve to expand tonic, first by V_3^4, then V_5^6, and finally by V_2^4. But one might go so far as to say that identifying roman numerals in this context identifies symptoms more than causes as to what motivates this passage's unfolding. Indeed, we seem to be missing the forest for the trees here, since an important melodic relationship between the bass and the soprano governs these measures.

EXAMPLE 5.21   Schubert, Impromptu in A♭ major, D. 935

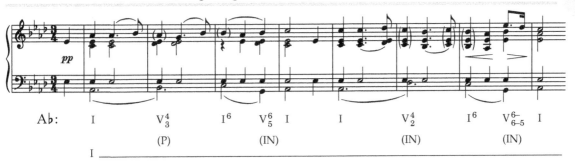

Example 5.22A shows a two-voice contrapuntal reduction that reveals a large neighbor figure (A♭–G–A♭) occurring over a large passing motion (A♭–B♭–C). These figures can be seen in the stemmed pitches, which represent the structural counterpoint.

EXAMPLE 5.22

A.   Mm. 1–8

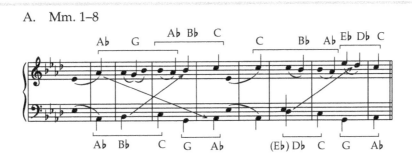

B.   Mm. 5–8

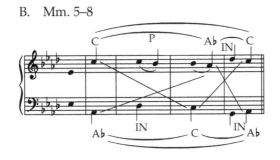

An understanding that invertible counterpoint holds together mm. 1–4 can bring new meaning to how we hear mm. 5–8 (Example 5.22B). First, the large A♭–C passing motion in the soprano from mm. 1–4 reverses direction in mm. 5–7. The descending portion is loosely mirrored by the bass (A♭–C), thus creating a large-scale voice exchange. Second, the use of V_2^4–I^6 in the bass (mm. 6–7) brings out the D♭–C motive, which is immediately imitated two octaves higher in the soprano.

CHAPTER 6

The Pre-Dominant, the Phrase Model, and Additional Embellishments

In this chapter we learn how composers incorporate the third and final harmonic function, the pre-dominant. Our composition exercises will be considerably enriched by incorporating the two harmonies that are used in this function. We will also learn new techniques for elaborating both melodic lines and harmonic functions, including a new type of melodic figuration predicated on metric accent and chromaticism.

The Pre-Dominant Function

Whereas tonic and dominant functions are sufficient to create coherent musical passages, a third harmonic function adds a new dimension to our sense of harmonic tension and resolution. Both excerpts in Example 6.1 contain independent chords that act as connective tissue between the tonic and the dominant. These chords are called **pre-dominants**, since they precede the dominant. The most important pre-dominant chords are IV and ii. Note that we now add the symbols T, PD, and D to represent the three functions of "tonic," "pre-dominant," and "dominant" in the second-level analysis.

EXAMPLE 6.1

A.   Meyerbeer, "Se non ti moro allato," *Sei canzonette italiane*, no. 5

B.   Foster, "Beautiful Dreamer"

Beau-ti-ful dream - er,   wake un-to me, _____   Star-light and dew-drops are wait-ing for   thee; _____

Eb: I   ii⁶   V⁷   I
    T   PD   D   T

EXAMPLE 6.2

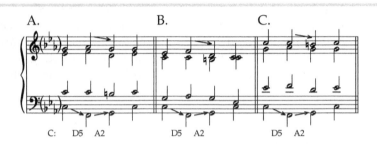

A.   B.   C.

C: D5   A2   D5   A2   D5   A2

The Subdominant (IV in Major, iv in Minor)

Composers frequently choose the subdominant as the pre-dominant chord because the I–IV motion proceeds by descending fifth (the most convincing root motion in tonal music) and the bass's ascent from $\hat{4}$ to $\hat{5}$ creates a smooth motion to the dominant (Example 6.2). As the bass ascends by step, the upper voices usually descend, to avoid voice-leading problems. Example 6.3 shows how IV can move to V^7. Note that the soprano's $\hat{4}$ prepares the seventh of the upcoming dominant.

EXAMPLE 6.3

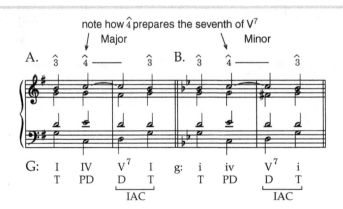

note how $\hat{4}$ prepares the seventh of V^7

         Major   Minor

A. $\hat{3}$ $\hat{4}$ ___ $\hat{3}$ B. $\hat{3}$ $\hat{4}$ ___ $\hat{3}$

G: I   IV   V⁷   I   g: i   iv   V⁷   i
     T   PD   D   T   T   PD   D   T
                 IAC   IAC

We can also approach V from above (i.e., $\hat{6}$ down to $\hat{5}$ in the bass) by moving from IV⁶ to V. Such a motion is especially common in the minor mode, where the powerful falling half step intensifies tonal motion to the dominant. This resulting special type of half cadence, in which iv⁶ moves to V, is known as a **Phrygian half cadence** (Example 6.4). Note that the upper voice moves from $\hat{4}$ to $\hat{5}$ against the bass's descent from $\hat{6}$ to $\hat{5}$.

EXAMPLE 6.4

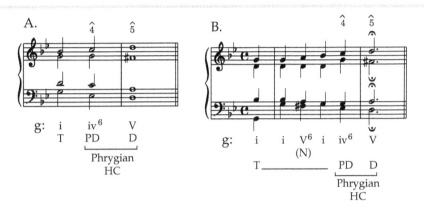

The Supertonic (ii in Major, ii° in Minor)

The supertonic is the most common pre-dominant chord; there are at least three reasons why composers consider the supertonic to be an effective pre-dominant:

1. The progression ii–V proceeds by descending fifth motion, the strongest root motion in tonal music.

2. ii introduces a striking sonority and modal contrast in progressions:
   a. In major keys, ii is minor. I and V are major.
   b. In minor keys, ii° is diminished. i is minor and V is major.

3. The progression ii–V–I is often set to $\hat{2}$–$\hat{7}$–$\hat{1}$ in the soprano, versus the less dynamic $\hat{1}$–$\hat{7}$–$\hat{1}$ when IV functions as the pre-dominant. This melodic motion encircles the upcoming $\hat{1}$, making the cadence especially powerful (Example 6.5).

EXAMPLE 6.5

Composers write both ii and ii⁶ in the major mode, but they almost always use the first-inversion ii°⁶ chord in the minor mode. This is because ii° is a dissonant diminished triad, and (as with vii°) any root-position diminished triad has an unsettling effect given its exposed tritone between the bass and an upper voice. The tritone is softened when first-inversion ii°⁶ is used and $\hat{4}$ occurs in the bass (Example 6.6).

EXAMPLE 6.6

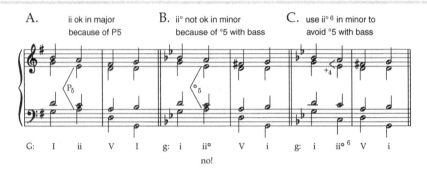

The use of ii in first inversion raises an important issue. Recall that root-position ii lacks the smooth melodic step progression to V in the bass that is enjoyed by IV (Example 6.3). The first-inversion supertonic (ii⁶) embodies the best attributes of ii and IV: the modal contrast from ii, the descending-fifth root relation of ii–V, and the smooth bass voice leading of $\hat{4}$–$\hat{5}$ from IV.

With the addition of pre-dominants, we can now write a stepwise line in the bass that ascends from $\hat{1}$ to $\hat{5}$, as shown in Example 6.7. The ascending bass line has an especially powerful effect in major-mode pieces, given that the bass of I⁶ ($\hat{3}$) lies only a half step from the pre-dominant on $\hat{4}$.

EXAMPLE 6.7   Chopin, Nocturne in F♯ minor, op. 48, no. 2

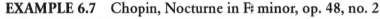

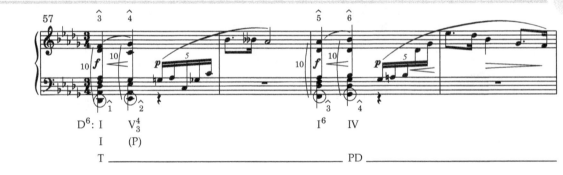

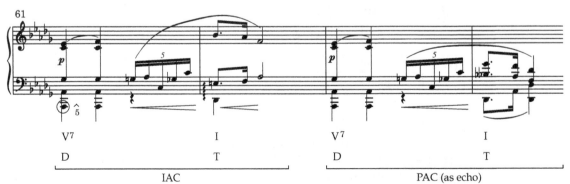

Part Writing Pre-Dominants

Keep the following in mind when writing pre-dominants:

1. Pre-dominants move to V: tonic→pre-dominant→dominant→tonic.
2. When the bass of a pre-dominant chord moves $\hat{4}$–$\hat{5}$ or $\hat{6}$–$\hat{5}$, the soprano moves in contrary motion with the bass (Example 6.8A–E).
3. Try to double the root of root-position pre-dominant chords (Example 6.8A–C).
4. When writing a ii⁶ chord, try to double the bass $\hat{4}$ (Example 6.8D).
5. In a Phrygian half cadence (iv⁶–V), the bass moves from $\hat{6}$ to $\hat{5}$, the soprano usually moves $\hat{4}$–$\hat{5}$, and the other voices double $\hat{1}$ to avoid voice-leading errors (Example 6.8E).
6. When writing in a minor key, approach the leading tone ($\hat{7}$) from above (Example 6.8F).

EXAMPLE 6.8

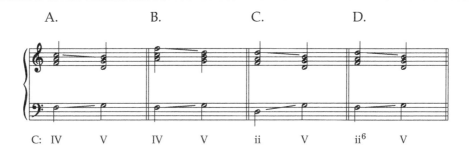

C: IV   V   IV   V   ii   V   ii⁶   V

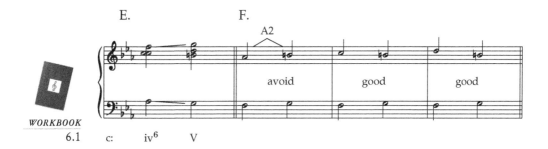

WORKBOOK
6.1   c: iv⁶   V

Extending the Pre-Dominant

Just as the tonic and the dominant functions may be extended by embellishing chords, so too may the pre-dominant. We will focus on two techniques that extend the pre-dominant function. The first technique involves the use of a chordal skip in the bass, that is, moving from ii to ii⁶ or vice versa. Example 6.9 illustrates this simple technique; notice the resulting voice exchange between the outer voices.

EXAMPLE 6.9 Beethoven, Piano Concerto in G major, op. 58, *Allegro moderato*

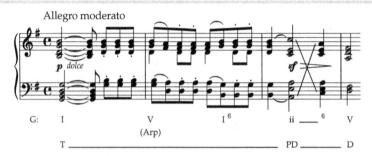

The second technique is subtler, yet arguably more important. We know that progressions whose roots move by step (e.g., IV–V) are especially vulnerable to parallel perfect intervals in voice leading, especially when the outer voices move in the same direction (Example 6.10A). In order to avoid poor voice leading, we can use a **voice-leading chord**, which breaks up the parallels. In Example 6.10B, the contrapuntal 5–6 motion above the bass avoids the parallel fifths in Example 6.10A.

The 5–6 motion above the bass is a common device that gives the impression that two chords (here, IV and ii⁶) are working together seamlessly to extend the pre-dominant function. This motion is interpreted in Example 6.10B as a melodic shift (IV with a 5–6 motion) rather than as a chord change from IV to ii. In Example 6.10C, the bass falls from $\hat{4}$ to $\hat{2}$, yet this chord change (IV to ii) is still motivated by the same voice-leading concerns as in Example 6.10B. Note that the goal-oriented melodic motion in the succession IV–ii⁽⁶⁾ is very common, but the weaker motion of ii–IV is not.

EXAMPLE 6.10

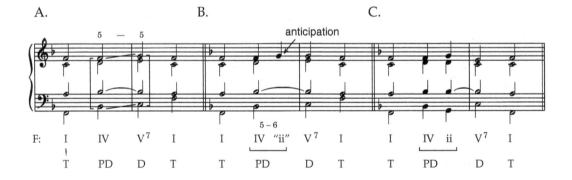

Introduction to the Phrase Model

Complete musical statements can rely exclusively on tonic and dominant chords. These units, called *phrases*, are always punctuated by strong closing gestures called *cadences*. Although there are many examples of phrases built exclusively on tonics and dominants, most phrases incorporate the pre-dominant function to create a richer harmonic progression. The harmonic motion of tonic (T), through pre-dominant (PD), to dominant and tonic at the cadence (D, or D–T), guides a phrase from its beginning to its cadence and is called the **phrase model (T–PD–D–T).**

EXAMPLE 6.11   **Haydn, String Quartet in D major ("Der Frosch"), op. 50, no. 6, Hob. III.49,** *Menuetto*

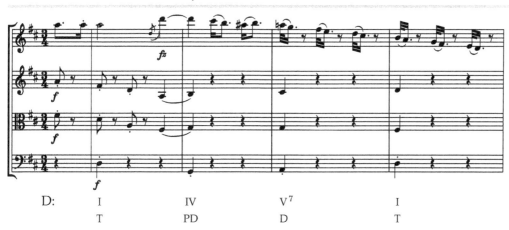

Although the phrase model can occupy any number of measures, four measures (or some multiple of four) is common, as seen in Example 6.11. Here, a balanced motion is clearly felt as the harmonic rhythm shifts once every measure. There is much room for variation in this model, however, and while the order of presentation of harmonic functions (T–PD–D–T) remains the same, their relative durations may vary considerably. For instance, the opening tonic often occupies at least as much time as the pre-dominant and dominant combined: Example 6.12A extends the tonic for three and one-third measures, with the PD and D occupying barely more than one beat. It is also common for the dominant to occupy two or even three times more time than the pre-dominant (Example 6.12B).

EXAMPLE 6.12

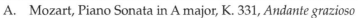

A.   Mozart, Piano Sonata in A major, K. 331, *Andante grazioso*

B.   Schubert, Violin Sonata No. 2 in G minor, D. 408, *Andante*

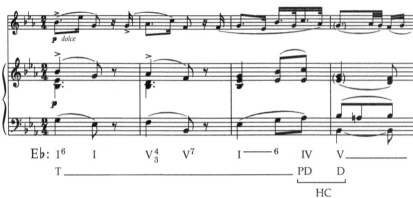

Four basic four-measure phrase models are given in Example 6.13. Models 3 and 4, which close with half cadences, are as grammatically complete as the first two models, yet their harmony implies an eventual resolution of the tension of the dominant.

EXAMPLE 6.13

					cadence
Four-measure phrase models					
measures:	1 _____	2 _____	3 _____	4 _____	*cadence*
model 1:	T _____	PD _____	D_____	T _____	authentic
model 2:	T _____	_____	PD___ D___	T _____	authentic
model 3:	T_____		PD___	D_____	half
model 4:	T_____			PD___ D___	half

Accented and Chromatic Dissonances

Tones of figuration enhance music's motion, grace, and drama. Their presence on the immediate surface of the music means that they are the first events to which the listener's attention is drawn. We group tones of figuration into two categories, based on their rhythmic placement. The first category includes **unaccented tones of figuration**, which include the chordal leap (CL), the passing tone (P), and the neighbor tone (N). We further categorize the unaccented tones of figuration into those that are consonant (chordal leaps) and those that are dissonant (most passing tones and neighbor tones). Consonant tones of figuration may appear without preparation or resolution; however, dissonant tones of figuration must be carefully controlled, nearly always occurring between consonances and moving by step.

Accented tones of figuration, by contrast, occur in metrically stressed contexts. Accented dissonances occur in many forms, but the most important are the accented passing tone (P̃), accented neighbor tone (Ñ), suspension (S), pedal (PED), and appoggiatura (APP). Since tones of figuration often fill the space between chordal members, by extension, **chromatic tones of figuration** fill the smaller intervallic space that occurs between stepwise motions. We will also explore such unaccented and accented chromatic figures.

Accented Passing Tone (P̃)

Just like a passing tone, an **accented passing tone** (P̃) fills in a melodic third; however, the accented passing tone occurs on, rather than between, beats. Example 6.14A shows an unelaborated SATB progression; Example 6.14B elaborates the progression with unaccented Ps. Note that consonance is aligned with metrical stress and dissonance is reserved for the metrically weak offbeat. Example 6.14C demonstrates accented passing tones; dissonance is highlighted since it occurs on the beat while the consonance now occurs on the offbeat. Accented passing tones impart a new level of tension since consonance and metrical accents do not align. Accented passing tones most often occur in descending lines, and they usually are part of either a 7–6 or 4–3 contrapuntal motion against the bass voice.

EXAMPLE 6.14

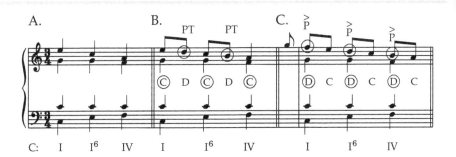

Chromatic Passing Tone

Chromatic passing tones fill the space between two diatonic pitches. Most often, the diatonic pitches are separated by a major second, creating a series of half-step motions. Like diatonic passing tones, chromatic passing tones occur in both unaccented and accented contexts (Example 6.15).

EXAMPLE 6.15   Mozart, Piano Sonata in B♭ major, K. 570

Accented Neighbor Tone (Ñ)

While not nearly as common as accented passing tones, the **accented neighbor tone** occurs with some frequency, especially in nineteenth-century music. Example 6.16A presents a neighboring expansion of the tonic without melodic embellishment. Example 6.16B contains unaccented neighbor and passing tones. In Example 6.16C, the neighbor and passing tones are accented, since they sound on the beat.

EXAMPLE 6.16

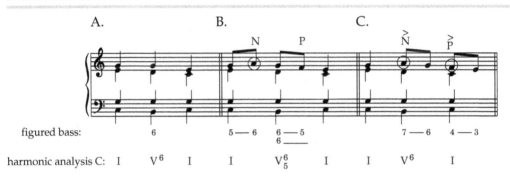

Chromatic Neighbor Tone

The chromatic neighbor is highly dissonant yet very beautiful. Example 6.17 recasts the diatonic neighbors from Example 6.16 into chromatic neighbors.

EXAMPLE 6.17

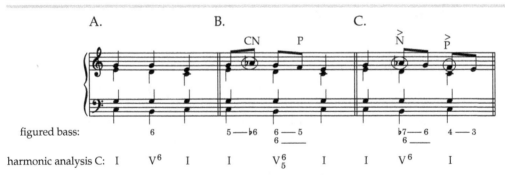

Appoggiatura (APP)

The appoggiatura is a striking type of figuration. Different than passing and complete neighboring tones (which are flanked by chord tones), appoggiaturas enter by leap, are dissonant, and are accented. They are related to other tones of figuration only in that they resolve by step to a chord tone (and usually in the direction opposite of their leap, in order to balance the melodic contour). Thus, the appoggiatura behaves very much like accented incomplete neighbor tones. We will tend to refer to accented incomplete neighbors as appoggiaturas. Example 6.18 illustrates appoggiaturas and their labeling.

EXAMPLE 6.18

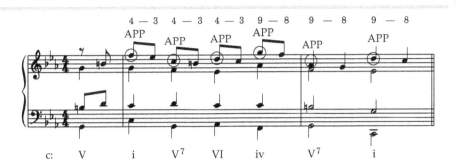

Suspension (S)

Example 6.19A presents a two-voice example, which we'll consider to be the outer voices of the implied progression whose roman numeral analysis is given. Example 6.19B presents a modified version of Example 6.19A; in four instances the soprano voice is sustained, where it intrudes into the following implied chord change. The accented dissonant pitch creates a great deal of musical tension, which is then discharged, or resolved as it falls by step to a chord tone. We refer to such expressive nonchord tones as **suspensions**, and they are the most important type of accented tone of figuration.

EXAMPLE 6.19

The contrapuntal setting and metric placement of suspensions is prescribed and should not be altered. Suspensions are composed of two pitches: The first pitch begins as a weak-beat *preparation* (P) and becomes a strong-beat *suspension* (S). The second pitch is a weak-beat *resolution* (R), one step lower than the first pitch. Each suspension in Example 6.19B illustrates the two-note figure and the three stages.

Labeling Suspensions

We use figured bass numbers to label the melodic motion of the suspension and resolution stages of the suspension figures: The four common suspensions are

7–6, 9–8, 4–3, and the bass suspension 2–3. The figured bass indications for the suspensions in Example 6.20 are 7–6, 9–8, 2–3, 7–6, and 4–3, respectively. Note that in bass suspensions, the numbers increase in size (2–3, sometimes accompanied by the figure 5–6) because the upper voices remain stationary while the bass, in its descending resolution, naturally increases the size of the interval.

EXAMPLE 6.20

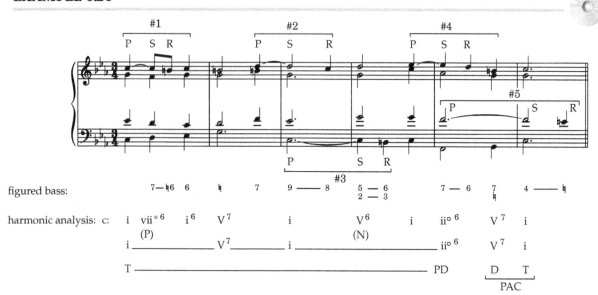

We show the melodic motion of the suspension by using the dash, so as not to confuse suspensions with inversions of chords. For example, a "7" appearing by itself indicates a root-position seventh chord; thus the "7" is a chord member. However, a "7–6" indicates a 7–6 suspension (such as in m. 1 of Example 6.20) in which the seventh above the bass displaces the sixth above the bass of a first-inversion chord.

Writing Suspensions

The only available upper-voice suspensions are the 9–8, 7–6, and 4–3. The only bass suspension is the 2–3. The following guidelines will help to write suspensions.

1. Suspension figures logically work best with chords whose intervals contain the interval of resolution. For example, 7–6 suspensions work well with first-inversion chords, given that chords with a sixth above the bass are most often first-inversion chords (e.g., vii°6, V6, and I6). Similarly, 4–3 and 9–8 suspensions work best with root-position chords. The bass suspension (2–3) works best with a first-inversion chord (especially in the progression I–V6).

2. Suspensions may occur in any voice at any time as long as the voice is moving down by step to the next chord tone. For example, in the chord

progression in Example 6.21A, the three upper voices in the first chord all lie a second above the corresponding voice in the second chord, which means that the resolution is already set up. Now we consider the second chord in order to find an appropriate voice to suspend. Given that the second chord is a first-inversion sonority, the 7–6 suspension would work best (see Example 6.21B).

EXAMPLE 6.21

3. Make sure that the resolution pitch is not doubled in any other voice, for if it were, it would be sounding against the dissonant suspension and thus would anticipate the suspension's tone of resolution and ruin its intended effect. The one exception to this rule is the 9–8 suspension, which falls to the octave, because the dissonance is far enough away from the sounding note of resolution. Finally, the duration of the dissonant suspended note should be at least as long as or longer than the preparation and the resolution.

Anticipation (ANT)

The **anticipation** is an unaccented nonchord tone. But given that it may be considered the "mirror opposite" of the suspension, it is included at this point. The anticipation appears before the chord to which it belongs actually sounds, usually creating a dissonance with the already-sounding chord. Because it occurs on a weak beat and is premature, it can be viewed as a tone of figuration that functions in the exact opposite manner of the suspension, which is an accented tone that delays a chord tone's resolution. It is most effective at cadences, when the final chord is strongly expected. Example 6.22 presents an example of a double anticipation.

EXAMPLE 6.22   Corelli, Violin Sonata No. 11 in D minor, op. 1, *Adagio*

Pedal (PED)

A sustained pitch or harmony that sits motionless during multiple harmonic changes is known as a **pedal** or **pedal point**. Derived from the organ's ability to sustain a pitch indefinitely, the pedal tone usually occurs in the bass and almost always is a tonic or dominant scale degree, which slows down the harmonic motion and firmly grounds the music on one static harmony. Pedals often occur in cadential situations (see Example 6.23), in which harmonic successions can unfold over a single held note. As the two levels of analysis in the Bach excerpt show, such harmonic successions are subordinate to the pedal.

EXAMPLE 6.23   Bach, Fugue in C minor, *The Well-Tempered Clavier*, Book 1, BWV 847

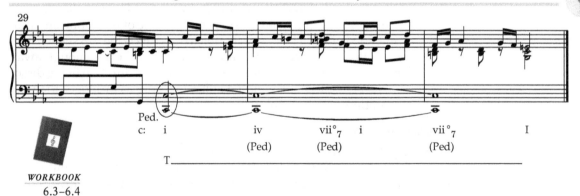

WORKBOOK
6.3–6.4

Analytical Extension: Revisiting the Subdominant

Contrapuntal Expansion with IV

The IV chord functions in two very different ways: In its root position or first inversion, IV occurs as a strong pre-dominant chord. In its first inversion, IV⁶ regularly occurs as a weak contrapuntal chord that expands either I or V. We now see how IV in root position also may be used to expand tonic. The root-position IV chord in Example 6.24 harmonizes the neighbor tones E♭ and G; thus, even though IV appears in root position, we hear tonic controlling the example. In the second-level analysis, we simply label IV as an **embellishing chord (EC)**, since it does fit into the other contrapuntal expansions we have seen (e.g., neighboring and passing chords).

EXAMPLE 6.24

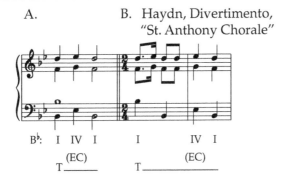

A.

B. Haydn, Divertimento, "St. Anthony Chorale"

Plagal Cadence

In addition to being an embellishing chord, IV sometimes has an important cadential function. In Example 6.25, IV participates in closing the hymn. The two-chord motion IV–I is called a **plagal cadence**; because it often appears in church music, it is also known as the *amen cadence*. Note how the plagal cadence immediately follows an authentic cadence, almost as if it were tacked on to the end of the piece. The plagal cadence is often a cadence in name only, since a strong authentic cadence usually precedes it.

EXAMPLE 6.25   Dykes, "Holy, Holy, Holy"

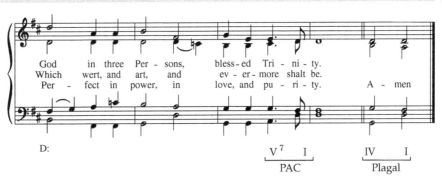

God	in three Per - sons,	bless - ed Tri - ni - ty.
Which	wert, and art, and	ev - er - more shalt be.
Per - fect in power, in	love, and pu - ri - ty.	A - men

CHAPTER 7

Six-Four Chords, Nondominant Seventh Chords, and Refining the Phrase Model

Six-Four Chords

We now explore six-four ($^6_4$) chords, a topic postponed until now because such chords occur much less often than root-position and first-inversion chords and in very specific contexts. Their paucity is explained by the dissonant interval of a fourth that lies above the bass; root-position and first-inversion triads contain only consonant intervals (octaves, thirds, fifths, and sixths). Although their intervals stack into second-inversion triads, six-four chords rarely function as do their root-position and first-inversion cousins. In fact, we will see that six-four chords are often only apparent harmonies resulting from the coincidence of passing and neighboring tones in two or more voices. Thus, six-four chords require careful contextual analysis and writing. Six-four chords occur in either unaccented or accented contexts; their discussion here will follow that order.

Unaccented Six-Four Chords

Unaccented six-four chords usually occur on weak beats within a measure or on weakly accented measures in four-measure groups. Listen to the short excerpt in Example 7.1, noting the six-four chord's function.

EXAMPLE 7.1   Gruber, "Stille Nacht"

These six-four chords arise through a neighbor figure exhibited simultaneously in two voices. Given the sustained bass over which the neighbor figure appears, we assign the name **pedal six-four chord** (Ped$^6_4$). We label pedal six-four chords as Ped$^6_4$ or with figured bass: $^{5-6-5}_{3-4-3}$.

EXAMPLE 7.2   Schubert, Minuet in D major, D. 41

Pedal six-four chords can prolong not only tonic, but also other harmonies, such as the dominant, as shown in Example 7.2. It is crucial to recognize that the apparent tonic harmony (I$^6_4$) in m. 3 arises as the byproduct of two upper neighbors that move in parallel motion.

So far, we have seen how pedal six-four chords can arise out of upper-voice neighboring motion. Pedal six-four chords can also arise from passing motion. The expansion of V^7 is often accomplished through a Ped$^6_4$, with the upper voices ascending or descending a third ($\hat{7}$–$\hat{2}$ and $\hat{2}$–$\hat{4}$), as shown in Example 7.3.

EXAMPLE 7.3   Mozart, Symphony in A major, K. 385, *Menuetto*

We learned that pedal six-four chords derive their name from a *sustained* bass and upper-voice motion. The **passing six-four chord** (P$^6_4$) derives its name from the bass *passing* motion that fills the interval of a third (Example 7.4).

EXAMPLE 7.4 Beethoven, Piano Sonata in C major, op. 2, no. 3, *Trio*

Measures 1–5 of Example 7.4 act as a tonic prolongation from i to i⁶ featuring an arch-shaped bass line (A–B–C–D–C). Within the arch, the passing six-four chord occurs in m. 2, where it connects i to i⁶ by the stepwise bass line A–B–C. Notice that this passing six-four chord functions identically to the passing vii°⁶ chord, which also fills the space between tonic and its first inversion. On the second level of analysis, we label the chord a P to reflect its passing function. Here, it is important to consider how this P$_4^6$ is unaccented. Unlike that of Example 7.2, which occurs on a weak *beat*, this chord occurs on a weak *measure* within a quickly moving four-bar group. Similarly, in very slow tempos, such chords may occur on weak *parts of beats*.

Passing six-four chords may be used to connect any root-position triad with its six-three inversion. Example 7.5 demonstrates a P$_4^6$ to extend both the tonic (d minor) and the subdominant (g minor). The Allegro opens with a series of restruck suspensions; once we remove them from the texture in Example 7.5B, we easily see the implied P$_4^6$ chords connecting i–i⁶ and iv–iv⁶.

EXAMPLE 7.5

A.   Beethoven, Piano Sonata in D minor, op. 31, no. 2

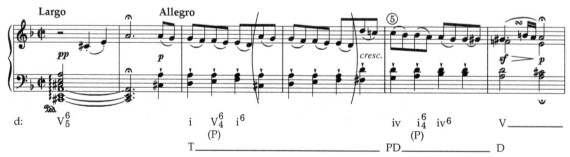

B.   Reduction

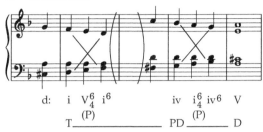

d: i   V⁶₄   i⁶   iv   i⁶₄ iv⁶   V
            (P)   (P)
      T_____   PD_____   D

Emerging from figurated textures and accompanimental patterns, the **arpeggiating six-four chord** (Arp⁶₄) is common in marches, waltzes, and folk tunes and is sometimes referred to as a *waltz six-four chord.* The arpeggiating six-four chords in Example 7.6 are consonant and merely part of arpeggiations of the harmony that controls each measure.

EXAMPLE 7.6   Schubert, Ländler, D. 336, op. 67, no. 16

G: I   IV   I   V⁷   I   IV   I   V⁷   I

In pieces such as waltzes, where one could easily imagine the first (low) bass note sustained through the entire measure, the (higher) apparent six-four chords are heard as completing a root-position harmony. Thus, when analyzing arpeggiating six-fours, you need not label the actual chords; it is sufficient to draw a dash after the initial roman numeral. This analytical method can be seen at work in Example 7.7, where the "filler" six-four chords on beats 2 and 3 of mm. 1 and 3 are effectively ignored.

EXAMPLE 7.7   Schubert, Waltz in A minor, *12 Grazer Walzer*, D. 924, no. 9

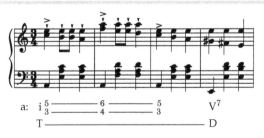

a: i⁵₃ ——————— 6 ——————— 5   V⁷
                 4   3
     T ———————————————————————   D

Example 7.7 contains not only the arpeggiated six-four (that occurs on the weak beats of mm. 1 and 3) but also a pedal six-four (m. 2), which expands the flanking tonic harmonies in mm. 1 and 3 through neighboring motion (see the left hand).

Accented Six-Four Chords

We will explore only one type of accented six-four chord, which is usually found at cadences. For that reason, we call it the **cadential six-four chord.** The cadential six-four chord was an outgrowth of two metrically stressed dissonant events: the suspension and the accented passing tone (Example 7.8).

- In Example 7.8A, the progression is I–I⁶–V–I, with each harmonic function occupying one measure. If we ornament the V chord with a soprano 4–3 suspension (Example 7.8B), we can link the tenor to the soprano by creating a $^{6-5}_{4-3}$ double suspension (Example 7.8C).
- In Example 7.8D, there are melodic gaps in the soprano ($\hat{2}$–$\hat{7}$) and tenor ($\hat{4}$–$\hat{2}$). If we fill these gaps with accented passing tones, we create a six-four chord on the downbeat of the second measure.
- There are different ways to label the cadential six-four chord, such as C$^6_4$ and I$^6_4$. Since the C$^6_4$ chord acts as part of the dominant function, the label that will be used for the remainder of the book is drawn from Example 7.8. In this manner, the cadential six-four chord is labeled as V, with the figure $^{6-5}_{4-3}$, and dominant appears in the second-level analysis.

EXAMPLE 7.8

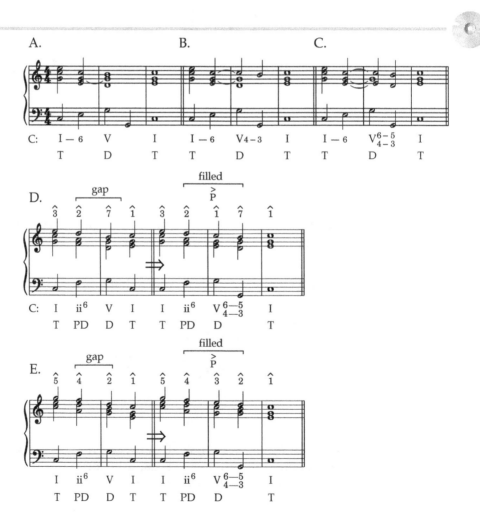

Cadential six-four chords can lead to V^7 chords, as in Example 7.9. The seventh typically appears as part of a melodic 8–7 motion above the bass; this motion is circled in the example.

EXAMPLE 7.9 Mozart, Concerto in E♭ for Horn and Orchestra, K. 447, *Larghetto*

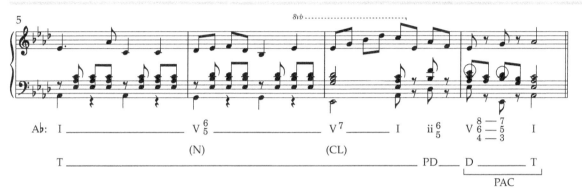

Writing Six-Four Chords

To summarize, the cadential six-four chord is a root-position dominant harmony whose chordal fifth and third are temporarily postponed by a dissonant fourth and sixth. These upper-voice, nonharmonic tones are both prepared (as a suspension or accented passing tone) and resolved (usually by downward step).

Based on the models of unaccented and accented six-four chords, we can now summarize their functions and formulate writing rules.

- *Unaccented six-four chords* are embellishing chords that prolong another harmony, usually the tonic. These include the pedal (Example 7.10A), passing (Example 7.10B), and arpeggiating six-four chords (Example 7.10C).
- The one type of *accented six-four chord* we have learned is the cadential six-four chord (Example 7.10D), which occurs over the root-position dominant and is formed by two nonchord tones above the root of V: the sixth and the fourth postpone the chordal fifth and third. The cadential six-four chord:
  - Occurs on a metrically accented beat (beat 1 in duple meter, beat 1 or 2 in triple meter, beat 1 or 3 in quadruple meter).
  - Does not usually follow another dominant-function chord (V or vii°), since such a chord weakens the impact of the cadential six-four chord's arrival.
  - May lead to V or V^7 at cadences.
  - May lead to V_2^4 within a phrase. In this case, the cadence is circumvented, creating an **evaded cadence** (Example 7.10E).
- Approach and leave six-four chords by step or common tone when possible, and double the bass note in all six-four chords.

EXAMPLE 7.10

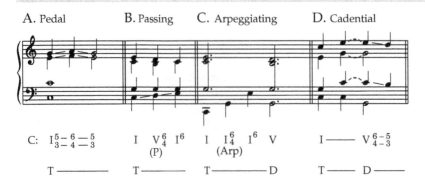

Summary of Contrapuntal Expansions

We have now completed our study of contrapuntal expansions. Although we have focused exclusively on ways that such embellishments expand the tonic and the dominant, we will see in later chapters that the principles can be applied to all of the other harmonies. The summary in Example 7.11 shows neighboring, passing and leaping bass motions, the possible contrapuntal chords used to harmonize them, and common soprano pitches used in setting these contrapuntal expansions. Progressions occur in major and minor, except those that involve vii°7, which (for now) occur only in minor.

EXAMPLE 7.11

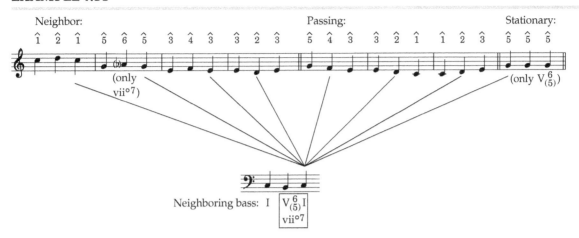

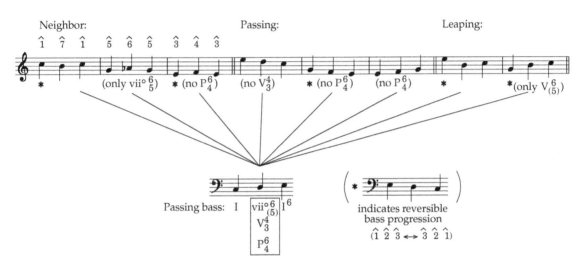

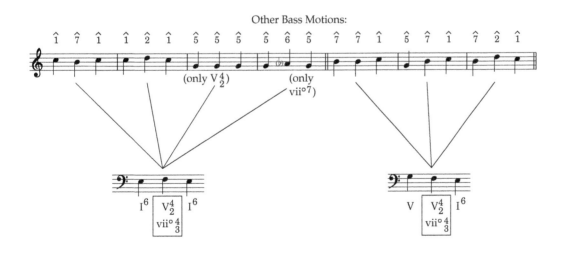

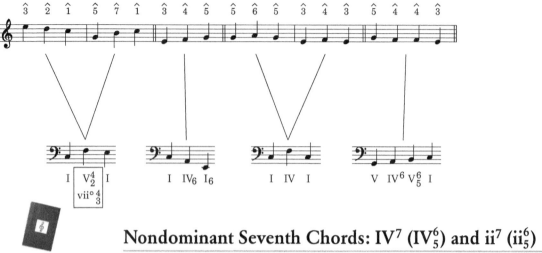

Nondominant Seventh Chords: IV^7 (IV$^6_5$) and ii^7 (ii$^6_5$)

Just as a diatonic seventh can be added to the V triad to create V^7 in both major and minor keys, so too can a seventh be added to the pre-dominant ii and IV triads. Example 7.12A shows how ii becomes ii^7 and IV becomes IV^7 in major. Example 7.12B shows how ii° becomes ii^{ø7} and iv becomes iv^7 in minor. Example 7.12C shows the first measures of one of Chopin's nocturnes, in which he presents the cadential progression ii^7–V^7–I. Notice the tension created by the abrupt and unprepared entrance of the ii^7 chord. Further, the following V^7 chord sounds more like a *resolution* that discharges the tension of the ii^7 than a *dissonance*.

EXAMPLE 7.12

These pre-dominant seventh chords fall into a broad category of **nondominant seventh chords.** The chords in this category do not have a dominant (major-minor) or leading-tone (diminished-diminished) seventh chord quality. Nondominant seventh chords, which are widely used throughout the common-practice period, provide color and contrast and are generally easy to implement.

Part Writing Nondominant Seventh Chords

1. You must *prepare* the seventh of the chord. The note that becomes the seventh of the chord must be approached (in the same voice) by the same note (or "common tone") or by the note one step higher.
2. You must *resolve* the seventh of the chord. As with the V^7 chord, the seventh of the nondominant seventh chord must step down in the next harmony.
3. Chords in inversion should be complete. Root-position seventh chords can omit the fifth (and double the root) in order to avoid parallels.

In general, pre-dominant seventh chords occur in all forms and inversions; however, ii^6_5 is the most common type and inversion of nondominant seventh chord. Example 7.13 illustrates ii^6_5 and the root-position ii^7 chord. Note how the seventh of the chord is prepared (marked with a P) and resolved (R); also note that the ii^6_5 chord is complete but that the ii^7 chord omits the fifth and doubles the root to avoid parallels with the preceding tonic chord.

EXAMPLE 7.13

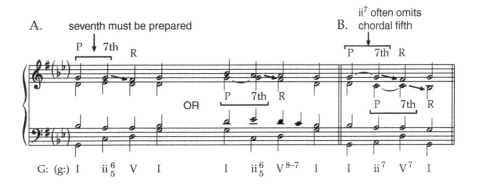

IV^7, not as common as ii^7, is a colorful sonority that may occur in root position. One must pay particular attention to the part writing from IV^7 to V; study Example 7.14A, where parallel fifths occur between IV^7 and V. To avoid this part-writing error, IV^7 is often followed by V^7 (Example 7.14B) or the cadential six-four chord (Example 7.14C). Doubling the root of IV^7 ($\hat{4}$) and omitting the fifth not only helps to avoid parallels, but also prepares the seventh of V. Finally, the IV$^6_5$ chord, shown in Example 7.14D, typically resolves to a V$^6_5$ chord.

EXAMPLE 7.14

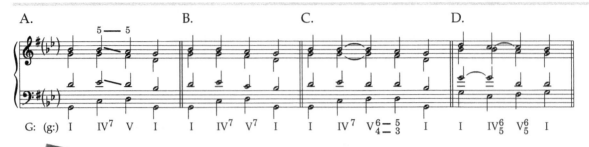

WORKBOOK
7.2–7.3

Embedding the Phrase Model

We have seen how musical events can coexist at various hierarchical levels. The tonal progression of the phrase model is no different. Composers often incorporate a mini "T–PD–D–T" model *within* a larger phrase model. The mini "T–PD–D–T" model begins and ends on tonic, thereby prolonging the tonic at the beginning of the phrase:

"mini" model:	T	PD	D	T		
phrase model:	T	——————		PD	D	T

In order to accomplish this, composers weaken the first PD–D–T progression through the use of inversions so that a listener will not confuse it with the actual cadence of the phrase model. This progression can be seen in Example 7.15, where the tonic expansion includes a mini, noncadential "T–PD–D–T" model.

EXAMPLE 7.15

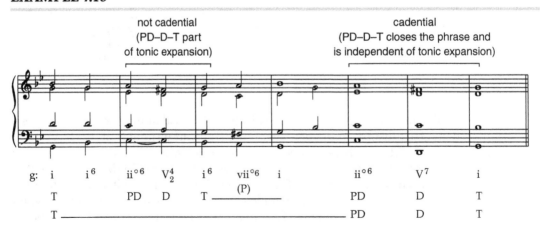

In Example 7.16A, we see a standard four-measure phrase model closing with a half cadence. Tonic and dominant alternate in mm. 1–2, until i⁶ appears at the end of m. 2 and signals the upcoming pre-dominant, which enters in m. 3 and moves to the embellished HC. This example is a recomposition of what Franz Josef Haydn *could* have done. However, Haydn extends his phrase to six full measures by evading the HC in m. 4 (Example 7.16B). He does so by sustaining the bass pitch (C), which becomes the dissonant seventh in a V$^4_2$ chord. The chord resolves weakly to i⁶, thus extending the tonic for two more measures before cadencing on V.

EXAMPLE 7.16

A.   Haydn, Piano Sonata in G minor, Hob. XVI/44, recomposed

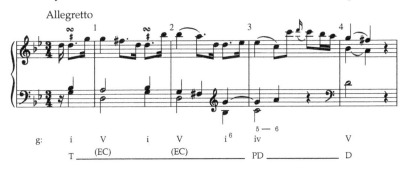

B.   Haydn, Piano Sonata in G minor, Hob. XVI/44, original

Such mini "T–PD–D–T" models, which we call **embedded phrase models (EPMs),** may occur anywhere within the tonic prolongation portion of the phrase. Keep the following in mind when analyzing a phrase with multiple T–PD–D–T progressions: A second-level analysis has just one overall T–PD–D–T progression for a phrase. Other occurrences of T–PD–D–T earlier in the phrase are not cadential—they are EPMs and expand tonic. Example 7.17 shows the following four important settings of EPMs:

- Example 7.17A places the dominant in a weak inversion and evades a cadence.
- Example 7.17B shows an EPM that affords great stability and balance between outer voices. The example has a neighboring motion in both of

the outer voices. It also includes a common and important use of the ii$_2^4$ chord, which prepares and resolves the seventh in the bass.

- In Example 7.17C, the bass leap of a third and stepwise return to $\hat{1}$ contrasts with the upper-voice neighboring motion.
- Example 7.17D shows the progression from 7.17C in minor. Note that $\hat{6}$ and $\hat{7}$ are raised to avoid awkward melodic intervals in the bass.

EXAMPLE 7.17

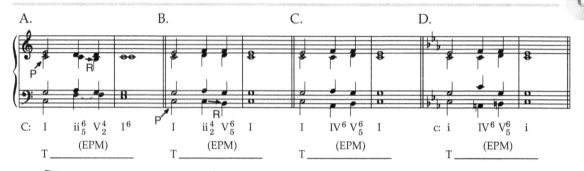

C:	I	ii$_5^6$ V$_2^4$	I^6		
	T _____	(EPM)			

B. P	I	ii$_2^4$ V$_5^6$	I	
	T _____	(EPM)		

C.	I	IV^6 V$_5^6$	I
	T _____	(EPM)	

D.	c: i	IV^6 V$_5^6$	i
	T _____	(EPM)	

Analytical Extension: Expanding the Pre-Dominant

We have seen how the pre-dominant may be expanded using such devices as inversion (ii–ii^6) and the 5–6 technique (IV–ii^6). We now observe several additional techniques that expand the pre-dominant. Pre-dominants may also be expanded through passing and neighboring chords, in the same ways we have expanded the tonic and dominant. We now look at three ways the pre-dominant can be expanded.

1. I^6 is an ideal choice for a passing chord between ii and ii^6 (Example 7.18). Note the voice exchange in the example.

EXAMPLE 7.18

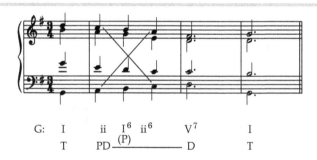

G:	I	ii	I^6 ii^6	V^7	I
	T	PD	(P)	D	T

2. A passing I$_4^6$ chord helps to expand the pre-dominant IV (Example 7.19). The P$_4^6$ chord usually occurs on a weak beat and is in the middle of a voice exchange.

EXAMPLE 7.19   Bach, "Gerne will ich mich bequemen," *St. Matthew Passion,* BWV 244

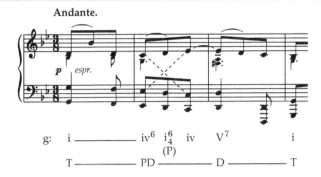

3. A passing I_4^6 chord can expand the pre-dominant by moving from IV_5^6 to ii_5^6 (Example 7.20). *Note that IV–ii motion is common but that ii–IV motion is rare.*

EXAMPLE 7.20

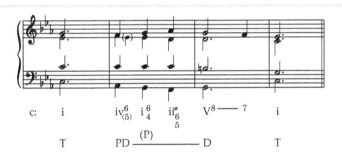

CHAPTER 8

The Submediant and Mediant Harmonies

We now explore the last of the diatonic harmonies: the submediant and the mediant. These chords always provide dramatic color contrast to the prevailing key and play important roles supporting the tonic, pre-dominant, and dominant pillars of the phrase model.

The Submediant (vi in Major, VI in Minor)

In a major key, the submediant harmony is a minor triad (vi). Because IV, V, and I are all major triads in a major key, the introduction of a minor sonority can provide a welcome relief from the prevailing harmonic color. In a minor key, the submediant harmony is a major triad (VI), so again it offers contrast to the minor and diminished harmonies i, iv, and ii°. The harmonic contexts in which the submediant typically occurs are inextricably tied to the three basic **root motions** of tonal music:

- The *descending fifth*, previously seen in the authentic cadence, V–I
- The *ascending second*, which we have seen in the progression IV–V
- The *descending third*

The Submediant as Bridge in the Descending-Thirds Progression

Our discussion of the submediant's first function arises out of the root motion by descending thirds. Example 8.1A demonstrates a progression that characterizes much of the rock and roll music of the 1950s and early 1960s. Take a moment to enjoy the voice leading of that style, which provides for a heavy dose of parallel perfect intervals. Example 8.1B illustrates the same progression but places it in the minor mode and uses common-practice voice leading to connect the chords. In these examples, the submediant is both attained and departed from by means of a descending third: I–vi and vi–IV. Taken together, the three roots $\hat{1}$–$\hat{6}$–$\hat{4}$ arpeggiate a triad of sorts. This progression is therefore often called a descending **harmonic arpeggiation**. The submediant in descending harmonic arpeggiations provides a way station, or bridge, connecting tonic to the pre-dominant. The submediant, therefore, has two seemingly contradictory functions: It is an extension of the tonic (with which it has two common tones), and it acts as a pre-pre-dominant chord (it prepares the PD). Although the submediant exhibits both qualities, we will tend to analyze vi as part of the tonic function in the second level; however, an arrowhead is added to show the bridging function of vi.

EXAMPLE 8.1

A.

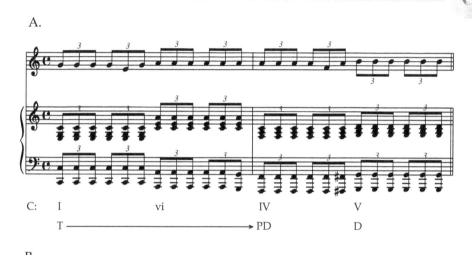

B.

The Submediant in the Descending Circle-of-Fifths Progression

Another function of the submediant arises from its participation in descending-fifths progressions. The vi chord appears twice in Example 8.2. First, it is part of an EPM that prolongs the tonic; then it prepares the PD at the phrase's structural cadence. Both times, vi is part of a descending-fifths progression.

EXAMPLE 8.2   Beethoven, Violin Sonata No. 5 in F major ("Spring"), op. 24

In Example 8.3, the vi–ii[6] progression blends the strong descending-fifths motion with a new means of obtaining a **melodic bass arpeggiation**: $\hat{1}$–$\hat{6}$–$\hat{4}$.

EXAMPLE 8.3   Schubert, "Frühlingstraum," *Winterreise*, D. 911, no. 11

The Submediant as Tonic Substitute in the Ascending-Seconds Progression

So far we have seen vi appear as a bridging harmony within a descending-thirds progression and as a harmony that initiates a descending-fifths progression. A third functional possibility is for vi to substitute for the tonic chord in the cadential progression V–I; the resulting progression is a root motion by ascending second (V–vi). This is shown in Example 8.4, where V moves to vi and the bass moves from $\hat{5}$ to $\hat{6}$. Haydn thwarts the arrival of the tonic by moving to vi; this is intensified by the fermata as well as by the florid ascent in the first violin to a very high register. In general, the progression V–vi is called a **deceptive motion** (also called *evaded cadence*), since the listener expects one outcome (V–I) but hears another (V–vi).

EXAMPLE 8.4   Haydn, String Quartet in D minor ("Quinten"), op. 76, no. 2, Hob. III/76, *Andante o più tosto allegretto*

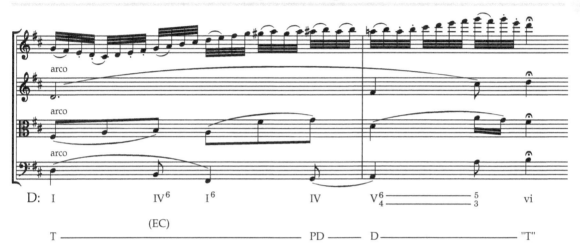

At the end of Example 8.4, we are suspended on vi and craving the tonic. In general, after a deceptive motion, the phrase model rewinds back to the pre-dominant and sometimes even the tonic, which is followed by an authentic cadence. In Example 8.5, the deceptive motion in m. 4 is followed by a return to pre-dominant harmonies, which leads to an imperfect authentic cadence (IAC) in m. 7.

EXAMPLE 8.5   Mozart, Clarinet Quintet in A major, K. 581, I

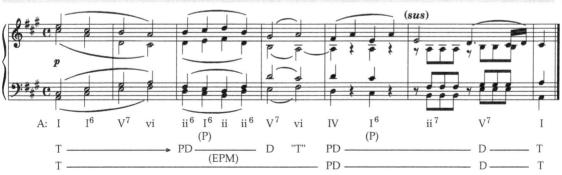

The Submediant as the Pre-Dominant

Occasionally, vi immediately precedes the dominant and, therefore, functions as the pre-dominant chord. Listen to Example 8.6; this famous opening features vi as a pre-dominant. As such, it allows for the motive of a descending second ($\hat{6}$–$\hat{5}$) to occur in the bass. Given the strong outer-voice counterpoint (with the contrary-motion intervals: 10–5–10) that undergirds the progression, composers often use this very progression in their works.

EXAMPLE 8.6 Mahler, Symphony No. 2 in C minor ("Resurrection"), "Urlicht"

Voice Leading for the Submediant

Voice leading for the submediant is simple in descending-thirds and descending-fifths progressions: Keep all of the common tones; any voice that moves should move up by step. Use the following guidelines for ascending-seconds progressions:

- To enhance the deceptive effect of the progression V–vi, use $\hat{2}$–$\hat{1}$ or $\hat{7}$–$\hat{1}$ in the soprano.
- The voice leading varies slightly for major and minor keys:
  - In major, if the soprano falls from $\hat{2}$ to $\hat{1}$, the remaining upper voices may all descend (Example 8.7A). Alternatively, the leading tone $\hat{7}$ can ascend to $\hat{1}$, in which case there will be a doubled third in the vi chord (Example 8.7B).
  - In minor, the leading tone $\hat{7}$ may only ascend, since falling to $\hat{6}$ creates an augmented second. Thus, all upper voices move downward except for the leading tone $\hat{7}$, which must resolve upward to $\hat{1}$ regardless of voicing (Example 8.7C). This will always result in a doubled third in the VI chord.

EXAMPLE 8.7

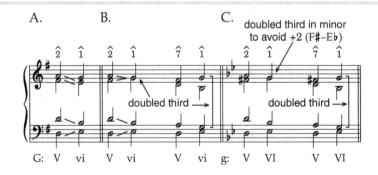

The Step Descent in the Bass

The most prevalent harmonic motion in phrases is from the tonic to the dominant. Previously, we have seen a way to embellish I–V motion by means of stepwise *ascent* in the bass (Example 6.7). It is now also possible to move from the tonic to the dominant by *descending* steps in the bass. There are numerous paths of descent, ranging from diatonic (1̂–7̂–6̂–5̂) to descents that are chromatic (with multiple expressive chromatic passing tones), to descents that even overshoot 5̂ and then return to the dominant. Some well-known examples include "Dido's Lament" from Purcell's *Dido and Aeneas* and the "Crucifixus" from Bach's *Mass in B minor*. Example 8.8 illustrates a characteristic stepwise descent.

EXAMPLE 8.8   Schütz, "Nacket bin ich von Mutterliebe kommen," *Musicalischen Exequien*, op. 7, SWV 279

Note that an especially strong gravitational pull downward to V is created by the descending melodic minor scale: This feel and the expressive half step ♭6–5 show why such descents occur more often in the minor mode than in the major. Note that in minor, v⁶ is used to precede minor iv⁶ since it avoids the augmented second between ↑7̂ and ↓6̂. First-inversion minor v and root-position v do not function as dominants; rather, they function as passing chords or voice-leading chords.

We call step-descent basses that fall directly from tonic to dominant (1̂–7̂–6̂–5̂) **direct step-descent basses.** When direct step-descent basses are cast in the minor mode they are known as **lament basses.** Lament basses often accompany melancholy texts, which are not historically confined to the seventeenth century; songs such as "Hit the Road, Jack," and "Erie Canal" are built on the same formula. The most common harmonic settings of these step-descent basses use the iv⁶ chord, which moves to V (Example 8.9A). Because of the lurking parallels, a root-position vi usually does not lead directly to V (Example 8.9B). It is first converted into a iv⁶ chord via a contrapuntal 5–6 motion in order to avoid parallels (Example 8.9C).

EXAMPLE 8.9

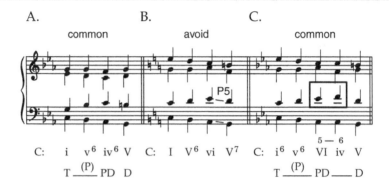

Step-descent basses may be extended by passing through the dominant to reach a pre-dominant on the bass note $\hat{4}$, which is harmonized by iv or ii⁶. Such **indirect step-descent basses** ($\hat{1}$–$\hat{7}$–$\hat{6}$–$\hat{5}$–$\hat{4}$ and then back to $\hat{5}$) create a descent by fifths. Composers often harmonize the first $\hat{5}$ with a passing $^6_3$ or $^6_4$ chord to avoid any feeling of arrival on dominant (Example 8.10)

EXAMPLE 8.10

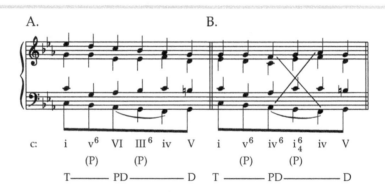

Mediant (iii in Major; III in Minor)

The mediant harmony occurs less frequently than any other diatonic harmony; this is not to say that the chord is unimportant, however. When we begin exploring the tonal plans of entire works, we will see that in minor-key pieces the structural significance of III is great—second only to that of tonic and dominant. The mediant harmony provides the same color contrast as the submediant: It is a minor triad in a major key and a major triad in a minor key. Within the phrase, the mediant usually appears in one of the following contexts: (1) ascending-bass arpeggiations and (2) descending-fifths progressions.

We have encountered the **ascending-bass arpeggiation** $\hat{1}$–$\hat{3}$–$\hat{5}$ under a I–I⁶–V progression, and we have seen how the contrapuntal motion of the bass can be filled with passing harmonies to create a stepwise ascent:

Bass:	$\hat{1}$	$\hat{2}$	$\hat{3}$	$\hat{4}$	$\hat{5}$
	I	vii^{o6}	I^6	IV	V
		or		or	
		V$^4_3$		ii^6	

Although $\hat{3}$ in the bass is most often harmonized by I^6, it can also be harmonized by a root-position mediant chord. In this way, iii substitutes for I^6 to create a tonic extension. Example 8.11 illustrates some common uses of the mediant within phrases. Just as we label vi's bridging function from T to PD with an arrow, so too will we use the arrow to show iii's bridging function leading from T to PD.

EXAMPLE 8.11

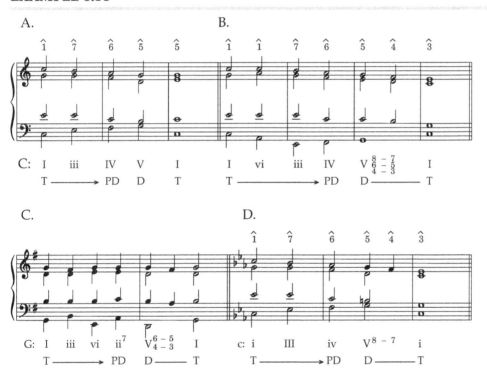

In Example 8.11A, the bass of the pre-dominant IV fills the space between $\hat{3}$ and $\hat{5}$. Note also how the soprano descends stepwise from $\hat{1}$ to $\hat{5}$, with $\hat{7}$ functioning as a downward passing tone rather than as a leading tone. Example 8.11B shows how vi can be inserted between I and iii, resulting in an effective descending arpeggiation. In many progressions, iii descends to vi, thus extending the descending-fifths progression back yet another notch (Example 8.11C). Example 8.11D recasts 8.11A in minor mode. Example 8.12 illustrates a prolongation of tonic: iii and IV harmonize passing tones in the soprano ($\hat{7}$–$\hat{6}$) and lead back to I.

EXAMPLE 8.12   Yarrow, "Puff the Magic Dragon"

A Special Case: Preparing the III Chord in Minor

The mediant appears in the minor mode more often than in the major mode.
Listen to Example 8.13. The second harmony that appears in all three examples is unfamiliar: a major triad built on ↓$\hat{7}$. Up to this point, we have seen
chords built from the leading tone (vii°⁶ and vii°⁷) and the subtonic ↓$\hat{7}$ (a passing v⁶ chord in the step-descent bass). In Example 8.13, the root-position "VII"
chord has a different function: It is the dominant chord of III. To reflect this
motion of the V–I sound of B♭–E♭, we label the B♭ harmony as "V of III" (or
"V/III"), indicating that B♭ is the dominant (V) chord that leads to E♭ (III). This
roman numeral symbol represents the sound of the triad built on ↓$\hat{7}$ far more
accurately than would the label VII, which fails to capture its dominant function at the immediate, local level.

EXAMPLE 8.13

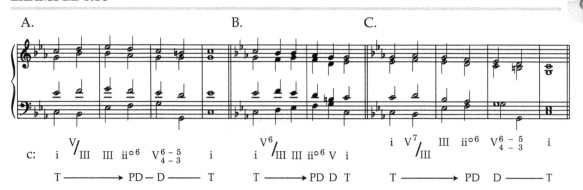

V/III often occurs in first inversion as V⁶/III (Example 8.13B). The use of
this inversion prominently places D—the temporary leading tone that leads to
E♭ (III)—in the bass, thus intensifying the motion to III. In Example 8.13C, a
seventh is added to create V⁷/III, which further intensifies motion to III (since
V⁷–I is more powerful than V–I). The use of chords such as V/III, which are
called **applied chords**, will be explored further in Chapter 11.

Voice Leading for the Mediant

Writing the mediant is easy as long as you remember these simple guidelines:

- Try to move the upper voices in contrary motion to the bass when approaching and leaving the mediant.
- Use the soprano line $\hat{1}$–$\hat{7}$–$\hat{6}$ when the mediant supports the passing tone $\hat{7}$.

General Summary of Harmonic Progression

The phrase model, composed of three ordered harmonic functions (T–PD–D–T) lies at the heart of tonal progressions. The tonic function usually occupies significantly more time and chords than the other two functions. Standing back and considering how harmonies function within a musical context—rather than haphazardly scattering roman numeral labels over a score—allows us to see deeper connections.

We will apply these global analytical ideas to compositions as well. However, we may find ourselves in a situation where we simply can't figure out which chord could come next. For example, after a basic tonic expansion using contrapuntal chords, we might wish to use other diatonic harmonies within the tonic expansion. In general, diatonic harmonies (such as dominants, submediants, supertonics, and mediants) tend to follow one another in one of the three root motions: descending fifth (D5), ascending (A2), and descending third (D3). These root motions may be combined in an infinite number of ways. For example, a series of falling thirds from the tonic, I–vi–IV, may be followed by two successive A2s (IV–V and the deceptive V–vi). From the submediant, a set of D5 motions might follow, which will return the progression to tonic (ii–V–I). The sum total of all this motion is a large goal-directed progression: I–vi–IV–V–vi–ii–V–I, which may be set in many ways, depending on the progression's meter and harmonic rhythm. Most musical settings of this progression would likely reflect the following second-level analysis:

WORKBOOK
8.1–8.4

$$\text{I–vi–IV–V–vi–ii}^7\text{–V}^7\text{–I}$$
$$\text{T}\text{———————— PD D T}$$

Analytical Extension: The Back-Relating Dominant

We know that a V chord may or may not function as a structural, cadential dominant. For example, in the preceding boxed progression, the structural dominant is most likely the second one, while the first dominant is part of an EPM that prolongs tonic and leads to the submediant chord. Another example of a nonstructural dominant occurs in the step-descent bass progression i–v⁶–iv⁶–V, where we observed that the minor v⁶ was far removed from its dominant function; it harmonized the passing tone lowered $\hat{7}$, connecting $\hat{1}$ and $\hat{6}$ in the bass. As always, contextual analysis is essential for understanding how harmony works as well as for interpreting which chords are structural and which are merely embellishing. Example 8.14 demonstrates an important way in which the dominant may appear in a nonstructural context.

EXAMPLE 8.14   Bach, Prelude in E♭ major, *The Well-Tempered Clavier*, Book 2, BWV 876

Heard as a single phrase, this progression presents us with an analytical dilemma: V does not progress to ii⁷. Such a backward motion from D to PD, called a **retrogression**, usually sounds awkward and weak; however, Bach's phrase doesn't sound weak at all. The V in m. 2 could be part of the structural dominant—this reading makes abstract sense—but the ii chord sounds as if it plays a harmonic role as a pre-dominant. To ignore the supertonic harmony is not a reasonable interpretation, since it clearly plays an important role in the excerpt. Given the prominence of ii, the harmonic importance of the first V now seems to wane. The melody begins on B♭, but in m. 2—where the problematic V appears—the melody leaps to E♭ and then descends to D. If we ignore the first dominant, the overall progression is I–ii⁷–V⁷–I, and each harmony supports the melodic descent B♭–A♭–G in the soprano (Example 8.15).

EXAMPLE 8.15

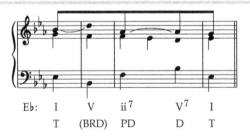

This analysis, which takes account of the phrasing and melodic continuity of the excerpt, reflects the perception of the music much better than the analysis that viewed the V in m. 2 as structural. The dominant chord in m. 2 prolongs the preceding tonic, but there is no connection between the dominant and the following ii chord. Dominants that prolong a previously sounding tonic without resolving to a following tonic are called **back-relating dominants (BRDs)**.

The concept of the back-relating dominant can be extended from a single phrase to multiple phrases, in which case we begin to account for more substantive events within a piece; and when we consider it to function at this deeper level, it carries possible performance implications. Example 8.16 illustrates.

EXAMPLE 8.16   Mozart, Piano Sonata in D major, K. 576, *Allegro*

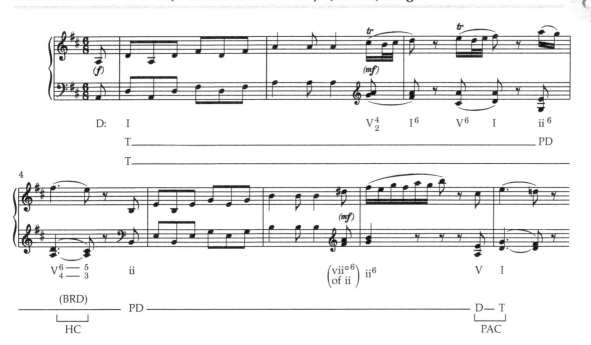

The first phrase (mm. 1–4) closes on a half cadence, strongly articulated by the powerful cadential six-four chord that helps to secure the dominant. The next phrase begins on the supertonic (ii). Because Mozart merely transposes the opening material of phrase 1 up a step (from D major to E minor), we can connect the *openings* of the two phrases rather than the *end* of the first phrase and the opening of the second phrase. (Recall that this is precisely the same tonal motion heard in Example 8.14, only now expanded to two phrases). Further, since Mozart extends the pre-dominant function, we see a single, large-scale tonal motion over two phrases: I (BRD)–ii–V⁷–I. Indeed, since the phrase with the HC is left harmonically open, the following phrase completes the incomplete tonal motion of the first phrase. The combination of the two phrases creates a single entity called a *period*, discussed in the next chapter.

CHAPTER 9

The Period, the Double Period, and the Sentence

We now learn how composers create larger formal structures by extending and combining phrases. We will also incorporate more fully in our analyses the psychological phenomena of expectation and fulfillment.

A phrase has a carefully balanced, goal-directed motion controlled by the outer-voice counterpoint and the pacing of the phrase model. According to the model, phrases often comprise one or more tonic expansions, one or more predominant chords, and a cadence. Larger musical structures, composed of multiple phrases, unfold logically as well. One of the best ways to create continuity is to call on a listener's expectations for continuation beyond the end of a phrase. If somebody telling you a story stops in midsentence, your immediate reaction is to want to know what comes next. We have observed a similar situation with deceptive motions: V to vi serves to heighten and thwart our expectations of tonic resolution. Few pieces—or even phrases—conclude with deceptive motions, because such motions create in listeners a desire to know what follows. The music continues so that its eventual completion satisfies expectations. Throughout the tonal era (and beyond), composers have relied on the pattern of incompleteness followed by completeness. Because a sense of incompleteness is crucial to the large-scale organization of tonal music, composers often avoid harmonically closed four-bar units. Instead, they rely on multiple four- or eight-bar phrases that hinge on each other. Listen to Example 9.1.

EXAMPLE 9.1   Beethoven, Symphony no. 3, in E♭ major, "Eroica," op. 55,
Allegro vivace: Trio

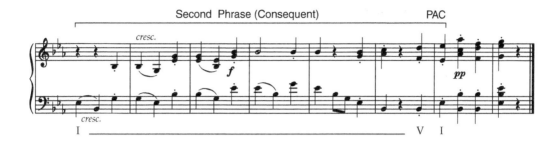

The phrases work well together. The first phrase ends on a half cadence (with $\hat{2}$ in the melody) that leaves us craving tonic and the resolution of the melody to $\hat{1}$—a resolution that is achieved at the PAC of the second phrase. Two phrases make a **period** when they relate to each other musically, and the second phrase resolves harmonic and melodic tensions left hanging at the end of the first phrase.

Types of Periods

The cementing of two separate phrases into a period depends on the interaction of melody and harmony. Listen to Example 9.2A–B.

EXAMPLE 9.2

A.   Mozart, Piano Concerto in D minor, K. 466, *Andante*

B.   Beethoven, Piano Sonata in B♭ major, op. 22, *Menuetto*

There are important thematic differences between these excerpts. The second phrase of the Mozart excerpt begins with the same thematic material as the first phrase, while the Beethoven excerpt has no thematic repetition of material from phrase to phrase. When two phrases begin with highly similar thematic material, as in Mozart's example, they create a **parallel period** (aa, or aa'). When two phrases are thematically dissimilar, as in Beethoven's, they create a **contrasting period** (ab).

Although the two periods in Example 9.2 have similar cadences (HC–PAC), there are important harmonic differences. Mozart's first phrase finishes on the dominant, and the second phrase starts over on the tonic. It is as if the harmonic motion is *interrupted* before finishing the first phrase. Only in the second phrase, after a restart of the phrase model, does the music push through the cadential dominant to attain the long-awaited tonic in m. 8. A pair of phrases with this harmonic structure creates an **interrupted period**. We indicate the interrupted harmonic motion with a double slash (//):

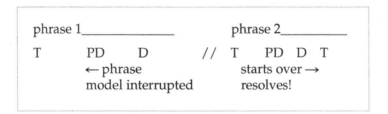

Beethoven's first phrase in Example 9.2B also finishes on dominant. The second phrase, however, does not begin again on the tonic. Instead, it begins with a V^7 chord and *continues* away from tonic. A pair of phrases with this harmonic structure—ending the first phrase and continuing the second phrase away from tonic—creates a **continuous period**:

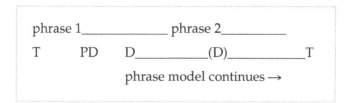

phrase 1_____ phrase 2_____

T   PD   D_____(D)_____T

phrase model continues →

In addition to interrupted and continuous periods, there are two other harmonic possibilities. Listen to Example 9.3.

EXAMPLE 9.3   Mozart, Piano Sonata in B♭ major, K. 281, *Allegro*

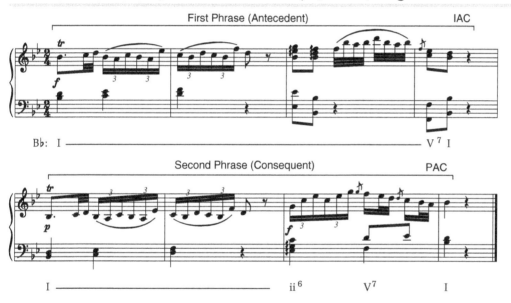

Both phrases in Example 9.3 close on the tonic, so we might wonder whether or not they form a period. It is indeed a period, because the melody is left incomplete at the end of the first phrase. The second phrase subtly completes the melodic motion by ending on $\hat{1}$. When two phrases have the cadences IAC and PAC—and each phrase is, in a sense, a closed harmonic *section*—they form a **sectional period**:

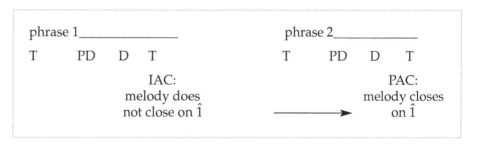

phrase 1_____   phrase 2_____

T   PD   D   T   T   PD   D   T

IAC: PAC:
melody does   melody closes
not close on $\hat{1}$ ⟶   on $\hat{1}$

As an introduction to the final type of period, listen to Example 9.4.

EXAMPLE 9.4   **Beethoven, Piano Sonata in D major, op. 28,** *Andante*

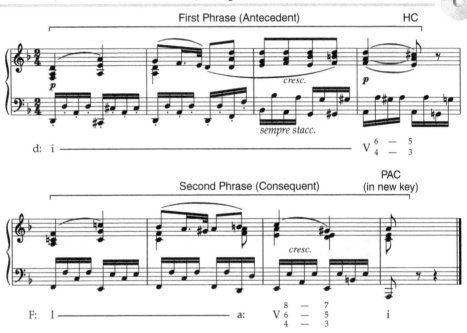

The cadence in Example 9.4 forms a weak–strong relationship (HC–PAC), but we are struck by the sound of the second cadence, which ends in the key of v. If two phrases have a weak–strong cadence relationship and there is a key change during the course of the phrases, they form a **progressive period**. It does not matter whether the cadences reflect any of the other periods (sectional, continuous, interrupted). The "progressive" label trumps all other labels, since it indicates a change of key.

Period Labels

We label a period with three words:

1. The phrases are either **parallel** or **contrasting**.
2. The harmonic motion is **interrupted**, **continuous**, **sectional**, or **progressive**.
3. The last word identifies the structure: **period**.

Thus, Example 9.2A is a parallel interrupted period and Example 9.2B is a contrasting continuous period. Example 9.3 is a parallel sectional period, and Example 9.4 is a parallel progressive period. See the following graphic summary of period types.

Period Diagrams and Their Labels

Period label	Abbreviation	Formal diagram
parallel interrupted period	PIP	a HC‖ I a′ PAC
contrasting interrupted period	CIP	a HC‖ I b PAC
parallel sectional period	PSP	a IAC I a′ PAC
contrasting sectional period	CSP	a IAC I b PAC
parallel continuous period	PCP	a HC, or AC somewhere other than tonic a′ phrase 2 PAC begins somewhere other than tonic
contrasting continuous period	CCP	a HC, or AC somewhere other than tonic b phrase 2 PAC begins somewhere other than tonic
parallel progressive period	PPP	a HC or IAC a′ phrase 2 ends with AC somewhere other than tonic
contrasting progressive period	CPP	a HC or IAC b phrase 2 ends with AC somewhere other than tonic

The Double Period

In Example 9.5, the 16 measures contain four phrases with distinct cadences. It feels as though mm. 1–8 and mm. 9–16 each divide into contrasting periods; however, the half cadence in m. 8 is not conclusive enough to close a period structure. As soon as we hear that m. 9 parallels the melody of m. 1, we gain a whole set of expectations for mm. 9–16: We anticipate that this second unit will take eight measures to close on the tonic. Indeed, mm. 1–16 appear to be one giant parallel interrupted period, with each half divided into period-like structures.

EXAMPLE 9.5 **Beethoven, Piano Sonata in A♭ major, op. 26,** *Andante*

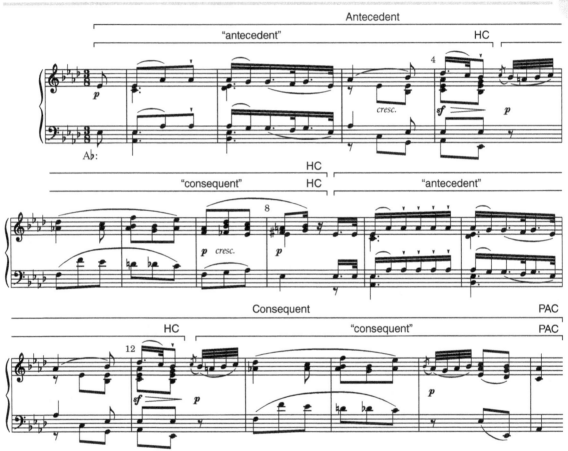

This type of structure is called a **double period**, and Example 9.5 is a parallel interrupted double period. In this structure, the cadential relationship in the first eight measures does not fit the requirements for a period, because the cadence in m. 8 creates a sense of inconclusiveness that requires closure in m. 16:

measures:	1–4	5–8	9–12	13–16
harmony:	I————HC	IV⁶————HC ‖	I————HC	IV⁶————PAC
smaller-level melody:	a	b	a′	b′
large-level melody:	A ------------------------------		A′ -------------------------------	
smaller-level period structure:	"antecedent"	"consequent"	"antecedent"	"consequent"
large-level period structure:	Antecedent	-------------------	Consequent	-------------------

The Sentence

Example 9.6 comprises a single phrase that closes with a half cadence. However, the phrase can be divided into units.

EXAMPLE 9.6   Beethoven, Piano Sonata in F minor, op. 2, no. 1, *Allegro*

The first half of the phrase contains two distinct yet closely related ideas (labeled A and A′); the second half of the phrase is one single unit. This pattern—a short statement followed by a similar repetition and then an elaboration of the statement that occupies twice as much time—is described as a **sentence** structure. Sentences exist concurrently with phrases and periods; that is, a sentence can exist within a phrase or a period. In Example 9.6, we saw a sentence that occurred over the course of a phrase. In Example 9.7, the sentence unfolds over the course of a period: The first phrase forms the A and A′ of the sentence, and the second phrase comprises the B.

EXAMPLE 9.7   Mozart, Horn Concerto in D major, K. 412, *Allegro*

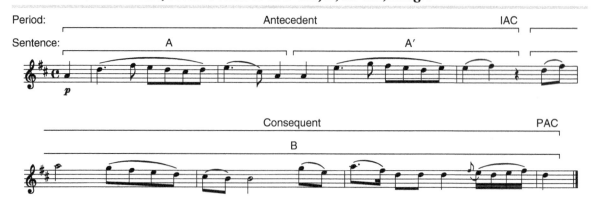

Let us return briefly to Beethoven's sentence in Example 9.6. Look at mm. 5–8. Measure 5 repeats a step higher in m. 6, and they are followed by the climactic gesture in mm. 7–8. We see a miniature sentence develop *within* the four-measure B of the larger sentence. Thus, sentences can occur in phrases and periods, and they can be **nested** inside the B part of other sentences:

measure:	1	2	3	4	5	6	7	8
larger sentence:	⌐A (2 mm.)⌐ +		⌐A′ (2 mm.)⌐		⌐B (4 mm.)			⌐
smaller sentence:					a (1)	a′ (1)	b (2)	

Analytical Extension: Modified Periods

Occasionally we encounter periods that do not exhibit the typical antecedent/consequent relationship. There are many ways composers alter the standard two-phrase model, three of which we will now discuss.

1. Composers may immediately repeat either the antecedent or the consequent (for example, *aab* or *abb*). Example 9.8 presents the opening of a rondo by Beethoven that has the structure antecedent–consequent–consequent. This type of period maintains a deeper-level two-phrase symmetry; the repetition of the consequent (which can also be considered an "extension" or "suffix" after the cadence in m. 8) is more of an echo than an independent entity.

EXAMPLE 9.8   Beethoven, Piano Sonata in C minor ("Pathetique"), Op. 13, Rondo

2. A series of phrases punctuated by weak cadences—none of which is strong enough to close a passage—does not constitute a period. Rather, it is just a phrase chain, or **phrase group**. Sometimes a composer writes a series of phrases, each of which contains new material, but the cadences in each but the final phrase are weak or even more like caesuras. Thus, we must consider the strength of the final cadence in order to discriminate a period from a phrase group. Consider Example 9.9. There are three distinct four-measure units, but only the third closes with a real cadence. The first unit, which alternates tonic and dominant, barely qualifies as a phrase, and the second unit merely elaborates tonic with a IV–I motion. Yet, given that the final cadence is so strong and brings closure to the previous "phrases," one could interpret the piece as a two-phrase period, with the middle unit acting as an extension of phrase one: A–extension–B.

EXAMPLE 9.9 Franz Gruber, *Silent Night*

3. Occasionally, composers write periods comprising an uneven number of distinct phrases, which create three-phrase, five-phrase, or even seven-phrase periods. We call these **asymmetrical periods**. Example 9.10 is an example of a three-phrase asymmetrical period (*abc*) that includes repeated phrases creating the pattern *aabcc*, which is detailed here:

EXAMPLE 9.10   Haydn, String Quartet in C Major, Op. 76, No. 3 ("Kaiser"), Hob. III, 77, *Poco adagio; cantabile*

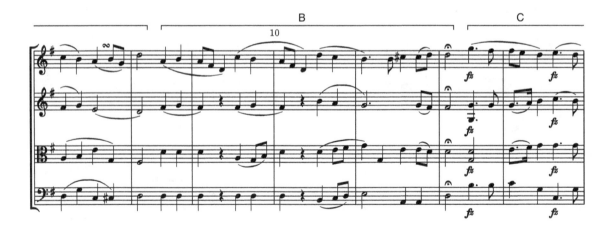

WORKBOOK
9.3

CHAPTER 10

Harmonic Sequences:
Concepts and Patterns

In this chapter we see how composers can draw from the full palette of diatonic harmonies to fill a single phrase. Listen to Example 10.1A, which presents the end of one phrase (with Phrygian cadence) followed by a complete four-measure phrase.

EXAMPLE 10.1

A.   Vivaldi, Concerto Grosso in C minor, F. 1, no. 2, "Il Sospetto," *Allegro*

B.   Vivaldi, recomposed

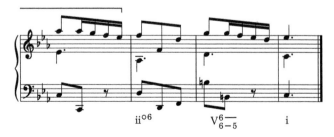

Example 10.1B presents the same structure as Example 10.1A, except that the final phrase of Example 10.1B contains twice as many measures. The added measures, bracketed and labeled in the example, are interpolated between the i⁶ that begins the final phrase and the ii°⁶–V⁶₅–I that closes the phrase. However, the added chords fit nicely within the phrase, and they serve both to prolong the tonic function and to connect the tonic to the predominant. Such patterns, called **harmonic sequences,** form seamless, goal-directed musical units that do not draw attention away from the underlying harmonic progression. Sequences first appeared during the Renaissance period (c. 1450–1600), but they played a much more important role in the Baroque (c. 1600–1750) and in successive musical periods, including in the popular and commercial music of today.

Components and Types of Sequences

One can divide a sequence into two parts: the **model** and its **copies** (which "copy and paste" the model at different pitch levels). The model presents the basic contrapuntal/harmonic pattern—this is usually two chords in length. Sequences typically have two or three copies of the model.

Sequence types are determined from harmonic and contrapuntal voice-leading patterns. Therefore, every chord in a sequence does not need a roman numeral. Sequences are analyzed according to the following criteria.

1. The first and last chords in a sequence receive roman numerals, since they participate in the harmonic progression of the phrase.

2. The sequence label consists of the distances between the chord's roots that make up the repeating pattern. In Example 10.2A, the distance from the root of the initial C major chord to the F major chord is a descending fifth (−5); the distance from the root of the F major chord to the B diminished chord is an ascending fourth (+4). This pattern of root motion repeats throughout the sequence −5, +4, −5, +4, −5, +4, −5. Therefore, the sequence label is (−5/+4), as in Example 10.2B.

EXAMPLE 10.2

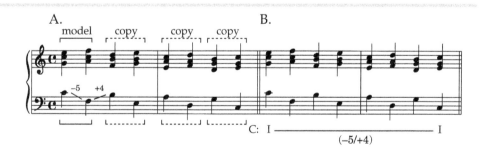

Although there are many types of sequences, they fall into two categories: **descending** and **ascending.** We will now examine two sequences that descend and two sequences that ascend.

The Descending-Fifths Sequence (− 5/+4)

The (−5/+4) sequence, as in Example 10.2, is called the **descending-fifths,** or **circle-of-fifths, sequence,** because the root motion from chord to chord follows the circle of fifths. We have seen this series of chords before. We began with V–I. Each time we added a new harmony, we backed up on the circle of fifths; the complete diatonic pattern of fifths is I–IV–vii°–iii–vi–ii–V–I. Range limitations preclude using descending fifths exclusively; therefore, we answer a descending fifth with an ascending fourth. Of course, composers might begin their sequences by rising a fourth and then falling a fifth—for simplicity, we will call any sequence whose roots fall a fifth and rise a fourth *or* rise a fourth and fall a fifth a (−5/+4) sequence. Notice that this sequential two-chord pattern creates a deeper-level step descent, as shown by the connecting beams in Example 10.3.

EXAMPLE 10.3

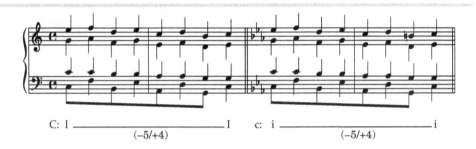

In your analysis, you may have noticed something unusual about the (−5/+4) sequence. First, the sequence has the potential for a tritone leap in the bass. Second, it is possible to have root-position vii° and ii° chords in major and minor modes, respectively. Although both of these are uncommon in traditional harmonic progressions, they are acceptable and necessary in the (−5/+4) sequence: Without the tritone in the bass, the sequence would spin off into chromatic areas and require six copies of the model to return to the tonic (for example, in the key of C major: C–F–[B♭–E♭–A♭–D♭–G♭]–B–E–A–D–G–C). Diminished triads are allowed in order to participate in the overall repeating pattern.

The (− 5/+ 4) Sequence in Inversion

Given the angular, disjunct bass that occurs in root-position (−5/+4) sequences, composers often place one of the chords of the model—usually the second chord—in first inversion. This technique, as we know, creates a more melodic bass. Notice that the outer-voice counterpoint of Example 10.4 consists exclusively of imperfect consonances (10–6), which enhances the smooth, melodic sound. We do not change the sequence label when there are inverted chords; instead, we add inversion symbols underneath the inverted chords.

EXAMPLE 10.4

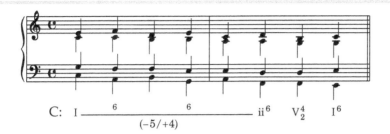

The Pachelbel, or Descending 5–6, Sequence (−4/+2)

The (−4/+2) sequence contrasts nicely with the (−5/+4) sequence, because it incorporates entirely different root motions. The Pachelbel Canon in D major is a well-known example of this sequence. Listen to Example 10.5A and note the miniature deceptive motion (V–vi) and the stepwise descending soprano line; these are common characteristics of the (−4/+2) sequence. Also observe the minor v chord in m. 1 of Example 10.5B, which is necessary to avoid the augmented second between A♭ and B.

EXAMPLE 10.5

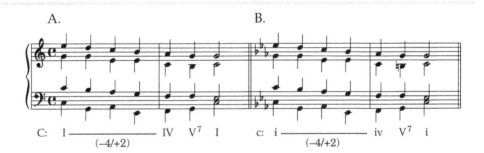

The (−4/+2) Sequence in Inversion

Composers often use first-inversion chords to smooth the bass line of the (−4/+2) sequence. Consider Example 10.6.

EXAMPLE 10.6

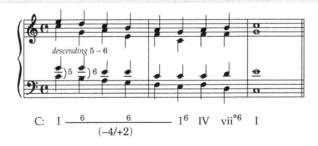

Notice the stepwise bass descent that moves in parallel tenths with the soprano. This sequence is also often called the *descending 5–6 sequence* because one voice (often the tenor, as in the example) remains stationary against the falling bass, forming first a fifth and then a sixth. The $(-4/+2)$ sequence is much more common in inversion than with only root-position chords.

The Ascending-Fifths Sequence $(+5/-4)$

This sequence, with ascending fifths and descending fourths, is much less common than the descending $(-5/+4)$ sequence, because it is not nearly as goal directed. Listen to Example 10.7.

EXAMPLE 10.7

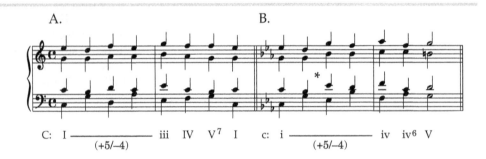

In the progression I to V, the dominant's natural tendency is to return to the tonic to create a strong progression; but V ascending a fifth to ii creates a weak retrogression. For two reasons, however, common-practice composers occasionally use the ascending $(+5/-4)$ sequence. First, given its overall ascent, it provides some sense of drive. Second, the second chord of the model (and each copy) again serves as a voice-leading harmony that prevents potential parallels that would occur in a progression moving up by step. The $(+5/-4)$ sequence—which typically occurs in root position only—results in a large-scale step ascent. Note that the ii° and VI chords are skipped in Example 10.7B (marked by the asterisk). This is typically done in order to avoid the tritone leap ($\hat{2}$–$\hat{6}$) in the bass.

The Ascending 5–6 Sequence $(-3/+4)$

Similar to the ascending $(+5/-4)$ sequence, the $(-3/+4)$ sequence is characterized by a large-scale step ascent to PD. The propulsion for this sequence comes from a springboard motion up a fourth to begin the next copy of the model, as indicated in Example 10.8.

EXAMPLE 10.8

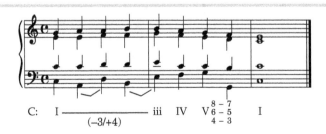

Look at Example 10.9. As with the other sequences that employ first-inversion triads, the addition of the $^6_3$ chords allows the $(-3/+4)$ to be much smoother. In fact, the bass is sustained as a common tone throughout the model (and in each copy). Parallels that would occur in a stepwise progression are averted by the intervening $^6_3$ chord, creating a 5–6 contrapuntal motion (which usually occurs in the outer voices); thus, this sequence is also known as the *ascending 5–6 sequence*.

EXAMPLE 10.9

WORKBOOK
10.1–10.2

Sequences with Diatonic Seventh Chords

It is common to add sevenths to harmonies that are involved in sequences, resulting in a stream of seventh chords. We will limit our study to the $(-5/+4)$ sequence. Listen to Example 10.10.

EXAMPLE 10.10

A.

B.   Francois Couperin "Les Nations" Premier Ordre: La Françoise, XIV, Chaconne

Example 10.10A contains a $(-5/+4)$ sequence composed entirely of triads. Example 10.10B, which reproduces the opening of a movement by Francois Couperin, illustrates a $(-5/+4)$ sequence that includes diatonic seventh chords. Notice the harmonic interest and richness in Example 10.10B compared with Example 10.10A, due in large part to the four different types of seventh chords used (mm, MM, dm, and Mm).

There is one important voice-leading point to bear in mind when including seventh chords in the (−5/+4) sequence: *Prepare and resolve each seventh.* Notice that the circled sevenths of each chord in Example 10.10B have been prepared by common tone and resolved down by step (the soprano-voice seventh moves to its upper neighbor before resolving down).

Diatonic sevenths are usually added to every other chord (Example 10.11A) or to every chord (Example 10.11B) in the (−5/+4) sequence.

EXAMPLE 10.11

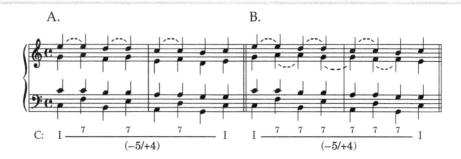

Note that every seventh is prepared by common tone (dotted slur in the example) and is resolved down by step. The soprano and alto in Example 10.11B have interlocking sevenths above the bass: As the soprano resolves its seventh, the alto prepares its seventh; as the alto resolves its seventh, the soprano prepares its seventh, and so on. Note that every other chord in Example 10.11B is incomplete (doubled root, omitted fifth).

Writing Sequences

In writing sequences, there are no new chords to conquer, nor are there any new voice-leading rules. In fact, given that each chord within a sequence must follow the voice-leading and doublings in the model, you will encounter doubled leading tones, dissonant leaps, and diminished triads in root position. All of these are frowned on in usual voice-leading situations, but they are perfectly acceptable within sequences (due to the overall repetition of the model). Following are three guidelines that will allow you to write successful sequences.

GUIDELINE 1 The voice leading in the model and first copy must be correct. Because the copies merely restate the model (at a different pitch level), any faulty voice leading in the opening will blemish every copy.

GUIDELINE 2 Write outer voices first. Try to incorporate contrary step motion between them and include at least one imperfect consonance (3, 6, 10). Example 10.12 shows various intervallic patterns between the outer voices of the (−5/+4) sequence. Although the soprano becomes more disjunct with the nonstop tenths in Example 10.12D, such a contrapuntal framework has occurred often in music, particularly in popular music of the twentieth century (including Bart Howard's *Fly Me to the Moon* and Jerome Kern's *All the Things You Are*).

EXAMPLE 10.12

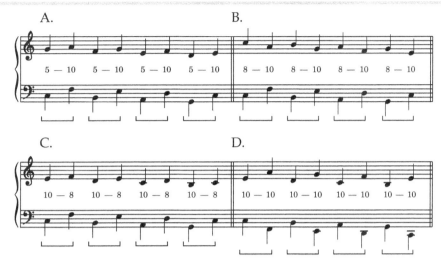

WORKBOOK
10.3

GUIDELINE 3 Prepare and resolve each chordal seventh.

Analytical Extension: Melodic Sequences and Compound Melody

One often encounters sequences in music written for single-line instruments, such as winds, brass, and strings. These may be purely melodic and will not be in concert with a sequential harmonic underpinning, such as in Example 10.13.

EXAMPLE 10.13

A.

B.   Pergolesi, "Se tu m'ami, se sospiri"

C.　Mozart, Symphony no. 29 in A major, K. 201, *Allegro moderato*

Example 10.13A presents a simple sequential tune that rises by step. Such common patterns arise as elaborations of stepwise ascending and descending lines. Example 10.13B contains a stepwise falling melodic sequence. Notice that the harmony that accompanies the vocal line is not sequential. Example 10.13C presents a much more elaborate ascending stepwise melodic sequence whose model occupies two full measures. Although the harmony does follow in lockstep with the melody, the chromatic passing tone figure D–D♯–E in mm. 3–4 is sequentially repeated in mm. 5–6. The melodically fluent ascending and descending line is shown by beams.

Very often one encounters sequences that unfold in such a way as to imply multiple voices that by themselves reveal a clear harmonic structure. Indeed, much Baroque music, particularly that of J. S. Bach, is presented through a single disjunct melodic line rather than by the harmonic combination afforded by multiple instruments playing simultaneously.

Numerous compositional techniques allow composers to imply harmonies without using a fully voiced chord. The most important technique, called **compound melody,** deploys a single melodic line in such a way that it implies two, three, or even four voices. This is achieved by means of registral leaps in the melody such that the single line splits into multiple voices delineated by register (Example 10.14).

EXAMPLE 10.14   Bach, Partita for Solo Violin in B minor, BWV 1002, *Corrente*

The solo violin plays an arpeggiated pattern with a few passing tones. As the analysis of the example shows, the harmonic rhythm moves at the speed of one chord per measure, unfolding a tonic in m. 1, a lower neighbor V_5^6 in m. 2, and a return to tonic in m. 3. In m. 4, a V^7/III harmony leads to D in m. 4. What is remarkable about this passage is not so much the logical harmonic progression that unfolds but, rather, that the chord members move by strict voice leading from harmony to harmony. The highest and lowest of these independent melodic strands form "outer voices," which move in note-against-note counterpoint (see the reduction in Example 10.15).

EXAMPLE 10.15

Notice the meticulous voice leading in Example 10.16. The three-voice lament bass contains 5 to 6 contrapuntal motions, which avoid the possibility of parallel fifths between the implied voices.

EXAMPLE 10.16   Bach, Cello Suite No. 1 in G major, BWV 1007, *Menuet II*

If standard harmonic progressions can unfold through the use of compound melody, then it follows that sequences can too. Example 10.17 contains two adjacent (-5/$+4$) sequences.

EXAMPLE 10.17   Bach, Sonata no. 2 for Violin in A minor, BWV 1003, *Allegro*

This passage, in E minor, begins with clear tonic and dominant harmonies. The (−5/+4) sequence with seventh chords follows, in m. 31. The D♯ in the preceding V chord prepares the D natural in the E⁷ chord, thus allowing the sequence to connect smoothly with the preceding tonic and dominant harmonies. The harmonies of the falling fifth sequence (E⁷–A⁷–D⁷–G⁷–C⁷–F♯⁷–B⁷) each occupy one beat, leading to a small arrival in m. 33 on i⁶. This short-lived tonic leads to A⁷ in the second half of the measure, and the second sequence unfolds, this time with each harmony occupying two beats. The sequence breaks off on C major (VI). Example 10.18 presents a harmonic reduction of the two sequences.

EXAMPLE 10.18

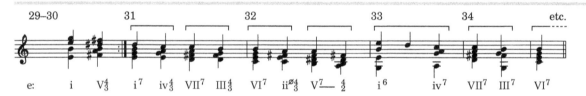

CHAPTER 11

Applied Chords and Tonicization

Chromaticism colors diatonicism; therefore, chromatic pitches are generally not integral to the underlying diatonic structure. One way to incorporate chromaticism into a diatonic progression is to alter diatonic pitches chromatically. Example 11.1A presents a typical harmonic progression, with the submediant chord between the I and ii chords. In Example 11.1B, the submediant chord has been altered with a chromatic C♯, creating an A-major sonority, which is not a diatonic chord in the key of C major.

EXAMPLE 11.1

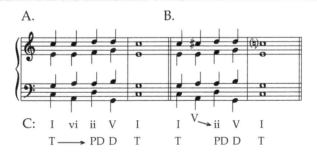

The A-major chord is chromatic in the key of C major, but it intensifies the harmonic motion towards the D-minor (ii) chord: In addition to a descending-fifth progression from A to D, the A-major triad is strongly directed to ii since it functions as the dominant (V) of D minor. This evokes the momentary impression that we have left C major and are in the key of D minor. This sensation of briefly experiencing a key other than the tonic (for a few beats or even for a measure or two) is called **tonicization**. Tonicization is accomplished through the use of chromatic chords that function as dominant chords in another key. These chromatic chords are called **applied chords** (also called **secondary dominant chords**). The essential feature of tonicization is that it elaborates a diatonic harmony with chromaticism, but it still participates in the underlying phrase model and harmonic progression (T–PD–D–T).

Applied Dominant Chords

For a chord to function as an **applied dominant chord**, it must behave like a dominant: It must be a major triad (V) or a dominant seventh chord (V^7), and it will usually move to its tonic. Since dominant chords resolve to tonic chords that are either major or minor, any major or minor chord—in any key—can be preceded by an applied dominant chord. For example, in the key of C minor, say we wish to find the applied dominant chord of V. V is a G-major chord, so we determine the applied dominant of G major to be D major. Note that we cannot determine applied dominant chords for diminished triads. Diminished triads are dissonant and cannot be tonic chords in major or minor keys.

In analysis, roman numerals are altered to reflect tonicization when writing applied dominant chords, since applied chords are chromatic and are not members of the prevailing key. In our example—with D major as the applied dominant chord to V in the key of C minor—we label the D major as the dominant of V, or "V/V." In Example 11.1B, the A-major triad is the applied dominant chord to ii in the key of C major. In this case, we label the A-major triad as the dominant of ii, or "V/ii." We have already seen this notation, with the "V/III" chord in Chapter 8.

To summarize, there are two different methods for creating applied dominant chords. One way is to take any major or minor triad in a key and precede it with its applied dominant. In Example 11.2, the diatonic progression I–vi–IV–ii–V–I is expanded with chromatic chords: V^7/vi precedes vi, V^7/IV precedes IV, V^7/ii precedes ii, and V^7/V precedes V.

Another way to explore the role of applied dominant chords is to alter diatonic chords chromatically, changing them into applied dominants and seeing where they lead to as dominant chords (Example 11.3). Note that IV (in major) cannot be altered to create V/vii°, because vii° is a dissonant, diminished triad. Similarly, VI cannot be altered to create V/ii° in a minor key.

EXAMPLE 11.2

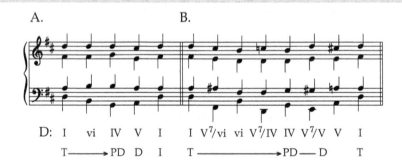

EXAMPLE 11.3

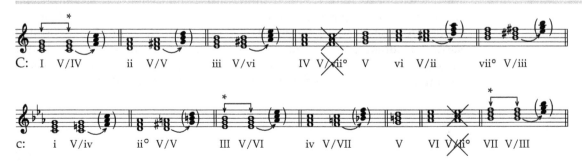

Notice that some diatonic chords are already major chords and can be used as applied dominant chords (see the asterisks and bracketed arrows). In major keys, V/IV is diatonic; in minor keys, V/VI and V/III are diatonic. In order to clarify their applied dominant function, these chords typically appear as V^7 chords.

Applied Chords in Inversion

EXAMPLE 11.4

D: I V^6/vi   vi V^4_3/IV   IV V^6_5/V   V   I
      T ———————————→ PD —— D   T

The bass line in Example 11.2B is rather angular, so we use inversions to make it more melodic (see Example 11.4). In the same way that inversions of V prolong I (e.g., V^6 usually expands I as a lower-neighbor chord), any other major or minor harmony in a key can be prolonged by its applied dominant chord. Example 11.5A reviews how tonic may be prolonged by any inversion of V^7. In Example 11.5B the supertonic is prolonged by its applied V^7 chord in precisely the same way. The only difference is the chromaticism: D must be altered to D♯ in order to function as the leading tone to the key of ii (E minor).

EXAMPLE 11.5

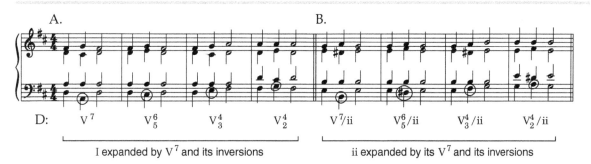

D: V^7 V^6_5 V^4_3 V^4_2 V^7/ii V^6_5/ii V^4_3/ii V^4_2/ii

I expanded by V^7 and its inversions   ii expanded by its V^7 and its inversions

Voice Leading for Applied Dominant Chords

Just as there are two tendency tones in V^7 chords, there are two tendency tones in every applied dominant chord. The third of *any* dominant chord acts as *leading tone*; in applied dominant chords, the leading tone is often chromatically raised. The other tendency tone is the seventh of the chord, which often needs to be chromatically lowered in applied dominant chords. The voice-leading rules and guidelines from our study of the V^7 chord pertain to applied dominant chords as well.

- Do not double the third (the *leading tone*) or the seventh of the chord.
- The leading tone resolves upward when in an outer voice.
- The seventh of the chord resolves downward in any voice.

Example 11.6 shows the proper voice leading for applied dominant chords to vi and IV in C major. Note that root-position applied dominant chords can be complete (Example 11.6A) or incomplete (Example 11.6B).

EXAMPLE 11.6

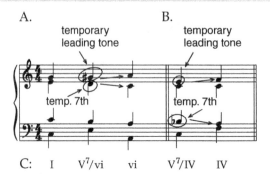

Look again at the soprano line of Example 11.6A. The leading tone (G♯) is a chromatic passing tone between G and A, which creates a smooth chromatic line: G–G♯–A. We **prepare chromaticism** by preceding a chromatic tone with its diatonic version in the same voice—in this case, resulting in a chromatic half-step line—because it softens the harsh aural effect of the chromatic tone.

When a chromatic tone is prepared by another voice (instead of the same voice), it results in a **cross relation**. For example, the chromatic G♯ in Example 11.7 is not prepared in the tenor; the diatonic G occurs in the soprano voice. This cross relation should be avoided, since it produces a harsh aural effect due to the awkward leaps in the soprano and tenor.

EXAMPLE 11.7

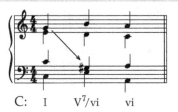

Despite the desirability of chromatic preparation, in some instances it is impossible for chromatic pitches to follow their diatonic forms in the same voice. Example 11.8A shows one such scenario: In a progression from I to V⁶/vi in C major, the bass leaps down from C to G♯, which resolves as it should, to A. A leap of a diminished fourth in the bass is acceptable and quite expressive; in Baroque music with text, this leap often accompanies words of great sorrow or pain. Clearly, the alto G cannot move to G♯ when the bass sounds that pitch (since G♯ is a leading tone in the applied V⁶/vi chord). A similar scenario occurs with a leap to the seventh of an applied dominant chord in the soprano (Example 11.8B).

EXAMPLE 11.8

WORKBOOK
11.1

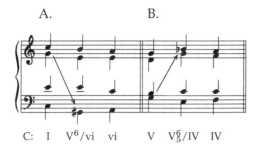

C: I   V^6/vi vi   V   V$^6_5$/IV IV

Applied Leading-Tone Chords

vii°⁶ and vii°⁷ (and to a lesser degree vii^{ø7}) are dominant substitutes that can participate in contrapuntal expansions of the tonic. Often, these harmonies are also used as applied dominant substitutes that lead to other scale degrees.

In Example 11.9, applied leading-tone chords help tonicize ii and V chords in the key of A major. Up to this point, we have used only diminished triads and seventh chords that are built on $\hat{7}$ of the minor mode. With the introduction of applied leading-tone chords, we now may use vii°⁷ and its inversions to tonicize major and minor triads.

EXAMPLE 11.9

A: I   vii°⁷ I   vii°⁷/ii ii vii°⁶/ii ii vii°$^4_3$/ii   ii⁶ vii°⁷/V V$^6_4$ – $^5_3$ I
      T ——————————— PD ————————————————— D ——— T

WORKBOOK
11.2–11.3

Extended Tonicization

A tonicization is extended when it involves multiple applied chords. For example, let's say we want to avoid the clutter of roman numerals in Example 11.10A, which has several chords in a row applied to D minor (ii). In order to show that there is an extended reference to another key—but the phrase remains in the original key overall, with a cadence in C major—we bracket where the tonicization occurs, label the temporary tonic chord under the bracket, and analyze the bracketed chords in the key of the underlying temporary tonic (Example 11.10B). Thus, the chords in the fifth measure—iv/ii and V/ii—become the progression iv–V in the key of ii. We are not changing the applied nature of the chords; we are providing a more holistic view of the chords' tonicizing function.

EXAMPLE 11.10

A. Schumann, "Talismane," *Myrten*, op. 25, no. 8

B. Measures 5–8 of the excerpt, with extended modulation

We will try out this method of analysis in the following examples from the literature, each of which demonstrates an extended tonicization.

EXAMPLE 11.11   Beethoven, Piano Sonata in E♭ major, op. 27, no. 1, *Andante*

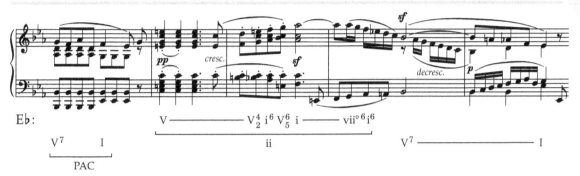

After a PAC closes a phrase in the first measure of Example 11.11, an unexpected and jarring C-major harmony appears in the second measure. When such an unusual event occurs, we must always look beyond individual harmonies to understand how it participates in the phrase. Given that the C-major chord becomes a dominant seventh in the third measure, it functions as an applied dominant chord leading to F minor. The tonicization of F minor (ii in the key of E♭ major) continues until the applied V^6_5/V chord. Thus, we see an expanded tonicization of ii.

The excerpt by Robert Schumann in Example 11.12 contains tonicizations of two harmonies, vi and ii, which are extended after the vocal entrance. As the second-level analysis reveals, over the course of the entire excerpt the tonicizations of vi and ii repeatedly expand the simple underlying harmonic progression, I–vi–ii–V–I.

EXAMPLE 11.12   Robert Schumann, "Mit Myrthen und Rosen," *Liederkreis*,
                    op. 24, no. 9

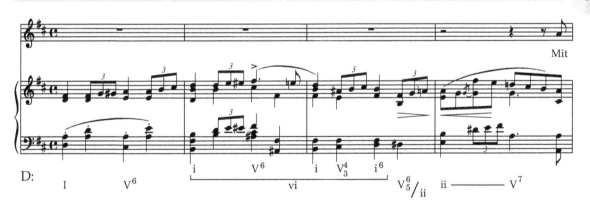

Continued

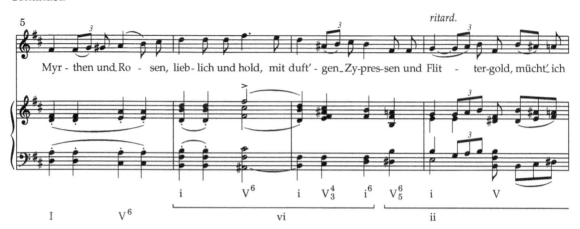

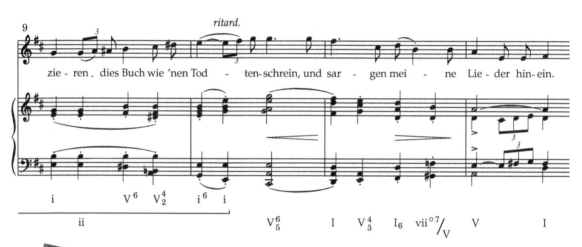

WORKBOOK
11.4

Analytical Extension: Sequences with Applied Chords

Applied chords are often incorporated within sequences. Such **applied chord sequences** greatly intensify sequential motion.

The (−5/+4) Sequence

Review the diatonic form of the (−5/+4) sequence in Example 11.13A, then note that a chromatic version of it appears when applied chords substitute for diatonic chords. The result is the sequence seen in Example 11.13B. The arrows are a visually helpful shorthand method for identifying applied chords and the chords to which they lead.

EXAMPLE 11.13

A. Diatonic   B. Applied V⁷

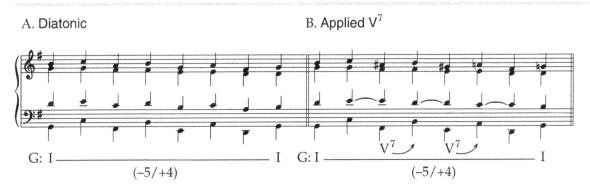

It is particularly common to add sevenths to the triads of the $(-5/+4)$ applied-chord sequence, thus enhancing the sequence's goal-directed motion (Example 11.14)

EXAMPLE 11.14

A. Applied V⁷ on every other chord   B. Applied V⁷ on every chord

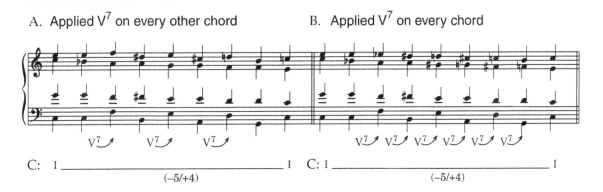

The $(-4/+2)$ Sequence

In the diatonic $(-4/+2)$ sequence, the second chord of each pair is a fourth below the first (Example 11.15A). A dramatic forward motion occurs in the applied-chord form of this sequence, seen in Example 11.15B. Note that the applied-chord version has different root motions than its diatonic counterpart. Thus, the diatonic $(-4/+2)$ is transformed into the $(+3/-5)$ applied-chord sequence. Applied chords in this sequence most often contain sevenths, as in Example 11.15B.

EXAMPLE 11.15

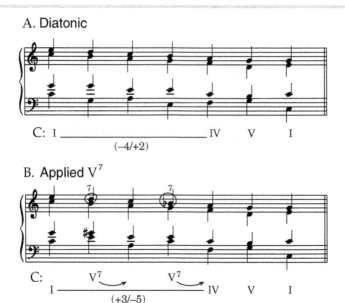

A. Diatonic

C: I _____ IV   V   I
              (−4/+2)

B. Applied V⁷

C:
I _____ IV   V   I
        (+3/−5)

Inverted chords help to smooth out the angular leaps created by root-position harmonies. Example 11.16 displays voice-leading variations on the (+3/−5) applied-chord sequence. Example 11.16C demonstrates that an applied leading-tone chord may also be substituted for the applied dominant chords in Example 11.16B, creating a (−4/+2) sequence.

EXAMPLE 11.16

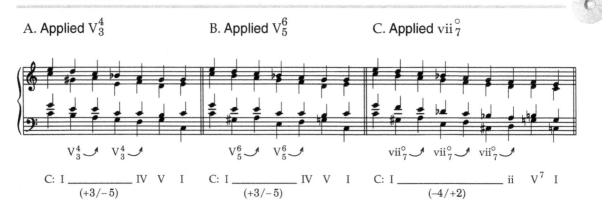

A. Applied V₄³   B. Applied V₅⁶   C. Applied vii°₇

C: I _____ IV V I   C: I _____ IV V I   C: I _____ ii V⁷ I
     (+3/−5)   (+3/−5)   (−4/+2)

The (−3/+4) Sequence

Of the two common sequences that ascend, (−3/+4) is much more likely to incorporate applied chords. The form of the sequence that includes first-inversion triads (Example 11.17A) may be converted into an applied-chord sequence simply by raising the bass a half step. This creates a powerful harmonized chromatic passing tone that functions as a leading tone in an applied dominant chord, which leads to the upcoming root-position triad (Example 11.17B). Example 11.17C adds the seventh to the applied chords.

EXAMPLE 11.17

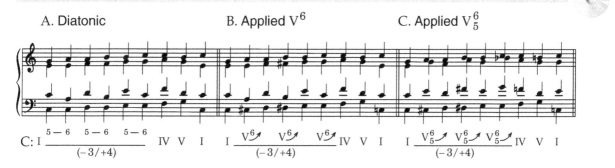

This sequence also employs root-position applied dominant chords. In this case, the chromatic passing motion appears in the soprano rather than in the bass (Example 11.18).

EXAMPLE 11.18

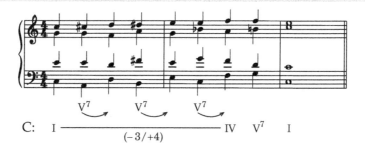

CHAPTER 12

Modulation and Binary Form

In Chapter 11 we reviewed applied dominant chords that led toward chords other than the tonic through tonicization. We will now explore modulations.

Modulation

Longer tonicizations, which can occupy entire sections of a piece, are called **modulations**. It is difficult to draw a firm line between tonicizations and modulations, since both lead to different keys. For our purposes, modulations include a cadence in the new key, which gives the feeling that a new key has usurped the home key (at least for the moment).

Listen to Example 12.1. The tonicization in this example evokes a different effect than in Chapter 11's examples of extended tonicizations. Here, the excerpt begins in E minor, and the second phrase closes in mm. 7–8 with a PAC in G major (III). The cadence in a new tonal area is an indication that the music has modulated.

EXAMPLE 12.1 Haydn, Piano Sonata no. 53 in E minor, Hob. XVI.34, *Vivace molto*

Closely Related Keys

Diatonic modulations usually move from a home key to any of its **closely re-lated keys**, which we define as those keys derived from consonant triads that occur on each scale degree of the home key. For example, the closely related keys to C major are D minor (ii), E minor (iii), F major (IV), G major (V), and A minor (vi). The closely related keys to C minor—using the natural minor scale—are E♭ major (III), F minor (iv), G minor (v), A♭ major (VI), and B♭ major (VII). Although it is possible to modulate to any major or minor diatonic key, our studies will focus on the most common modulations. They are listed in or-der of importance:

1. Major keys tend to modulate to V, vi, and iii.
2. Minor keys tend to modulate to III, v, and VI.

Analyzing Modulations

Here is a method for analyzing modulations.

1. *Look for the pitches that differ between the old and the new keys.* Consider Example 12.2, which modulates from D major to A major. What pitches are exclusive to these keys? D major has G, and A major has G♯. The G♯s begin in m. 6, which means that A major is already in effect in that measure.
2. *Identify the last chord that is diatonic in both keys. If this is not a second-inversion ($^6_4$) triad, then it can be a **pivot chord** between the two keys.* In Ex-ample 12.2, the final chord in m. 5 is the last possible chord that is dia-tonic in both the old and the new keys. It is vi⁶ in D major and ii⁶ in A major; therefore, it is a good candidate to be a pivot chord. The rare na-ture of vi⁶—and its spelling as the common ii⁶ in the new key—is one indication that the key is already changing.

EXAMPLE 12.2   Mozart, Piano Sonata in D major, K. 284, Thema, *Andante*

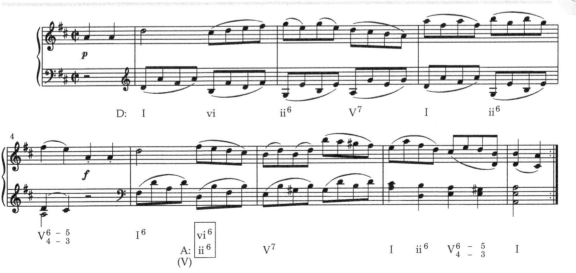

Continued

3. *Second-inversion ($^6_4$) triads are not good candidates for pivot chords, since they are unstable.* For example, the cadential six-fours in Example 12.3 are not standalone I^6_4 chords in the new keys—they function fully in the new keys as part of the dominant. In these cases, we back up one chord and attempt again to find a suitable pivot chord.

EXAMPLE 12.3

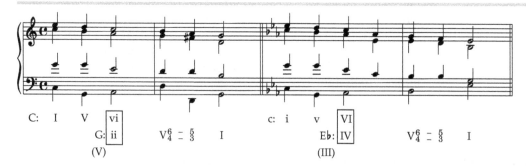

Writing Modulations

Modulations must be tested with performance; often, what looks like a successful pivot chord may in actuality not work at all. This is because in addition to following voice-leading rules, we must establish two keys in a convincing manner. To review the guidelines for writing modulations, let's set ourselves a task: *Create a phrase that modulates from F major to D minor.*

Identify the potential pivot chords. One easy method is to write out the roman numerals for F major and to line up the tonic of D minor with the vi chord in F major.

F major	I	ii	iii	IV	V	vi	vii°
D minor						i	

Now write the roman numerals for the key of D minor, starting on the given tonic chord. Where the chord qualities match between keys, you have a potential pivot chord. (In this case, modulating from major to relative minor, all chords are potential pivot chords.)

F major	I	ii	iii	IV	V	vi	vii°
D minor	III	iv	v	VI	VII	i	ii°
Best (PD in new key)		•		•			•
Good	•					•	
Poor			•		•		

For our example, we will use a B♭-major chord as the pivot. At the same time, it will be IV in F major and VI in D minor. When establishing the two keys, make sure that the durations of the tonal areas are balanced. Place the pivot chord about halfway into a phrase that modulates, and use at least a few chords in each key. For our task, we will start the progression with the descending bass arpeggiation, I–IV⁶–I⁶, and move to the pivot chord and a strong cadence in the new key. (See Example 12.4.)

EXAMPLE 12.4

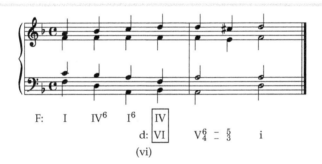

WORKBOOK
12.1–12.3

Modulation in the Larger Musical Context

Very few compositions end in a different key from the one in which they begin. In fact, considering a work as a whole, modulations will never displace the prevailing tonic. Thus, modulations in tonal music participate in a single overall harmonic motion. Listen to Example 12.5 and note the cadences and keys.

EXAMPLE 12.5   Handel, Prelude in G major

The first eight measures include a modulation from G major to D major. Starting at m. 9, we have a modulation to E minor, followed by a return to G major. Therefore, the overall harmonic motion is as follows:

m. 1	m. 8	m. 16	m. 21	m. 22	m. 25		m. 26
G: I	V	vi	V	I	ii$^6_5$	V	I
I ———————————		vi	V	I	ii$^6_5$	V	I
T ————————————————————————————————					PD	D	T

The keys participate in the overall harmonic motion. The modulation to V in m. 8 is subordinate to the larger I–vi–V–I that leads to m. 22; this progression is embedded within a larger I–ii$^6_5$–V–I that occurs over the entire example. We will not address the effect of the repeat signs on the harmonic progression here.

The Sequence as a Tool in Modulation

The function of a pivot is not limited to a single chord. Often, several chords that function in two keys will work together to create a **pivot area**. For example, a pivot chord might be expanded or tonicized. Or a group of chords that share the same harmonic function (such as pre-dominants IV and ii) might be coupled through a voice exchange, creating a pre-dominant complex that works in both the starting and the ending key.

Sequences, too, make terrific pivots. In fact, we have seen that one of the two functions of a sequence is transitional: It frequently takes the music from one harmonic area to another. There are many strategies of using sequences to modulate, given that a sequence touches on many chords, sometimes every chord, within a key. Therefore, by prematurely quitting a sequence and reinterpreting one of its chords as a pre-dominant that moves to a dominant, one can effectively move to a new key. Listen to Example 12.6.

EXAMPLE 12.6   Vivaldi, Trio Sonata in C minor, *Allegro*

Continued

Vivaldi invokes a (−5/+4) sequence that stops on VI (c–f–B♭–E♭–A♭). The A♭ chord functions as IV in the new key of E♭ (III of C minor).

Example 12.7 demonstrates how easy it is to modulate to a variety of keys from within a sequence. Example 12.7A presents a (−5/+4) sequence in G minor, and Example 12.7B presents a (−3/+4) sequence in B♭ major. Each sequence contains at least two repetitions of the model, marked by brackets. Beneath each sequence are progressions that modulate to several different keys, accomplished by incorporating some, but not all, of the given sequence. The G-minor example modulates to III (two examples), VI, and v (two examples). The B♭-major example modulates to iii, vi, and V.

EXAMPLE 12.7

Binary Form

Binary form, a term describing a complete work that is parsed into two sections, can be traced back to well before 1700. The Baroque suite, for example, comprises numerous dance movements, ranging from slow sarabandes to lively gigues, each of which is cast in binary form. One of these dance movements, the **minuet**, was maintained in compositions of the Classical period, where it may be found in instrumental sonatas, string quartets, and symphonies. It, too, is cast in binary form, as are the theme and subsequent subsections of many variation sets. Throughout the common-practice period, repeat signs almost always mark the two sections of pieces in binary form; for this reason, binary form is also known as **two-reprise form**. Listen to Example 12.8 and ask the following questions.

1. How many sections does the work contain, and what differentiates these sections musically?
2. What is the overall tonal structure?
3. Does material recur?

EXAMPLE 12.8   Hummel, Bagatelle in C major

Most likely, your senses led you to consider this piece in two parts; the double bars indicate two sections. When we describe binary form, we apply a label in the same manner as a period label. We consider the melodic structure (or thematic design), which can be **simple** or **rounded**. We also consider the harmonic structure, which can be **sectional** or **continuous**. These terms are defined in the following discussions.

Notice that no thematic material recurs in Example 12.8; in cases like this, when the two sections of a binary form share no melodic material, the melodic design is called **simple**. As for the harmonic label, our first step is to consider the cadence that occurs at the end of the *first* section. When the cadence at the end of the first section ends on the *tonic*, the harmonic structure is called **sectional** (since both *sections* of the binary form are tonally closed). Thus, we can say that Hummel's Bagatelle is in **simple sectional binary form**.

Now listen to Example 12.9, which illustrates a different type of binary form.

EXAMPLE 12.9 **Carl Maria von Weber, No. 1, Six Ecossaise, J. 29**

Melodically, this binary form is simple (*ab*). Harmonically, the tonicization of the dominant at the end of the first section clearly presents a significant difference from the previous example. The dominant continues after the double bar but is weakened by the addition of the seventh, which forces it back into the orbit of G major. In cases like this, when the first section closes *away from the tonic*, and the following section *continues* away from the tonic, the binary form's harmonic structure is called **continuous**. Thus, Weber's piece is in a **simple continuous binary form**.

Listen to Example 12.10. In what ways does it differ from Examples 12.8 and 12.9?

EXAMPLE 12.10   Haydn, Sonatina no. 4 in F major, Hob. XVI.9, *Scherzo*

The first section closes on tonic; therefore, the piece's harmonic structure is sectional. However, we see a distinct HC in m. 16 that divides the second half. After the HC, there is a literal restatement of material that began the piece. Thus, the second section of Haydn's binary form is more complex than in Examples 12.8 and 12.9. It features a new compositional tactic: Begin the second section with fragmented and unstable material that leads to a HC. We call this small development section a **digression**, since it wanders from the preceding material but then quickly leads back to a restatement of the original material. We call the HC in m. 16 an **interruption** (marked with a double slash, //), since this is the point where the underlying harmonic progression is interrupted and begins again in the tonic.

When all or part of the *opening* material of a binary form returns in the second section after the digression, the binary form's thematic design is called **rounded** (*a-dig.-a'*). This name derives from the cyclical effect created by the return of the opening material. The scherzo by Haydn is in a **rounded sectional binary form**. Look back at Example 12.2. The harmonic structure is continuous, since the first section ends away from the tonic. Thematically, there is a digression in mm. 9–12 that leads to an interruption; this is followed by a repetition of part of the opening theme in the tonic. Thus, Mozart's piece is cast in **rounded continuous binary form**.

Balanced Binary Form

Binary forms—whether sectional or continuous, simple or rounded—can have an additional characteristic: They can be **balanced** if the closing material in the first section is restated as the closing material in the second section. "Balanced" does not always refer to an exact repetition, because, in many binary forms, the first section closes in a nontonic key. To provide convincing tonal closure at the end of the piece, the restatement of this material will naturally occur in the tonic. Look back at Example 12.5.

The first section closes in V (D major) in m. 8, making the harmonic structure continuous. In the digression (mm. 9–21), Handel develops the piece's opening gesture by reversing the order of scale and broken chord and placing them within two sequences. Handel is in a quandary: The extensive, 13-measure digression creates an imbalance with the first section, which occupies only eight measures, yet he must provide convincing melodic and harmonic closure. He does not return with the opening harmonic and melodic material as in rounded binary form; instead, his solution is to draw material that closes the piece from an analogous point in the close of the first section, to create a **(balanced) simple continuous binary form**. Balanced is in parentheses to show that it is an additional element of the form that does not disrupt the other melodic and harmonic aspects of the label.

Summary of Binary Form Types

The feature common to all two-reprise binary forms is the presence of two sections, often marked by double bars. We look at cadences to determine the harmonic structure:

sectional:	‖: ----------------------- ends on tonic :‖: -------------------- ends on tonic :‖
continuous:	‖: ---------------- ends away from tonic :‖:------------------- ends on tonic :‖

Like many specimens of tonal music, binary forms do not always fall neatly into one of our established theoretical categories. Categorization is merely an attempt to deal with the many and varied stimuli with which we are confronted at every moment of our lives. As such, categories are more general than specific. Given that music is an art form capable of multiple interpretations, we must be flexible and open-minded in our attempts to come to grips with it. In your analysis of form, always be sensitive to the music.

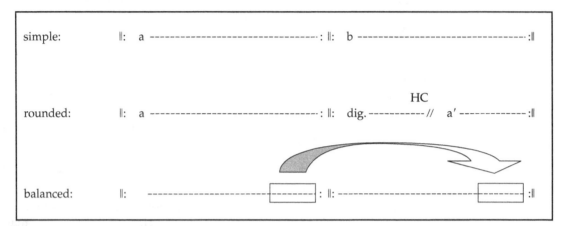

WORKBOOK
12.4–12.5

Analytical Extension: Binary Form in Baroque Dance Suites

One of the most important types of instrumental solo and ensemble pieces in the Baroque era is the **dance suite**, which is a collection of usually four to six separate contrasting movements cast in binary form and based on the meters, rhythms, tempos, and moods of various dances of the time. The typical suite begins with an Allemande (of German descent, usually rather stately, in quadruple meter, with running sixteenth notes), Courante (French, usually in a triple meter and rather spritely), Sarabande (Spanish, also usually in a triple meter, but slow, and set in a syncopated rhythm that stresses beat 2), Minuet (French, in a moderate triple meter), and Gigue (French or English, usually in a compound meter, quite fast, and often imitative). Many other dance movements can be included between the outer movements just listed, including the Corrente, the Bourrée, the Gavotte, the Louré, the Siciliano, and the Air, among others.

These pieces are usually constructed in simple continuous binary form (*ab*) and include a repetition of the cadential material at the end of the A section at the end of the piece, but transposed to the tonic. However, it is just as common to have no material return, as in Example 12.11.

EXAMPLE 12.11   Corelli, Violin Sonata in D minor, op. 5, no. 7, *Sarabanda*

This short movement achieves its symmetry from the two eight-measure phrases, neither of which explicitly repeats material. Thus, this would be a typical simple (*ab*) continuous binary form.

Often, traces of the A material can underlie the B material, thus blurring the contrast in the two sections. Such structures are still considered simple, given that no B material is a literal restatement of the beginning of the A material (the condition necessary for a rounded binary). Recomposition is accomplished in countless ways. For example, in Bach's Sarabande from the D-minor French Suite (Example 12.12), the slowly moving bass voice in the first half of the piece is activated in the second half with what turns out to be the exact same soprano melody from the first half.

EXAMPLE 12.12   Bach, French Suite in D minor, *Sarabande*

Corelli creates an explicit connection between the sections of a Sarabande (Example 12.13) by incorporating melodic material from the A section. Given that the opening of the A material reappears at the dominant in the second section (where it answers the opening I–V with V–I), it would be more accurate to label this type of simple continuous piece A–A'.

EXAMPLE 12.13   Corelli, Chamber Sonata in A major, op. 2, no. 10, *Sarabanda*

Finally, in Handel's Suite in G minor (Example 12.14), the Allegro's A section is literally transposed to III in the A' section. Such "cutting and pasting" techniques for these simple continuous A–A' binary forms are important to recognize.

EXAMPLE 12.14   Handel, Keyboard Suite in G minor, *Allegro*

CHAPTER 13

Expressive Chromaticism: Modal Mixture and Chromatic Tonicization

Chromatic harmony in the form of the applied dominant chord has existed essentially from the beginning of tonality: Examples of V/V can be found in the output of early sixteenth-century composers such as Josquin. Yet, as music moved into the late Classical and Romantic eras, composers began to focus on exploring the potential of pre-dominant, rather than dominant, harmony. For example, the off-tonic beginning—which typically involves starting a piece on a ii or IV chord and only eventually revealing the home sonority—is a hallmark of Schumann, Brahms, Wolf, and Mahler. A natural outcome of this new interest in pre-dominant harmony was that composers began investing pre-dominants with their own forms of chromaticism. We now explore how pre-dominants function both as expressive devices in local contexts and as stepping-stones to remote tonicizations at deeper levels.

Modal Mixture

When we listen to music of the late eighteenth and early nineteenth centuries, we frequently encounter a type of chromaticism that cannot be said to derive from applied functions and tonicization. In fact, the chromaticism often appears to be nonfunctional—a mere coloring of the melodic and harmonic surface of the music. Listen to the two phrases of Example 13.1.

EXAMPLE 13.1   Mascagni, "A casa amici," *Cavalleria Rusticana*, scene 9

1

Continued

The first phrase (mm. 1–8) contains diatonic harmonies in the key of F major, but the second phrase (mm. 9–20) is full of chromaticism. This creates sonorities that appear to be distant from the underlying F-major tonic. The chords in mm. 11–20 share one important feature: All but the cadential V–I are in the key of F minor—the parallel mode of F major. Viewing these measures through the lens of F minor reveals a simple progression that briefly tonicizes III (A♭), then moves to PD (ii°$^4_3$) and D (V), followed by a final resolution to T (I) in the major mode. This excerpt is quite remarkable in its tonal plan: Although it begins and ends in F major, a significant portion of the music behaves as though written in F minor. This technique of borrowing harmonies from the parallel mode is called **modal mixture** (sometimes known simply as **mixture**).

Although harmonies may be borrowed from either the parallel major or minor, *it is much more common for elements of the minor mode to be imported into the major mode.* A quick review of the possible pitch material in the major and minor modes reveals why: In the minor mode, $\hat{6}$ and $\hat{7}$ each have two forms, depending on whether the melodic line ascends or descends. Consequently, the importation of natural $\hat{6}$ into a minor piece results from good voice leading and is not surprising. By contrast, the major mode does not include the altered forms of $\hat{3}$, $\hat{6}$, and $\hat{7}$; thus, if a musical passage is forging ahead in a major key but then introduces ♭$\hat{6}$, the result can be quite shocking and effective.

Altered Pre-Dominant Harmonies: iv and ii°

The most common scale degree involved in modal mixture is $\hat{6}$. There are four reasons why this is so.

- $\hat{6}$ is least likely to undermine the integrity of the home key and mode.
- Lowering $\hat{6}$ permits a strong half-step motion to the dominant.
- Modal mixture invoked on $\hat{6}$ colors all PD harmonies.
- $\hat{6}$ is the only scale degree outside of the tonic triad that may be consonantly supported by a harmony with $\hat{1}$ in the bass. Thus, it is a component of the contrapuntal 5–6 motion that figures prominently in music.

Example 13.2 shows how ♭$\hat{6}$, which is drawn from the parallel minor, alters the most common pre-dominants, ii, ii^7 and IV; the supertonic harmony becomes a diminished triad (ii°), ii^7 becomes a half-diminished seventh (ii^{ø7}), and the subdominant becomes a minor triad (iv). This type of chromatic alteration—which changes the *quality* of a chord but *does not alter its root*—is called **melodic mixture**. The labeling of chords to reflect melodic mixture is easy: We label the chord as if it were in a minor key.

EXAMPLE 13.2

C: ii°   ii^{ø7} iv

In Example 13.3, melodic mixture appears on the downbeat of m. 3 as the PD seventh chord incorporates ♭6̂ to become ii°⁷. One way to view this melodic mixture is to interpret the A♭ in the voice—a heartbreaking cry—as a surprising foreign tone to C major. When A♭ enters the melody in m. 3, it has a highly poetic function. Schumann is able to underscore the speaker's pain ("I bear no grudge, even if my heart breaks") by introducing dissonance through modal mixture. The jarring entrance of the A♭ shatters the major mode, just as the poet's heart ("Herz") is broken. Schumann leads the phrase to its high point on the word *heart*, extending the word for most of m. 3. The A♭ continues to intensify the pain by forming an even more dissonant minor ninth when the A♭ is sustained over the dominant (G).

EXAMPLE 13.3　Schumann, "Ich grolle nicht," *Dichterliebe,* op. 48, no. 7

Melodic mixture harmonies work very well in contrapuntal expansions of the tonic, especially as embedded phrase models (EPMs), as shown in Example 13.4.

EXAMPLE 13.4

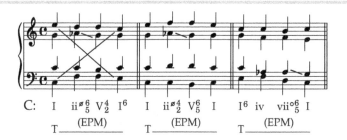

Altered Submediant Harmony: ♭VI

In melodic mixture, ♭6̂ appears as the *third* or the *fifth* of a mixture chord. A different situation occurs when ♭6̂ appears as the *root* of a mixture chord: In this case, the root of the chord has been shifted down from where it usually occurs. We describe this as **harmonic mixture**, and we write our roman numerals to reflect the change in the root. In Example 13.5, the A♭ major chord, with ♭6̂ as the root, is analyzed as a ♭VI chord.

EXAMPLE 13.5

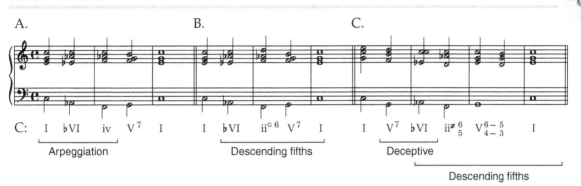

We use the generic "♭VI" to refer to all major triads built on the lowered form of 6̂ and when generally describing the chord, even if a natural rather than a flat is used to notate the chord (e.g., in A major, the ♭VI chord is built on F natural, not F flat). Despite its new roman numeral and chromatic inflection, ♭VI continues to function as a submediant chord.

- It participates in descending-thirds progressions (Example 13.5A).
- It participates in descending-fifths progressions (Example 13.5B).
- It follows the dominant (and substitutes for the tonic chord) in deceptive motions (Example 13.5C).

Altered Tonic Harmony: i

Scale degree ♭3 creates melodic mixture in altered tonic harmonies. Eighteenth-century composers were keenly aware of the ambiguity that can result from making a major tonic minor. Because this modal juxtaposition calls the mode of an entire piece into question, a minor tonic is more often only implied rather than literally stated. For example, in Example 13.6, the long chromatic line—which extends the dominant (before it returns to the tonic) and includes F—implies the parallel mode, D minor.

EXAMPLE 13.6   Mozart, Menuett in D major, K. 94

Despite this destabilizing effect, some eighteenth-century composers—including not only Bach but also Classical composers such as Haydn and Mozart—invoked modal mixture on the tonic. By the nineteenth century, some composers (such as Schubert) began to saturate their major-mode pieces with elements of the minor to such a degree that the 24 major and minor keys could be said to have fused into 12 major-minor keys. For example, it would be impossible to tell if a piece were in D major or D minor if it had equal numbers of Fs/F♯s and Bs/B♭s. In Example 13.7, the key of F major is pervaded with elements of F minor, including a tonicization of ♭III (A♭).

EXAMPLE 13.7   Schubert, "Schwanengesang," op. 23, no. 3, D. 744

Altered Mediant Harmony: ♭*III*

The ♭III chord arises from harmonic mixture, with ♭3̂ as its root. As Example 13.8 shows, ♭III continues to function as a mediant chord.

- It divides the fifth between I and V into two smaller thirds (Example 13.8A).
- It is a bridge between T and PD (Example 13.8B).
- It participates in descending-fifths motion (Example 13.8C), although less often than the diatonic iii chord.
- It is a PD chord (Example 13.8D).
- It can be preceded by its dominant (in minor keys, V/III leads to III; in major keys, this progression becomes V/♭III to ♭III) (Example 13.8E).

EXAMPLE 13.8

Voice Leading for Mixture Harmonies

The following guidelines restate and slightly develop the rules we used when writing applied dominant chords:

> GUIDELINE 1 Avoid doubling a chromatically altered tone unless it is the root of a chord (as in ♭VI).

> GUIDELINE 2 When possible, prepare and resolve the chromatically altered tones by step motion. Keeping the chromatic line in a single voice (as the neighboring 5̂–♭6̂–5̂ or the passing 6̂–♭6̂–5̂) helps to avoid cross relations.

> GUIDELINE 3 Once we introduce ♭VI, iv, or ii° mixture chords, continue to use mixture chords until we reach a dominant chord. This is because ♭6̂ possesses such a powerful drive downward to 5̂ that any intrusion of the diatonic 6̂ not only would create a jarring cross relation but would also ruin the drive to the dominant (Example 13.9).

EXAMPLE 13.9

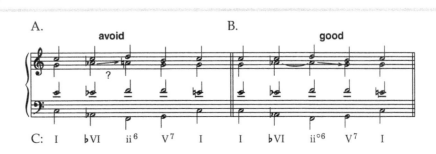

Plagal Motions

During the nineteenth century, the role of the dominant harmony gradually changed. For the most part, progressions still led to the tonic, but the dominant was often conspicuously absent from the cadence. This is due largely to nineteenth-century composers' obsession with creating novel harmonic combinations along with a general distaste for commonplace formulas such as V⁷–I. The growing acceptance of mixture harmonies partially accounts for this change, since their dramatic effects made them popular substitutes for the dominant.

For example, iv leads convincingly to the dominant in both major and minor modes. In a way, though, because ♭$\hat{6}$ strongly desires resolution by half step to $\hat{5}$, iv also can move directly to the tonic at a plagal cadence (Example 13.10A). Plagal motions are not restricted to the iv chord; both ii° and ♭VI may also move directly to tonic (Example 13.10B and C). The **Hollywood cadence** in Example 13.10B is commonly heard in popular music of the 1920s through the 1950s and in films today.

EXAMPLE 13.10

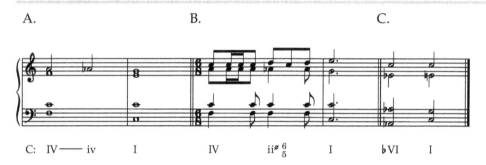

Example 13.11 presents a passage that uses plagal motion and lacks dominant harmony entirely. The excerpt begins with an expansion of tonic harmony through an upper-neighbor figure G–A–G in the alto. Although a repetition of this figure is expected in m. 3, ♭VI instead participates in the upper-neighbor figure, now chromaticized (G–A♭–G). The mixture continues with ♭VI and minor iv resolving to the tonic in a plagal cadence.

EXAMPLE 13.11   Brahms, Symphony no. 3 in F major, op. 90, *Andante*

Modal Mixture, Applied Chords, and Other Chromatic Harmonies

Two tonal processes account for chromaticism in tonal music.

1. Tonicization is intimately associated with *dominant* function, as new chromatic tones act as *leading tones*.
2. Modal mixture usually occurs within the *pre-dominant* function, as the new chromatic tones retain their scale degree function, but in an *altered* form.

Occasionally, composers use two other modal mixture harmonies on $\hat{3}$ and $\hat{6}$ of a major key, but these harmonies are not borrowed from the parallel minor key. The first is a major mediant chord whose root is an unaltered, diatonic $\hat{3}$. This major "III" chord is sometimes labeled "III♯" to distinguish it from the mixture chord ♭III that we have already seen. Like the diatonic iii and the mixture ♭III, the major III♯ chord most often is part of a rising bass line that often includes a pre-dominant. In Example 13.12A, the D-major chord in the first measure leads to the pre-dominant ii⁶ chord; in this case, D major acts as a mediant chord and is labeled III♯. Compare this with Example 13.12B, where the same D-major chord leads to a G-minor chord (vi). Now, the D-major chord has a different function—it is the applied dominant chord to G minor—and is therefore analyzed differently (as V/vi). It is important to discern between III♯ and applied V/vi chords!

EXAMPLE 13.12

B♭:   I ——————— III♯   ii⁶   V   I   I ——————— V/vi   vi   ii⁶   V   I

The second chromatic harmony that one occasionally encounters is a major submediant chord whose root is an unaltered, diatonic $\hat{6}$. This major "VI" chord, sometimes labeled "VI♯," is shown in Example 13.13A, where it leads to the pre-dominant IV chord as part of a I–VI♯–IV progression. Example 13.13B has the same A-major chord, followed by D minor. As in Example 13.12, we must discern the function of this chord: Since it is the applied dominant chord to D minor, we label the chord V/ii.

EXAMPLE 13.13

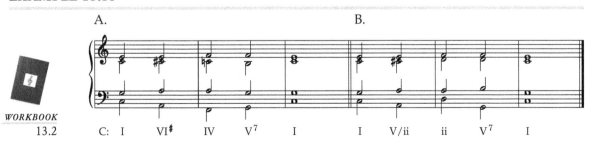

WORKBOOK
13.2   C: I   VI♯   IV   V⁷   I   I   V/ii   ii   V⁷   I

Expansion of Modal Mixture Harmonies: Chromatic Modulation

♭VI and ♭III are the most commonly tonicized chromatic harmonies in eighteenth- and nineteenth-century music. We now explore the means by which composers move smoothly from diatonic harmonies to keys based on chromatic harmonies. We will then see how **chromatic modulations** function logically within the harmonic progression of entire works.

Chromatic Pivot-Chord Modulations

In order to move smoothly from one key area to another, composers usually employ a pivot harmony that is common to both keys. When we search for a suitable pivot for chromatic modulation, however, we encounter a problem: Often, there are no triads common in both keys. For example, there are no chords in common between C major and A♭ major, the key of ♭VI (Example 13.14A). However, the knowledge that a major key often borrows from its parallel minor allows us to reenvision our move from C major as one from C major/minor to A♭ major (Example 13.14B). Permitting modal mixture to enter into the equation causes four potential pivot chords to emerge.

EXAMPLE 13.14

A.

triads in C major:

I   ii   iii   IV   V   vi   vii°

triads in A♭ major:

iii   IV   V   vi   vii°   I   ii

B.

triads in C:

major:
I   ii   iii   IV   V   vi   vii°

minor:
i   ii°   III   iv   v   VI   VII

triads in A♭ major:

iii   IV   V   vi   vii°   I   ii

Since **chromatic pivot-chord modulations** typically use mixture chords in the original key, the presence of modal mixture in nineteenth-century music often signals an upcoming chromatic modulation. In Example 13.15A, the modal shift from E major (I) to E minor (i) in m. 3 nicely prepares the overall motion from the key of E major (I) to the key of C major (♭VI). This same strategy is used in Example 13.15B, although it is considerably—and artfully—expanded.

EXAMPLE 13.15

A.

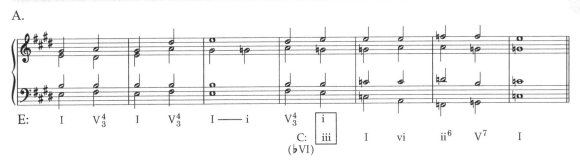

B.   Beethoven, Piano Sonata in E major, op. 90

Writing Chromatic Pivot-Chord Modulations

1. Add the necessary accidentals in the new key, or change the key signature.
2. The pivot chord must always result from modal mixture.
3. In order to create a seamless musical process and allow listeners to get acclimated to the new tonal environment, do not hurry to the cadence in the new key. Expand PD, or use an EPM, in order to postpone the cadence.

Example 13.16 shows one way to modulate from C major to A♭ major (♭VI), using the following steps.

- C major is established with an EPM. Note that mixture is already hinted with the ii$^{\varnothing 4}_{2}$ chord.
- The pivot chord is a mixture chord in the original key (iv^6 in C major) and a diatonic chord in the new key (vi^6 in A♭ major).
- In the new key, the submediant is elaborated (with a V$^4_3$/vi chord) in order to postpone the cadence.
- This is followed by the cadential dominant and tonic, with a PAC in A♭ major.

EXAMPLE 13.16

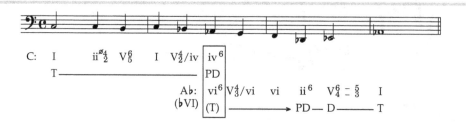

Unprepared and Common-Tone Chromatic Modulations

Unprepared chromatic modulations (sometimes referred to as *direct modulations*) occur without the aid of a pivot chord (Example 13.17). The change of key is abrupt and instant, with no strong audible connection between keys.

EXAMPLE 13.17 Haydn, String Quartet in C major, op. 54, no. 2, Hob. III. 58, *Allegro*

Most chromatic modulations are not as abrupt as that of Example 13.17. In Example 13.18, Schubert juxtaposes D major (I) with B♭ major (♭VI). The D in the violins at the beginning of the Trio is common to both keys: It is 1̂ in D major and 3̂ in B♭ major. This creates a **common-tone modulation**, a modulation that strips away all but one pitch from the original key—this pitch also exists in the new key and becomes the thread that connects the two keys.

EXAMPLE 13.18   **Schubert, String Quartet no. 3 in B♭ major, D. 36, *Minuetto/Trio***

Continued

Trio

Bb:

Analytical Extension: Modal Mixture and Text–Music Relations

We now look at songs written by two of the most important composers of the nineteenth century: Franz Schubert and Robert Schumann. We see how modal mixture functions in larger contexts, and we explore how composers control the interaction of music and poetry to project underlying poetic meaning in their vocal compositions.

In nineteenth-century Germany, the genre of song (*Lied*, pl. *Lieder*) became an important laboratory for experimentation. The idea was to develop musically expressive forces that would be capable of meeting the needs of communicating the emotionally rich poetry of the time. Modal mixture was often at the heart of these innovations. For example, the juxtaposition of mixture tones and harmonies against diatonic ones is almost always a sign of emotional conflicts, tensions, or contradictions. Consider the role of $\hat{6}$ (in both raised and lowered forms) in Schubert's song "Laughter and Tears" (Example 13.19).

EXAMPLE 13.19 Schubert, "Lachen und Weinen"

Etwas geschwind

Ab:

In m. 21, the shift from A♭ major to A♭ minor prepares the listener for the substitution of ♭6̂ for 6̂ at m. 25; this is where the new expressive tone underscores the melancholy text, "and why I weep now." The specific placement of the sigh on F♭–E♭ (mm. 25–26) strongly highlights the word *weep*. The next development of F♭, at m. 27, transforms the pitch ♭6̂ into the chord ♭VI. The ♭VI chord captures the protagonist's wonder at love's ability to arouse conflicting feelings of pain at twilight and joy at daybreak by means of a strange and wondrous-sounding chromatic harmony. In summary, the diatonic and mixed forms of 6̂ represent these two sides of his emotions. Both forms of 6̂ are neighbors to 5̂; that they share a common genesis in 5̂ may be analogous to the fact that love is the source of both his pain and his joy.

Robert Schumann also used modal mixture to project poetic drama. In his song "Waldesgesprach" (Example 13.20), what appears at first as a simple chromatic tonicization is revealed through analysis to be an important dramatic moment. As the song gathers momentum, we will see how the motion to ♭VI reverberates throughout the song, foreshadowing and directing the surprising turn of events that follow.

The story begins traditionally enough: A horseman comes across a beautiful woman deep in the forest, and after informing her of the dangers of the woods and extolling her beauty, he offers to guide her home. The unsettling chromatic departure to C major (♭VI of E major) to herald the woman's entrance is curious. This abrupt juxtaposition of E major and C major, coupled with the man's inability to complete the final word of his phrase, *heim* ("home"), in his key rather than in her foreign key not only enhances the strangeness of this woman, cloaking her in tonal mystery, but also plants the seeds for his later demise.

The woman informs the man that she has been hurt in love before and by a hunter. Apparently, from her past unsuccessful encounters, she has now gained some sort of strength, intimating an otherworldly power, and warns the man that he does not know with whom (or what) he is dealing. She gives him one—and only one—chance to flee. Foolishly, the man stays and continues his flattery. But just as there was an abrupt shift in the first section, so too is there one here. As he realizes she is the infamous Lorelei, a demon in the form of a beautiful woman who lures men to their death, placid E major is thrown over by its parallel minor, the stark modal shift enhancing this terror-filled moment. In the final verse, the woman informs the man that he is ensnared and will never again leave the forest: He is hers.

EXAMPLE 13.20   Schumann, "Waldesgesprach," *Liederkreis*, op. 39, no. 3

Es ist schon
It   is   late,

Continued

aug. 6th ⟶ V (as IV/E)   ii⌀⁶₅   V

her ____ und hin,   o flieh',_   o flieh'._   du weisst   nicht, wer ich bin.
here   and there   Oh flee!   You do   not   know   who   I am

So reich ge - schmückt_ist Ross__ und Weib,_ so wun - der-schön, so wun-der-schön der
So richly   covered   are horse   and   woman,   so   beautiful   her

jun - ge Leib;_ jetzt kenn' ich dich, Gott steh mir bei,   du bist die He-xe Lo - re - lei!
young   body   Now I   know who you are—God save me!   You are the witch, Lorelei!

Du kennst   mich wohl,   du kennst__ mich wohl, von ho-hem
Indeed   you know me—from rock's height

The introduction to the song captures an out-of-doors feeling with its sprightly triple meter. The simple alternation of tonic and dominant in the bass lends a folklike quality to the song, while the syncopated upper voice of the left hand—with the emphasis on beat 2—creates a fifth drone and rhythmically suggests the feel of folk dances such as the mazurka and polonaise. The lilting right hand also supports the rustic character of the introduction. In fact, the two-voice intervallic progression in the right hand with stepwise motion (E–F♯–G♯) occurring over leaps (G♯–B–E) is used by Schumann because of its connection with the sound of hunting horns. This trick of invoking the idea of the hunt has a double meaning in the song: Not only do we think immediately of the dense forest, its fauna, and the hunter's horn, but we are also reminded of another meaning of the hunt—that of seduction. By the end of the poem, however, we discover that our original expectations are shattered as the roles of hunter and prey are reversed.

The form of the song is dependent on the interaction of its two characters:

A (he speaks)—B (she speaks)—A' (he speaks)—B' (she speaks)—Coda

A number of musical features reinforce hearing the piece in this way: The piano interludes separate the sections; there is highly contrasting melodic, accompanimental, and tonal material in the B section; and motion from E major to C major (♭VI) powerfully separates the A and A' sections from the B section. This motion to ♭VI is initially quite surprising, but in retrospect we see that it is a deceptive motion (V→♭VI) in E major, which turns C major into the tonic.

Analytical Payoff: The Dramatic Role of ♭VI

By virtue of its surprising arrival at m. 14 and its otherworldly sound, ♭VI plays an important role in creating mystery and distance. Its appearance, like a rock thrown into a pond, creates musical ripples that extend to the outer reaches of the song. This strange, new harmony seems to characterize the speech of the unknown woman in the piece's B section. Now let us turn to the moment in which he realizes who she is. The hunter begins his A' section (m. 33) pretty much as his A began, seemingly oblivious to the woman's warnings. But at the moment of the modal shift to E minor (m. 41), the man's tune moves in a new direction. His melody is strongly reminiscent of the Lorelei's tune, with her ascending line G–A–B–C recurring in his ascending motion. The effect is more than simple association: The witch's seductive powers have begun to permeate his being, and the decomposition of his melodic independence represents his loosening of will.

On the other side, the modal shift from E major to E minor, which places the Lorelei's key of C major within easy reach, further suggests that he is slipping into her tonal power. E minor is part of her tonal domain: It is diatonic to her C major, making his eventual abduction almost certain. The final step in his demise occurs in the Lorelei's closing strophe (m. 46). Her musical texture returns unchanged, save for one crucial alteration: It is recast in his key, E major. His tonal foundation of E major, a metaphor for his physical being, has now been secured by the Lorelei; indeed, even his opening words, "Es ist schon spät, es ist schon kalt," are now possessed and sung ironically by the victor. It is clear that the man is ensnared in her forest arms, never to return home. That the postlude reprises the introduction—lilting, happy, and naive—shows that the forest returns to its placid and amiable state, but the Lorelei, like a Venus flytrap, awaits her next victim.

CHAPTER 14

Two Important Chromatic Harmonies: The Neapolitan Chord and the Augmented Sixth Chord

Listen to the excerpt from one of Schubert's songs in Example 14.1. Keep a tally of particularly striking chromatic harmonies—where are they, and what contributes to their novel sound?

EXAMPLE 14.1   Schubert, "Der Müller und der Bach," *Die schöne Müllerin*, D. 795, no. 19

Continued

A new chromatic harmony first appears in m. 8 (and again in m. 16 and m. 25). We have seen previously that there are two main types of chromaticism: (1) applied chords, which alter the function (and roman numeral) of diatonic chords in order to tonicize other keys; and (2) mixture, which alters the quality of a diatonic chord but does not change its roman numeral or function. What kind of chord do we have here? The chord in m. 8 is a major triad; its quality suggests that it may be an applied chord. However, as such it would be the dominant of D♭ (♭V of G minor), and we certainly have not encountered "♭V"!

Clearly this is a pre-dominant function chord, with the bass C ($\hat{4}$) and the pitch E♭ ($\hat{6}$) both pulling toward D ($\hat{5}$). The A♭ ($\flat\hat{2}$) is a chromatic pitch that substitutes for the diatonic A. As a result, instead of a ii°6 chord (C–E♭–A), we have a major triad in first inversion, a ♭II⁶ chord (C–E♭–A♭). This chord, commonly called the **Neapolitan chord,** occurs more often in minor-mode pieces than in major-mode pieces (Example 14.2A), and it usually occurs in first inversion in order to have a smooth bass motion to $\hat{5}$ rather than an awkward tritone leap from $\flat\hat{2}$ to $\hat{5}$ (Example 14.2B). In the major mode, both the supertonic and the submediant are lowered ($\flat\hat{2}$ and $\flat\hat{6}$, respectively), as in Example 14.2C.

EXAMPLE 14.2

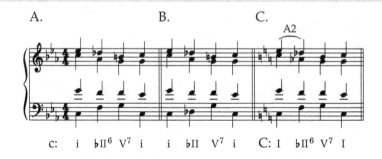

Writing the Neapolitan Chord

- ♭II⁶–V progressions will have a ♭$\hat{2}$–$\hat{7}$ motion in one of the upper voices—usually the soprano (Example 14.2A).
- Double the bass, $\hat{4}$. (See Example 14.2A.) If necessary, you may double $\hat{6}$.
- In minor, any chord that would precede ii°⁶ can also precede ♭II⁶.
- In major, the common chords before ♭II⁶ are tonic (I) and mixture chords (♭III, ♭VI, iv). When writing in major, avoid the augmented second that occurs between $\hat{3}$ and ♭$\hat{2}$ (Example 14.2C).
- The ultimate goal of the Neapolitan chord is to move to V. However, there are two common ways to move from ♭II⁶ to V, both of which harmonize a passing $\hat{1}$ (Example 14.3).

EXAMPLE 14.3

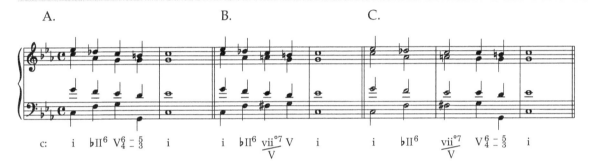

Other Uses for the Neapolitan Chord

The Neapolitan can be part of a sequence—a bonus of incorporating the Neapolitan in sequences is that it allows for root-position ♭II. Example 14.4 uses a (−3/+4) sequence with applied chords that continues all the way to V. The use of ♭II in the (−3/+4) sequence is much more common in minor-mode works.

EXAMPLE 14.4

WORKBOOK
14.1–14.3

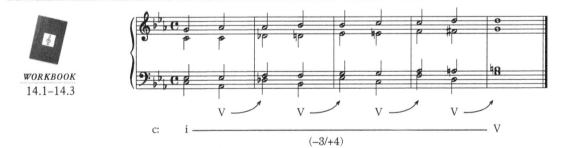

The Neapolitan is also effective as a pivot chord when modulating to diatonic as well as chromatic keys.

The Augmented Sixth Chord

Listen to the excerpt in Example 14.5 and focus on the second-to-last chord. Can we assign a roman numeral to this chord? What is its root? D♯? If so, then the chord is D♯–F–A–B, which is not a quality of chord we can label easily with a roman numeral. Since this chord doesn't lend itself to a roman numeral analysis, let's focus on the melodic motion. $\hat6$ and $\sharp\hat4$ play important roles in this chord: Both $\hat6$ (bass) and $\sharp\hat4$ (soprano) push outward by half step to $\hat5$. The $\hat6$ and $\sharp\hat4$ create the strongly directed interval of the **augmented sixth**. Therefore, we call this chord an **augmented sixth chord.**

EXAMPLE 14.5   Handel, "Since by Man Came Death," *Messiah,* HWV 56

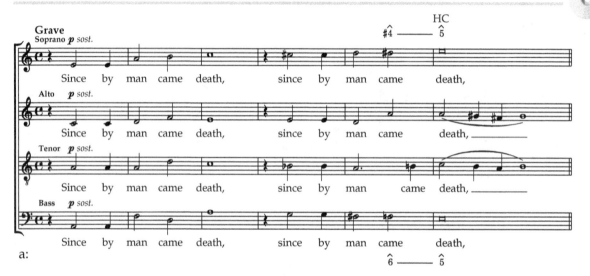

Is an augmented sixth chord an example of an applied chord or a mixture chord? To answer this question, consider the diatonic progression in Example 14.6A. Then study the progression in Example 14.6B. There is a mixture iv⁶ chord in Example 14.6B, which introduces ♭$\hat6$, a bass note that is a half step above $\hat5$. Compare Examples 14.6A and 14.6C; the difference this time is in the chord's function, with IV⁶ changed into the applied vii°⁶/V through the use of the soprano $\sharp\hat4$.

EXAMPLE 14.6

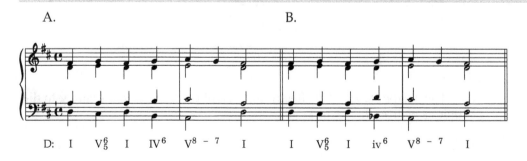

C.   D.

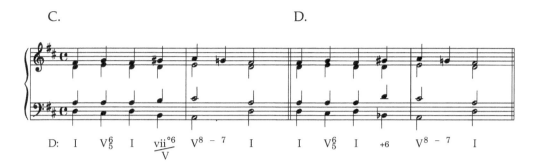

D: I   V⁶₅   I   vii°⁶   V⁸ ⁻ ⁷   I   I   V⁶₅   I   +6   V⁸ ⁻ ⁷   I
                         ───
                          V

Thus, the mixture iv⁶ uses ♭$\hat{6}$ in the bass, and the applied vii°⁶/V uses ♯$\hat{4}$ in the soprano. So how do we describe the augmented sixth chord that has both pitches (Example 14.6D)? It is the ultimate chromatic chord, combining mixture (bass ♭$\hat{6}$) and tonicization (♯4) to create the augmented sixth that pushes toward the dominant. The augmented sixth chord is typically preceded by a tonic chord, a subdominant chord, (♭)VI, or (♭)III; it is almost always followed by V or the cadential $\frac{6}{4}$ chord.

Types of Augmented Sixth Chords

There are three basic components of all augmented sixth chords we will study.

1. The bass is a *half step above* $\hat{5}$.
   a. In minor keys, the bass is the diatonic $\hat{6}$ and does not need an accidental.
   b. In major keys, the bass is ♭$\hat{6}$, requiring an accidental.
2. One of the upper voices—often the soprano—is a *half step below* $\hat{5}$, on ♯$\hat{4}$.
3. Another upper voice has *the tonic,* $\hat{1}$.

We distinguish three types of augmented sixth chords, based on the pitch in the final upper voice (Example 14.7). We label augmented sixth chords using their "regional" names followed by their figured bass (without chromatic alterations).

- If the final upper voice doubles $\hat{1}$, it creates an **Italian augmented sixth chord,** It⁶ (Example 14.7A).

- If the voice has $\hat{2}$, it creates a **French augmented sixth chord,** Fr⁴₃ (Example 14.7C).

- The **German augmented sixth chord,** Ger⁶₅, includes $\hat{3}$ in minor keys (Example 14.7B and D).

  - In major keys, this added pitch is ♭$\hat{3}$. When a Ger⁶₅ occurs in the major mode and leads to a cadential $\frac{6}{4}$ with a *major* sixth above the bass, composers often notate ♭$\hat{3}$ using the enharmonic equivalent ♯$\hat{2}$ (Example 14.7E).

EXAMPLE 14.7

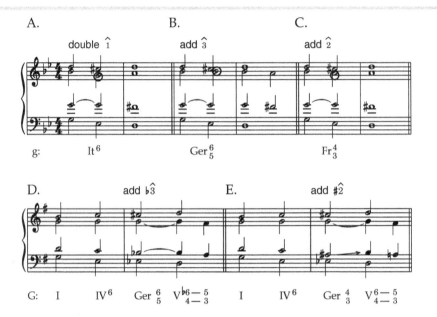

Writing Augmented Sixth Chords

The voice leading after an augmented sixth chord is straightforward, due to the number of tendency tones in the chord. The bass moves down by half step to $\hat{5}$, the upper voice with $\sharp\hat{4}$ moves up by half step to $\hat{5}$, and the other voices move as smoothly as possible (usually by step). The most common chord after the augmented sixth is V; however, the progression Ger$^6_5$–V involves parallel fifths and is often avoided (Example 14.8A). Instead, a Ger$^6_5$ is followed first by the cadential $^6_4$, before resolving to the V; this results in no forbidden parallel motions (Example 14.8B).

EXAMPLE 14.8

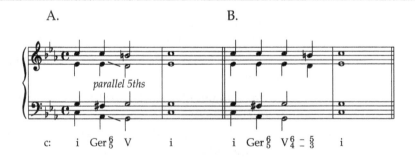

If an augmented sixth chord moves directly to V^7, $\sharp\hat{4}$ does not resolve to $\hat{5}$ but instead slides down to the diatonic $\hat{4}$ (Example 14.9).

EXAMPLE 14.9

#̂4 resolves down to 4̂

g: i   Fr $\frac{4}{3}$ V^7 i

(♭)VI and the Ger$^6_5$ Chord

There is a special relationship between VI and Ger$^6_5$ in a minor key (and between ♭VI and Ger$^6_5$ in a major key). The Ger$^6_5$ contains all of the pitches in the (♭)VI chord, plus #̂4. This relationship is particularly helpful when VI moves to the dominant. In Example 14.10, the tonicized ♭VI (mm. 10–12) is destabilized by the F♯, which converts ♭VI into Ger$^6_5$, and the music moves smoothly to a V–I cadence.

EXAMPLE 14.10   Schubert, Waltz in C major, *Valses sentimentales*, D. 779, no. 16

♭VI ----------→ Ger $^6_5$ V$^8_{6 \atop 4}$ ══════ $^{7 \atop 5 \atop 3}$ I

The Augmented Sixth Chord as a Pivot Chord

You may have already discovered that the It⁶ is enharmonically equivalent to an incomplete V⁷ (Example 14.11A) and that Ger$_5^6$ is enharmonically equivalent to a complete V⁷ chord (Example 14.11B).

EXAMPLE 14.11

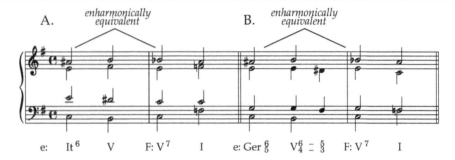

We can take advantage of this enharmonic relationship by treating this sonority as a pivot chord. Such **enharmonic reinterpretation** permits certain chromatic modulations, as in Example 14.12. Beethoven's enharmonic reinterpretation of the Ger$_5^6$ chord (E♭–G–B♭–C♯) as a V⁷ chord (E♭–G–B♭–D♭) allows him to tonicize A♭ (♭II) effortlessly.

EXAMPLE 14.12   Beethoven, "Rage Over a Lost Penny," op. 129

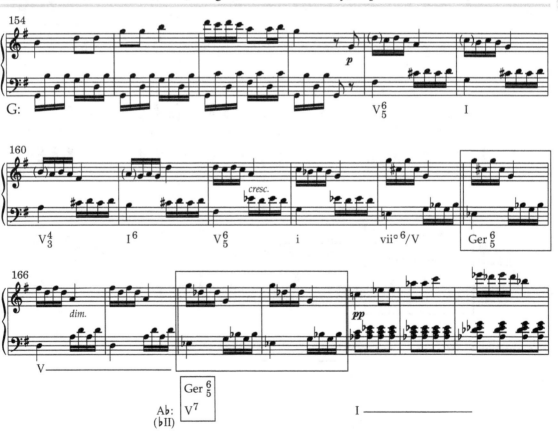

Instead of notating the Ger_5^6 and V^7 chords successively in their two forms, one form is sometimes used as a pivot chord between the two harmonic areas (Example 14.13).

EXAMPLE 14.13

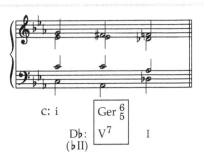

The excerpt in Example 14.14 shows another enharmonic reinterpretation, this time from B♭ major to B minor—an enharmonically respelled C♭ minor—the distant key of ♭ii.

EXAMPLE 14.14   Strauss, *Serenade*, Op. 7

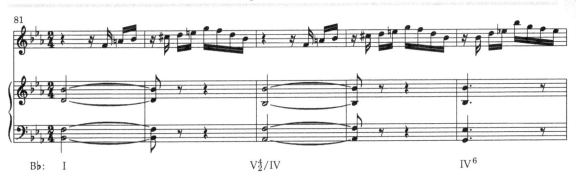

WORKBOOK
14.6

Analytical Extension: Prolongation with ♭II and +6 Chords

The Neapolitan chord is like any other major chord. It can be prolonged with a chordal leap in the bass (Example 14.15A), by tonicization (Example 14.15B and C), and by extended tonicization (Example 14.15D).

EXAMPLE 14.15

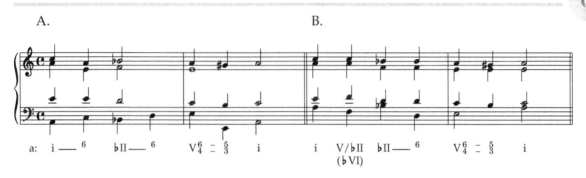

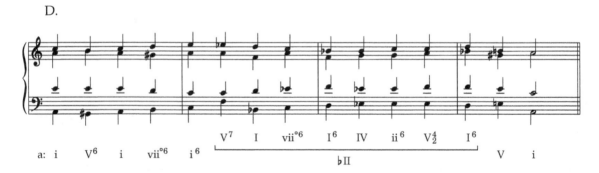

Sometimes composers tonicize ♭II merely by restating material up a half step—from I to ♭II—which is a common procedure in middle-period Beethoven pieces, such as Example 14.16. The root-position Neapolitan of mm. 6–7 occurs when the opening tune of mm. 3–4 is transposed a half step higher in m. 6. Melodically, this presents an important motive, B–C, which is highlighted within mm. 3–6. Note that this example—and the preceding examples—demonstrates the Neapolitan's pre-dominant function within the overall progressions.

EXAMPLE 14.16 **Beethoven, String Quartet in E minor, op. 59, no. 2,** *Allegro*

Listen to Example 14.17. The Neapolitan in m. 24 is contrapuntally prepared in the previous measure by the 5–6 motion from I, over the bass D♭/C♯.
A♭ moves to A (the enharmonic spelling of ♭$\hat{6}$, B♭♭), creating a V$^6_5$/♭II. When the
Neapolitan arrives at the downbeat of m. 24, Chopin spells it enharmonically as D major rather than as E♭♭ major. Chopin's *ppp* dynamic marking at
this moment helps the performer interpret this special harmonic coloration.
The Neapolitan's bass motion up to V is accomplished by the vii°$^4_3$/V chord
in m. 25; this chord is pivotal, because it sounds like a mixture coloring of the
right-hand B-natural in m. 24, yet the vii°$^4_3$/V also leads to V^7 (A♭) as an applied chord.

EXAMPLE 14.17   Chopin, Nocturne in B♭ minor, op. 9, no. 1

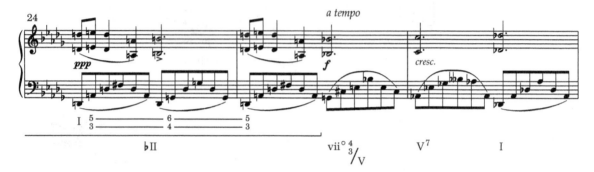

Augmented Sixth Chords as Part of PD Expansions

Augmented sixth chords frequently combine with other pre-dominant harmonies to expand the pre-dominant function. Given that two of its voices are
so goal-directed toward $\hat{5}$, an augmented sixth chord is usually the last event
before the dominant, following either iv$^{(6)}$ or VI. Augmented sixth chords often appear in chromaticized bass descents as the final step before the dominant (Example 14.18A). One of the most important techniques for expanding
the PD is to move from iv through a passing $^6_4$ chord to iv^6 (Example 14.18B);
it is also common for iv to move to a different PD harmony, such as the ii$^{ø6}_5$ in
Example 14.18C. In both cases, the expansion of the PD involves a prominent
voice exchange between the bass and one of the upper voices.

EXAMPLE 14.18

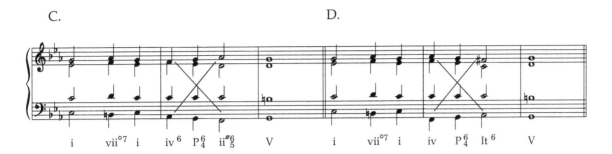

C.   D.

i   vii°⁷ i   iv⁶ P⁶₄ ii°⁶₅ V   i   vii°⁷ i   iv   P⁶₄ It⁶   V

Since the augmented sixth chord is structured similarly to iv⁶, it often participates as the final chord in PD expansions of the type shown in Example 14.18B. However, when chromatic augmented sixth chords occur with other diatonic pre-dominants (such as iv and ii⁶), the resulting voice exchange is not exact. This can be seen in m. 2 of Example 14.18D, in which the F and A♭ of the iv chord swap to become the A♭ and F♯ of the It⁶ chord. This special type of swapping of cross relations is called a **chromatic voice exchange.** Example 14.19 illustrates both a diatonic voice exchange (m. 108 to downbeat of m. 109) and a chromatic voice exchange (m. 109).

EXAMPLE 14.19   **C.P.E. Bach, Flute Sonata no. 6 in G major, Wq 134 H548,** *Allegro*

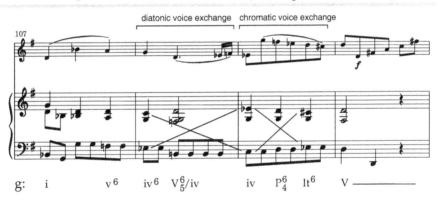

diatonic voice exchange   chromatic voice exchange

g: i   v⁶   iv⁶   V⁶₅/iv   iv   P⁶₄ It⁶   V ——————

In rarer cases where the PD expansion involves only an augmented sixth chord, the resulting voice exchange is literal, as in Example 14.20A. The chord on the downbeat of m. 1 in Example 14.20A is a Ger⁶₅. The chord on beat 3 of that measure sounds like—and contains the same pitches as—a Ger⁶₅, although the pitches have been reordered such that ♯4̂ appears in the bass and ♭6̂ in an upper voice. The resulting chord is therefore an inversion of the augmented sixth and is called a **German diminished third chord.** Since the figure for this chord would be "7," we label the German diminished third chord as **Ger⁷**. The individual voices of this chord behave identically to those in any augmented sixth chord—$\hat{6}$ descends to $\hat{5}$ and $\sharp\hat{4}$ ascends to $\hat{5}$—but given that the pitches are switched from the traditional Ger$^6_5$ arrangement, the voices contract on resolution instead of expand (see Example 14.20B).

EXAMPLE 14.20

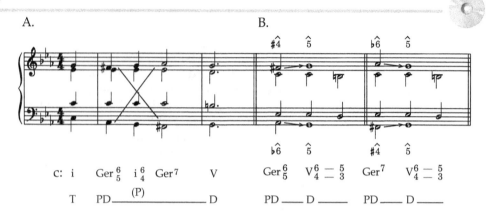

CHAPTER 15

Ternary and Sonata Forms

In this final chapter we explore two important large forms: ternary form and sonata form. Taken together, these forms fittingly describe the structure of vast numbers of instrumental and vocal works composed throughout the eighteenth and nineteenth centuries. Learning to recognize these forms and their local and large-scale harmonic procedures will be a major step toward comprehending the design of classical works.

In addition to exploring formal strategies, we will look at musical processes that unfold throughout a piece and that provide musical narratives for both listener and performer. Generally these processes are motivic, and they range from simple repetitions that are slightly obscured by the musical surface to significant transformations in which the motive is expanded at the very deepest level of structure.

Ternary Form

Ternary form is a three-part form whose sections are self-contained. The three independent sections feature strong melodic contrast (ABA or ABA') and a three-part tonal structure (original key–contrasting key–original key) with sections that usually begin and end conclusively in the same key (see Example 15.1A). Binary form is different from ternary form, since its sections are tonally dependent on one another and can be viewed as being more organic in construction. Contrast the design of ternary form with rounded binary form, which has a three-part melodic design (a-dig-a') but a two-part tonal structure (Example 15.1B).

EXAMPLE 15.1

A. Ternary form

A	B	A or (A')
° original material	° contrasting material	° literal repetition of A (or altered restatement, labeled A')

° original key	° contrasting key:
	  (major mode: IV, vi, iv, ♭VI, i)
	  (minor mode: III, iv, VI, I)
		° original key

B. Rounded binary form

: a   :|: digression   a'   :
° in one key   I _____V // | I _____V I

The three distinct and autonomous parts in Example 15.2 may be labeled ABA'. The fast, folklike B part in the parallel major key highly contrasts with the brooding A and A' parts. The piece is in ternary form because each of the three sections is harmonically and thematically closed, and the B section is self-standing. If each of the three sections of a ternary form closes in its respective tonic, as in Example 15.2, we call the form a **full sectional ternary form** (A. B. A'.—periods represent closed sections). If the A section were to close away from its tonic chord (A B. A'.—not common), or if the B section were to close away from its tonic chord (A. B A'.—common), then we refer to these as examples of a **sectional ternary form**. When both A and B close away from their respective tonic chords (ABA'.), we call the form a **continuous ternary form**.

Sometimes it may not be easy to distinguish a continuous ternary form from a rounded binary form. To decide whether a form is rounded binary or continuous ternary, consider how much the B part is dependent on the A part. If there is little connection, a ternary form is indicated. By contrast, if there is a thematic or motivic connection and little or no change of key, it is better termed a binary form. Like much of your musical analysis, you must interpret such works according to how you hear them and then support your answer.

EXAMPLE 15.2   Grieg, "Hjemve," *Lyric Pieces*, Book VI, op. 57, no. 6

Continued

Continued

Transitions and Retransitions

Composers sometimes write *bridging* sections in order to create a sense of continuity in a ternary form. Material that bridges between tonic and a new key (from A to B) is called a **transition**. Bridging material that leads from a contrasting key back to tonic (from B to A') is a *returning transition*, or a **retransition**. Note that a ternary form may have a transition and a retransition, a transition without a retransition, a retransition without a transition, or no bridging material at all. We will see that retransitions occur much more frequently than transitions.

Transitions and retransitions make for some of the most exciting music in a piece, because their material is completely unpredictable. They may be as simple as presenting the dominant of the upcoming key, or they may be considerably more involved, delicately foreshadowing motives and harmonies of the upcoming section. Consider the relationship between the A and B sections in Example 15.3. The outer parts of Brahms' *Romanze* are in F major, and the contrasting B section (beginning in m. 17) is in the remote key of D major (VI). The B part is further distinguished from A by a faster tempo and a meter change. If we view the transition as the final measure of the A section (m. 16), then it is present but quite short. Here, a bass arpeggiation of D minor prepares the upcoming D-major section. All that is required is a modal shift to the parallel major.

EXAMPLE 15.3 Brahms, Romanze in F major, *Six Piano Pieces*, op. 118, no. 5, mm. 1–19

Continued

A retransition prepares for A′ after the B section (Example 15.4). The retransition begins by shifting to the lullaby-like $\frac{6}{4}$ meter of the A section and by reprising the A section's two-note slurred chords in parallel sixths (m. 45). Yet elements of the B part are retained in the retransition, the most obvious of which are the key of D major and the trills that close the retransition. In m. 46, D major moves to D minor, which functions as diatonic vi in F major; this is followed by a cadential six-four chord in F major that resolves directly to the tonic (mm. 47–48). Thus, Brahms' work is a sectional ternary form, with a transition and a retransition.

EXAMPLE 15.4   Brahms, Romanze in F major, *Six Piano Pieces*, op. 118, no. 5, mm. 37–50

Da Capo Form: Compound Ternary Form

The ABA structure of da capo works is realized by following the marking at the end of the score, "Da Capo (al 𝄐)," which in literal translation means "from the head to the fermata sign," telling the performer to return to the beginning of the piece and to play to the fermata sign. It is the return that creates the final balancing A section; the da capo instruction merely saves space and ink. Example 15.5 is in **da capo form**.

EXAMPLE 15.5   Haydn, Divertimento in G major, Hob. XVI/11, *Presto*

Continued

Haydn's Divertimento (Example 15.5) is much like Grieg's work in Example 15.2. Both are full sectional ternary forms, and both include smaller binary forms within the larger ternary form. These are **compound ternary forms**, because larger parts divide into smaller forms (Example 15.6).

EXAMPLE 15.6

A.   Grieg (Example 15.2)

measures:	1–8	9–18	19–27	28–67	68–75	76–85	86–94
large parts:	A _____			B	A' _____		
small parts:	*a*	*dig*	a'		*a*	*dig*	a'
	(rounded binary)				*(rounded binary)*		

B.   Haydn (Example 15.5)

measures:	1–8	9–16	17–24	25–32	33–40	41–48	1–8	9–16	17–24
large parts:	A _____			B _____			A'_____		
small parts:	*a*	*dig*	a'	b	*dig*	b'	*a*	*dig*	a'
	(rounded binary)			*(rounded binary)*			*(rounded binary)*		

Minuet-Trio Form

The Baroque **minuet** was a type of dance that remained popular in the following Classical period, when it became a standard inner movement in symphonies and chamber pieces such as serenades, divertimentos, and sonatas. In the hands of first Haydn and Beethoven, the minuet was often transformed into a more spirited piece called the **scherzo**. The Classical minuet is followed without pause by a companion piece of lighter texture, called a **trio**, after which a "da capo" marking indicates that the minuet is to be repeated. The result is a large ternary form called **minuet-trio form**.

As with many composite forms, the minuet-trio form is often a compound ternary, with nested binary forms. Example 15.7 is a full sectional ternary form, and both the minuet and the trio are rounded continuous binary forms. The minuet, in F minor, moves from i to III in the first *a* section. The digression is characteristically more transitory, tonicizing iv briefly in mm. 19–25 before the V and interruption in m. 28. The underlying tonal progression of the minuet is i–III–iv–V ‖ i–V–i.

EXAMPLE 15.7   Beethoven, Piano Sonata in F minor, op. 2, no. 1, *Menuetto/Trio*

Continued

WORKBOOK
15.1–15.2

Sonata Form

Sonata form is a process on which many of the greatest compositions from the later eighteenth and nineteenth centuries are based. We explore its history, trace the evolution of its form, and analyze two examples from the literature.

Originally, in the sixteenth century, the term *sonata* was used as a signal that a given musical work was to be performed instrumentally and not sung. To a large degree, this meaning has held constant for centuries. The term applies to multimovement works for solo instrument or a small ensemble of instruments (there are almost no sonatas for voice). Over the years, musicians also have extended the word *sonata* beyond its original meaning and have applied it to discussion of movements with a very particular form. This form is as important (and just as common) as variation, binary, ternary, and rondo.

Since the 1770s all of the important genres of art music, including symphonies, concertos, operas, and instrumental sonatas, have featured movements written in sonata form. The two terms often used as synonyms for sonata form—*sonata-allegro form* and *first-movement form*—are misnomers, because movements cast in sonata form may be in any tempo and occur in any movement of larger works. Furthermore, the first movements of these works may not even be in sonata form.

At a deeper level, even the term *sonata form* itself is problematic, given that it implies a rigid formal mold governed by a series of compositional rules that composers are required to follow. However, sonata form is essentially a way of composing, one that is the outgrowth of a large-scale musical process that is dependent on a powerful yet simple tonal strategy:

- State the opening material in the tonic.
- State additional material in a contrasting key.
- Restate all of the material in tonic.

This very general model harks back to binary form. It is from the merging of rounded and balanced elements of binary form that sonata form arises.

The Binary Model for Sonata Form

Sonata form may be seen as arising from a combination of balanced and rounded continuous binary forms:

A.   Balanced rounded continuous binary form (major mode)

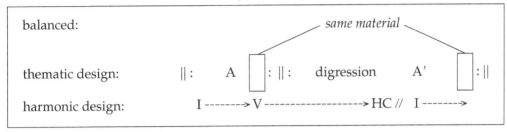

B.   Sonata form (major mode)

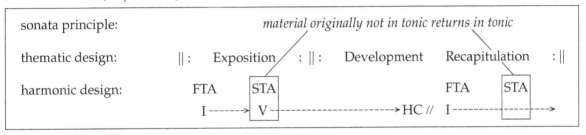

In the **first tonal area (FTA)**—the initial part of a sonata's first section, the **exposition**—material is presented in the tonic key. The FTA is dependent on the rounded binary characteristics, returning with the original material (**recapitulation**) after a digression (**development**) and a half cadence with an interruption. In the **second tonal area (STA)**, material is presented in the exposition in a contrasting key (usually V in major mode and III in minor mode). The STA is dependent on balanced binary characteristics: Material (STA, usually with a new theme) presented at the end of the first section (exposition) returns at the end of the piece (recapitulation) in the tonic key.

The FTA and STA may contain similar or contrasting thematic material; they may also contain multiple themes. To avoid confusion and ambiguity, each theme will be labeled with its tonal area and a number to indicate order. For example, given three themes in the FTA and two in the STA, the labels would be FTA_1, FTA_2, FTA_3, STA_1, and STA_2.

The small sonata movement in Example 15.8 blends and expands aspects of rounded and balanced binary forms, but only the exposition repeats. The following diagram reveals why only the exposition is repeated: The development and recapitulation together are over twice as long as the exposition. Beethoven achieves a proportional balance by repeating only the exposition. *("x" designates a new melody in the development, not based on FTA_1 or STA_1.)*

```
measure:                   1      16         34           64      80
thematic design:  ||: Exposition   :|| Development   Recapitulation ||
                     FTA₁  STA₁       STA₁  x  STA₁    FTA₁    STA₁
harmonic design:  i ———→ III ———→ VI ———→ V // i ———→
```

EXAMPLE 15.8   Beethoven, Piano Sonata in G minor, op. 49, no. 1, *Andante*

Continued

Transition

Now that we have determined the large-scale tonal and formal sections in Beethoven's movement, let's return to those passages that seem not to belong to the sections in Example 15.8. Between the FTA and the STA (mm. 9–15) is a passage that begins identically to the opening of the piece. Given that this passage follows a half cadence, we might expect this to be a consequent phrase that makes a period in the FTA. Instead, there in an alteration in m. 13, and the passage modulates to B♭ major (III), ending on a half cadence and preparing for the entrance of the STA. This seven-measure passage that leads to the STA is called a **transition** (Tr). There are two types of transitions.

1. A **dependent transition (DTr)** begins with a restatement of the initial theme from the FTA.
2. An **independent transition (ITr)** uses new thematic material.

Both types of transition modulate to the STA and end on either the new tonic or the new dominant (in which case the actual statement of the tonic is reserved for the opening of the STA). The pause that very often occurs between the end of the transition and the beginning of the STA, and which marks the approximate midpoint of the exposition, is called the **medial caesura**.

Transitions often reappear in the recapitulation even though there is no need for a transition, since the FTA and STA remain in the tonic. Since the ending key for the "transition" is now the original key, this passage is often altered (harmonically and/or melodically) to create a sense of motion. In Example 15.8, the transition returns at m. 72. This time, there is more activity (in the right hand) and a quicker movement to III before a half cadence in the original key (m. 79).

Closing Section

The contrasting tune of the STA ends with a PAC (in III) in m. 29 of Example 15.8. The following cadential section, which closes the exposition, is called the **closing section (CL).** The closing section follows the appearance of contrasting thematic material in the STA and a conclusive cadence of that material. Because the closing section's purpose is to reinforce the new key, it usually contains multiple cadential figures that are cast in two or more subsections that may even contain new thematic material. As such, the closing section is often longer than the STA, which may occupy eight or even fewer measures. A double bar (or repeat sign) usually marks the end of the exposition, just as it marks the close of the A section in a binary form. Thus, the exposition for Beethoven's sonata has the following form:

measure:	1	9	16	29
thematic design:	FTA	DTr	STA	CL
harmonic design:	i	i ⟶ III		III

Development and Retransition

The development is usually the freest section in a sonata form and is analogous to the digression in a binary form. Material presented in the exposition is transformed, although composers are free to introduce one or more new themes, explore new and often remote harmonic areas, and develop thematic and motivic material through transformations that include thematic fragmentation and sequence. Given the improvisatory character of the development, there is often a lapse of regular phrasing and periodicity. Thus, developments are often the most complex and dramatic sections of the movement. Underneath the chaotic surface, however, lies a logical unfolding of tonal and melodic events that imbue the form with a sense of coherence.

Beethoven begins his development in Example 15.8 with a variation of STA_1, followed by a new melody in E♭ major (VI) that enters in m. 38. The melody from the closing section enters in m. 46, ushering in a tonally unstable section that drives to the dominant and the interruption in m. 54. The **retransition (RTr)** is the final area of the development, where the dominant prepares the return of the tonic in the recapitulation. In major-mode sonata forms, the dominant would be secured much earlier (in the STA), and from that point is implicitly prolonged through the development; in this case, the retransition explicitly restates and expands the dominant at the end of the development and moves to the interruption that precedes the recapitulation.

Recapitulation and Coda

Although the recapitulation almost always repeats many events of the exposition, there are crucial changes. The most important change is the return of STA and CL material *in the tonic key*. Transitions are also altered so that they lead back to the tonic. Other changes may include a compressed statement of thematic material from the FTA, brief tonicizations that use modal mixture, or reversing the order of the themes from the expositions's FTA and STA.

Example 15.8 could have ended in m. 97, but Beethoven instead concludes the movement with cadential material—from the STA—in a **coda**. Codas occur after the recapitulation; they also can occur at the end of the exposition, where they are called **codettas** since they are typically shorter and end away from the tonic key. Codas are optional, as their name implies (in English, "tail" or "appendage"). They serve to confirm the closing key and often incorporate material from the FTA or STA. Material is often stated over a pedal point, which creates a strong cadential feeling. Finally, codas often emphasize the subdominant, which provides a large plagal motion that extends the prevailing key.

The following diagram provides a complete summary of the prototypical events that occur in a sonata form written in either major or minor modes.

Sonata form

thematic design:	‖: Exposition					:‖: Development		Recapitulation		Coda:‖
harmonic design:	FTA Tr	STA	CL	(Codetta)			RTr	FTA "Tr"	STA CL	
keys (major mode): I	→	V	V	V		⟶ V //		I →	I	I
keys (minor mode): i	→	III	III	III		⟶ V //		i →	i	i

WORKBOOK
15.3

Analytical Extension: Motivic Expansion

The first movement of Mozart's Piano Sonata in B♭ major, K.333 (Example 15.9) presents what appears to be a random series of harmonies and keys in the development. Our goal is to seek an underlying compositional logic for these curious excursions.

The formal structure is clear in this movement. The exposition, demarcated by the double bar and repeat signs, occupies mm. 1–63. The FTA closes at m. 10, the DTr begins at m. 11 and closes on the arpeggiating dominant of the new key, and the STA in F major (V) occupies mm. 23–38. The CL section divides into two smaller sections (mm. 38–50 and mm. 50–58), and a codetta closes the exposition (mm. 59–63). The recapitulation and coda (mm. 94-165) unfold in the same manner as the exposition.

EXAMPLE 15.9   Mozart, Piano Sonata in B♭ major, K. 333, *Allegro*

Continued

Continued

Continued

The following chart shows the main formal sections of the movement; notice that the harmonic progression in the development (mm. 64–93) remains to be interpreted.

measure:	1	11	23	39	59	64	87	94	104	119	135	161
thematic design:	Exposition					Development		Recapitulation				Coda
harmonic design:	FTA	DTr	STA	CL	Codetta		RTr	FTA	"DTr"	STA	CL	
	I	⟶V	V	V		???⟶V //		I	⟶I	I	I	

Exposition

We will now explore the thematic and motivic materials in Mozart's sonata. Let's make a contrapuntal reduction of the outer voices of the FTA theme in order to understand the underlying voice-leading framework from which motivic figures might emerge. A clear I–ii–V^7 progression opens the piece and is followed by a contrapuntal elaboration of the tonic (mm. 5–6). This movement does not initially appear to contain any clear-cut motives based on surface contours, except for the descending scalar sixth (comprising a fifth, preceded by an upper-neighbor grace note that should be played as a sixteenth note) that begins the piece.

Although the B♭ in the upper voice of m. 1 is clearly an arrival point, the E♭ (m. 2) that eventually moves to D (m. 4) seems to be more important, given those pitches' durational, metrical, and registral prominence. Might the initial scalar descent be emerging and expanded over many measures? This is the interpretation given in Example 15.10; note that the overall descent of a fifth (the same fifth that opened the movement) is bisected into thirds by range: F–E♭–D and D–C–B♭. The F in the upbeat of m. 1 is prolonged through the downbeat of m. 2 before it descends to E♭ (m. 2) and D (m. 4). The continuing C–B♭ in mm. 5–6 is not a strong arrival on tonic, because the tonic chord is in inversion and is not preceded by a PD–D motion. The chords in mm. 5–6 act as part of a voice exchange that prolongs tonic, which further indicates the subordinate nature of the B♭ in m. 6. The strong structural arrival of C–B♭ in mm. 9–10 completes the fifth descent.

EXAMPLE 15.10

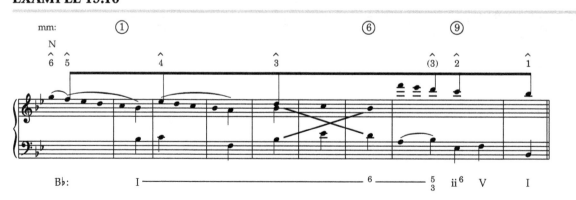

The theme in the STA literally repeats the same fifth-plus-neighbor descent from the FTA, in the key of F major (V). However, this time Mozart develops the upper neighbor to $\hat{5}$ by harmonizing $\hat{6}$ with B♭ major (IV) in m. 24, thus stabilizing the upper-voice D. Just like the FTA's fifth-plus-neighbor descent, the STA's descent is interrupted by a pause on $\hat{3}$ (in F major, m. 26). The complete descent does not occur until m. 38.

Development

The development contains unusual modal shifts and curious tonicizations that make it difficult to determine any underlying harmonic progression. It begins with a simple right-hand restatement of the initial tune in F major (V), with the upper-neighbor D. A bass ascent begins with F in m. 64 and moves through G, A, B♭, and C; the line continues with the D (m. 69) and resolves to C (m. 70). This results in another setting of the familiar motive of a stepwise fifth-plus-neighbor, this time in exact retrograde (reversal) of the opening gesture of the STA and expanded over seven measures. The chord in m. 69 sounds out of place, as if Mozart has marked it for our consciousness. Could he be preparing us for other hidden statements of the motive?

The unexpected cadence on F minor (rather than major) in m. 71 and motion to a G^7 harmony in m. 73 implies a tonicization of C minor; however, the "arrival" on C minor is greatly weakened when the bass is left unresolved on G, resulting in a six-four harmony (m. 75). G♭ descends to an F^7 harmony (mm. 76–78), implying the possible beginning of the retransition. However, once again our expectations are thwarted when F rises to F♯ in the left hand (m. 79) and resolves to G minor (m. 80). There is no strong cadence in G minor; instead, the retransition suddenly appears in m. 87 (with the progression V$^4_3$/V–V). The recapitulation begins in m. 93.

We now step back and interpret these events. F major (V) controls the opening of the development, and C minor (ii) and G minor (vi) follow. Thus, a series of ascending fifths (F–C–G, and D, as V of G) underlies the development until the motion to F at m. 87. But many questions remain unanswered. For example, why are the tonal areas so weakly tonicized? And how can we explain the odd shift from the unusually long and unresolved D-major harmony that moves to the weak V$^4_3$/V chord in m. 87? Let's look to the eight-measure motivic expansion of the fifth-plus-neighbor motive for clues.

The bass F ascends to G in m. 73; the sustained G is followed by the chromatic passing tone G♭, which returns to F in mm. 76–77. Again, the bass rises to F♯ and G, followed this time by a rapid descent to D (mm. 81–86). D falls to C—transferred up an octave at the V$^4_3$/V chord in m. 87. Finally, there is a leap to F (m. 88) and a return to B♭ at the opening of the recapitulation.

From this bass-line summary, we see that Mozart is projecting the small opening gesture (G–F–E♭–D–C–B♭) over the entire development (Example 15.11). The very first expanded statement of the descent (mm. 1–10) stopped on D for five measures. We now can understand why Mozart extended D major for so long (mm. 81–87) and didn't resolve it to its tonic. We also know why Mozart did not resolve the G to C in m. 75, for to have done so would have obscured the remarkable parallelism. Finally, in light of the controlling nature of the motive, we understand why Mozart used the V$^4_3$/V chord in m. 87 rather than the expected and much stronger root position: The inversion (with C in the bass) preserves the motive's stepwise descent.

EXAMPLE 15.11

The goals of the preceding analyses were to understand the mechanics of sonata form, to show how sonata form is an outgrowth and expansion of binary form, and to demonstrate how sonata form is a flexible and fascinating vehicle that composers employ to express uniquely personal musical statements. Discovering and interpreting hidden and transformed manifestations of motives are some of the rewards of analysis.

Additional Formal Procedures

Subphrases and Composite Phrases

A complete phrase may comprise two or more smaller units called *subphrases*. A **subphrase** is a relatively independent part of a phrase that is marked by a pause (called a **caesura**) and/or by the repetition and variation of short melodic gestures. The eight-measure phrase in Example A.1 divides into three subphrases: The first two subphrases are both two measures long, and each ends with a caesura. The final subphrase is four measures long and ends with a half cadence (thus ending the overall phrase).

EXAMPLE A.1   Haydn, Symphony No. 100 in G major ("Military"), *Allegretto*

The presence of a caesura does not guarantee the presence of subphrases. For example, in the opening of Example A.2, the vocal line is clearly divided into two gestures, where the initial gesture restarts in m. 3. However, a glance at the harmony reveals a single continuous harmonic motion over the four-measure phrase. The V_3^4 harmony in the second measure functions as a bass passing tone between $\hat{1}$ in m. 1 and $\hat{3}$ in m. 3. This I^6 then leads to the pre-dominant–dominant in mm. 3 and 4. The contiguous stepwise-fifth ascent combined with a goal-oriented harmonic progression and cadence in m. 4 results in a phrase that contains no subphrases.

EXAMPLE A.2   Schubert, "Des Müllers Blumen," *Die Schöne Müllerin*, D. 795

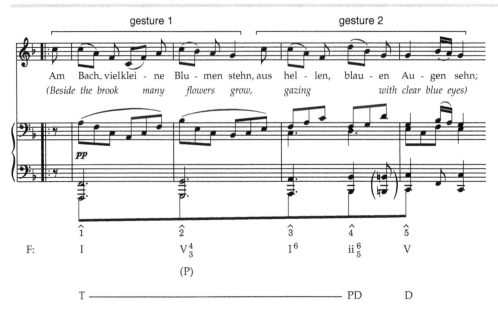

Conversely, there may be subphrases within a phrase even if no caesuras are present. The eight-measure phrase in Example A.3 moves from the tonic to a half cadence. Despite the nearly continuous movement, the phrase contains three subphrases, the first two of which are two measures long (delineated by their motivic structure), and the third of which is four measures long.

EXAMPLE A.3   Schubert, Symphony No. 4 in C minor ("Tragic"), *Andante*

Phrases that comprise three or more subphrases are called **composite phrases.** The phrases in Examples A.1 and A.3 are both composite phrases. Composite phrases—like all phrases—contain only one structural harmonic progression and one cadence, but they are often longer than the more common four-measure phrases that we have encountered. Composite phrases are usually eight or more measures in length, and they give the aural impression of being composed in an additive, stage-by-stage process rather than a single sweeping motion. There are two common types of composite phrases, distinguished in the way their harmonic motion unfolds.

1. The harmonic progression unfolds gradually, with each subphrase's melody supported by a new harmonic function, as illustrated in Example A.4. The 14-measure phrase contains three subphrases, and a single goal-oriented I–ii⁶–V–I progression underlies the entire structure.
2. The harmonic progression stays on the initial tonic through most of the subphrases, changing to PD, D, and T only at the very end of the phrase. Projecting this structure in performance enhances the musical drama considerably. The first two subphrases in Example A.5 close on the tonic. Subphrase 1 ends in parallel tenths, surely a weak conclusion, and subphrase 2, while featuring a ii–V⁷–I ending, still feels more like the beginning of a new phrase that is cut short with a T–PD–D gesture that is more a harmonization of the soprano melody $\hat{3}$–$\hat{4}$–$\hat{3}$ than an actual cadence. It is only with the deceleration of the melody to quarter notes and the trill that the final subphrase brings the entire structure to a close in m. 8.

Identification and interpretation of both subphrases and composite phrases is often, if not usually, a subjective enterprise. In fact, the interpretations of Examples A.1–A.5 are all debatable to some extent, and alternate viewpoints are certainly possible.

EXAMPLE A.4   Haydn, String Quartet in B♭ major, op. 64, no. 3, Hob. III.67, *Menuetto*

Continued

EXAMPLE A.5   Haydn, Piano Sonata No. 30 in D major, Hob. XVI.19, *Moderato*

Variation Techniques

Continuous Variations

One of the most difficult and important tasks for a composer is to balance unity with variety. Fulfilling that task raises a central question in composition: How do you handle repeating melodic material? As master listeners, composers are keenly aware of the potential stasis that is created by literal restatement, on the one hand, and of the potential for aural chaos when a listener is constantly assailed with new material, on the other. One of the most important genres for exploring and developing this relationship between unity and variety is the *variation set*. Variation sets usually begin with an initial idea, or theme, from which a series of variations unfolds. These variation sets may be independent pieces, or they may be members of larger, multimovement works such as suites and sonatas. Variation sets are found in just about all instrumental combinations, including works for solo instruments, chamber works, symphonies, and vocal pieces.

The two common types of variation sets are continuous variations and sectional variations. The difference between the two is based on how strong the division is between variations and how smooth the progression of events is from the opening to the close of the piece. We focus here on continuous variations.

In a **continuous variation set**, the theme is relatively short (usually a phrase), and it gives the effect of being incomplete in order to permit each variation—there are usually many—to flow seamlessly into the next. This is often accomplished by an overlapping process whereby the ending tonic of one variation simultaneously acts as the beginning of the next.

Listen to Example A.6, which is the beginning of a continuous variation set. Note the repeating bass pattern (bracketed in the example) that forms the foundation for the variations (note also the brackets above the staves showing how some repetitions of the pattern are overlapped, as the initial arrival on V can be heard as part of an authentic cadence).

EXAMPLE A.6   Monteverdi, "Lamento della ninfa" ("Lament of the Nymph"), *Madrigali guerrieri, et amorosi*

Continued

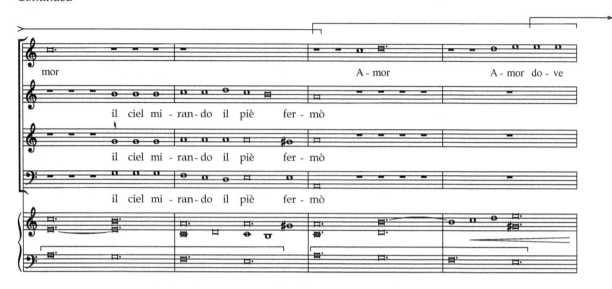

Continuous variations are most often constructed through the use of a repeated idea, called an *ostinato*, rather than a lyrical tune. Ostinati provide the backbone of the variations, over which changes in register, texture, and motivic design occur. Ostinati generally appear in the lower voices and can be as simple as a repeating bass pattern, called a **ground bass**, a repeating harmonic pattern, called a **chaconne**, or both a repeating bass and a harmonic pattern, called a **passacaglia**, as in the case of Monteverdi's "Lamento."

Often, all three terms are used interchangeably. The distinction between the repeating bass line of the ground bass and the repeating harmonic pattern of the passacaglia and chaconne is often artificial; composers use repeating harmonies to accompany a repeating bass, and vice versa. In Example A.7, Purcell harmonizes his eight-measure ground bass (circled notes) with a harmonic pattern that is used in each repetition.

EXAMPLE A.7   Purcell, Ground in G, theme and two variations

Examples A.8 and A.9 illustrate how composers merge the two types of ostinati. Bach's famous Chaconne is based on a repeating series of harmonies (see Example A.8). That the ostinato begins in midmeasure helps to maintain continuity between repetitions. Furthermore, the variations overlap, with each ending dovetailed with the beginning of the next statement; only the theme is not overlapped.

EXAMPLE A.8   Bach, Partita no. 2 in D minor for violin solo, BWV 1004, Chaconne

In Example A.9, Beethoven's eight-measure theme—a repeating harmonic ostinato—traverses an indirect step-descent bass to iv, followed by a two-measure cadential gesture. Although the theme is tonally closed and there is no dovetailing between repetitions, continuity is preserved by the continuous figurations.

EXAMPLE A.9   Beethoven, *Thirty-two Variations on an Original Theme,* in C minor, WoO 80, theme and two variations

Chaconnes and passacaglias often employ sequences. For stepwise bass descents the (−5/+4) sequence works well. Recall that the underlying structural motion is by step, usually leading to the pre-dominant function on $\hat{4}$. Thus this sequence preserves the common step descent. For example, in the key of G minor the progression i–iv–VII–III–VI–ii°–V–I creates a direct step descent to the dominant, as shown in bold: **G**–C–**F**–B♭–**E**♭–A–**D**–G. Example A.10, from a Handel Passacaglia, demonstrates.

EXAMPLE A.10   Handel, Suite no. 7 in G minor, *Passacaglia*

Indeed, Pachelbel's Canon is a good example of a continuous variation set: Its nonstop $(-4/+2)$ sequence leads to the subdominant IV and rises to the dominant, preparing for the next statement of the pattern (Example A.11).

EXAMPLE A.11   Pachelbel, Canon in D major

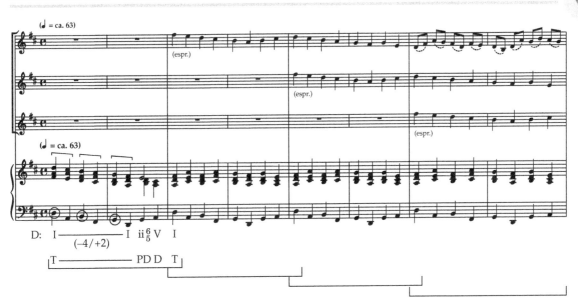

Sectional Variations

Continuous variation sets flow seamlessly from one variation to the next. We now explore the **sectional variation** set, where the theme and variations are usually in binary form (often a rounded continuous binary form) and are separated from one another. There are often more substantive changes among variations in a sectional variations set: In addition to changes in texture and figuration, there may be reharmonization, tonicization of diatonic and chromatic keys, and changes between major and minor modes.

In general, composers strive to balance musical unity with diversity in each variation by retaining one or more characteristic elements presented by the theme. For example, if a composer significantly alters the theme's melody by adding figuration or ornamentation, the harmonic underpinning will most likely not stray too far from its thematic presentation. If the harmony is dramatically altered, the melody will often remain unchanged. One musical element that tends not to be altered is the form of the theme, including its general proportions and length. When we analyze variations, it is precisely the degree and types of changes in the variations that interest us. It is particularly rewarding to find the seeds for such alterations sown in the theme itself, seeds that lie dormant until a particular variation provides the environment for it to germinate and flourish.

By their very nature—that of repeating some musical idea—variation sets clearly run the risk of being merely a string of connected ideas devoid of any larger, goal-oriented musical process or development. To avoid such problems, composers use two common strategies. In the first strategy, a sense of drive leads to a musical climax. The most common means of achieving such a drive is to use ever-smaller note values (sometimes referred to as a *rhythmic crescendo*) or increasingly elaborate textures and expanded registers and dynamics (in which there may be one or more arches of intensity). In the second strategy, groups of two or more variations create another level of organization. This procedure creates a large-scale ebb and flow in the unfolding of the entire set. For example, in a set of 12 variations, a composer might create three larger groups of five, two, and five variations, respectively, with each group distinguished from the other by mode change (e.g., the central group may be cast in the parallel minor if the work is in major) and with each group unfolding in one of the processes described in strategy 1.

The following excerpts provide a clear and simple example of sectional variations. The theme (Example A.12) lacks the typical double-bar signposts that are symptomatic of binary forms; nonetheless, it meets the requirements for a sectional simple (and balanced) binary form. The theme opens with an eight-measure contrasting interrupted period. The first phrase's initial descent is followed by a series of leaps that highlight $\hat{6}$ and $\hat{5}$ (E and D). The second phrase precisely balances these features by reversing the contour: It ascends by step to $\hat{6}$ and then descends to close on $\hat{1}$. Measures 9–12 are primarily sequential, though the bass's static E–D neighbor motion is reminiscent of the melody in the first eight measures.

EXAMPLE A.12   Beethoven, *Variations on the Duet "Nel cor più non mi sento,"* WoO 70, Theme

Fast-note chromatic lower neighbors characterize the first part of Variation I (Example A.13), while broken-chord figures characterize the second part (mm. 9–11). Both melody and harmony remain faithful to the theme, save for minor deviations (e.g., a shift from root-position harmonies to more stepwise motion in the opening), followed by a compensating alteration in the sequence. Contrapuntal features that were only implied in the theme are now made explicit, including the striking parallel-tenth motion in mm. 25–26. A small flourish follows the fermata, in which the lower-neighbor motive from the opening of the variation becomes a trill; C♯ eventually leads to C natural in order to destabilize the dominant.

EXAMPLE A.13   Beethoven, *Variations on the Duet "Nel cor più non mi sento,"* WoO 70, Variation I

Continued

Beginning in Variation II (Example A.14), Beethoven intensifies the musical drama. By swapping the material that occurred in the right and left hands of Variation I, both textural density and register are expanded. The sixteenth-note motion now occurs in the left hand, and the right hand's large leaps create compound melody, giving the impression that a third voice has been added to the texture. The added applied chord (V_5^6/V in m. 44) intensifies motion to the dominant to close the first phrase. The applied chord is also a reminder of the preceding variation's C♯–D neighbor motive and trill extension.

EXAMPLE A.14   Beethoven, *Variations on the Duet "Nel cor più non mi sento,"* WoO 70, Variation II

Variation III, the midpoint of the variation set, is climactic, in that Beethoven continues to expand the register (by a full octave in the bass and by dwelling in the high register of the right hand rather than merely touching those notes as he had done previously). Further, the hands are equal: They share all textural material and create the impression of a dialogue.

Variation IV (Example A.15) provides a momentary respite from the mounting tension of the preceding figuration variations. However, the shift to the parallel minor mode combined with the accented dissonances and an added fourth voice creates a dark and introspective mood. This variation also contains the most significant harmonic departure: The subdominant—rather than the dominant—becomes the harmonic focus in each section. The harmonic tide turns already at the beginning of the second phrase (m. 86), where tonic becomes V^7/iv. Unlike the sequence in the theme, the sequential passage in mm. 90–93 turns to the subdominant through a diaologue-like play between soprano and bass that is reminiscent of Variation III. The theme's D–E motive appears at the climax of Variation IV (m. 95). Sighlike echoes of the motive immediately follow in the inner voice (mm. 96–98).

EXAMPLE A.15   Beethoven, *Variations on the Duet "Nel cor più non mi sento,"* WoO 70, Variation IV

Variation V's sudden shift to the high register projects the tune, which is accompanied by rapid scalar sixteenth-note triplets. Outdoors, pastoral horn calls in the left hand contrast dramatically with Variation IV. Variation V also provides what feels like a giant upbeat to the final variation.

Variation VI rounds out the set by restating crucial features of the theme. Then Beethoven adds a 24-measure coda, which presents the opening gesture of the theme (5̂–3̂–2̂–1̂) in imitation and in the extreme upper and lower registers (Example A.16). Such a drive to the end is fitting, given that it also summarizes events presented in earlier variations. The brief tonicization of IV beginning in m. 156 serves three purposes. First, it signals the close of the piece, since codas often touch on the subdominant to create a plagal effect. Second, it is reminiscent of the tonicization of minor iv that took place in variation IV, and third, the IV–I motion permits one last statement of the E–D neighbor motive that played a central role in the variation set.

EXAMPLE A.16   Beethoven, *Variations on the Duet "Nel cor più non mi sento,"* WoO 70, Variation VI

Continued

Ternary Form and the Nineteenth-Century Character Piece

Some of the species of ternary forms from the eighteenth century, such as the minuet-trio, continued to serve composers throughout the nineteenth century. Others, such as the da capo, fell out of favor and were replaced with new—or at least hybrid—forms whose very titles suggest the intense Romanticism that begot them. One new addition, the **character piece**, was a short, expressive work often written for solo piano. Examples of some important nineteenth-century character pieces include the bagatelles of Beethoven, the impromptus and *Moments musicaux* of Schubert, and the ballades, nocturnes, polonaises, and mazurkas of Chopin. In addition, composers who were influenced by the literature of the time wrote entire cycles of piano pieces with highly descriptive titles, such as Robert Schumann's *Papillons* and *Carnival*. Character pieces continued to be composed throughout the nineteenth century by Liszt, Brahms, Scriabin, and Grieg, whose "Hjemve" ("Homesickness") we have already encountered in Chapter 15.

In the following short examples from the cusp of the nineteenth century and onward, we explore how composers used motives to link independent sections of ternary works—in particular, how apparently new musical material may be seen to be a concealed repetition or a transformation of earlier material. Although it reaches its apogee in the music of Liszt and Wagner, motivic transformation is not new to the nineteenth century. One often encounters instances of transformation in the music of late-Classical composers such as Mozart and Haydn, some of whose string quartets are unified through the recurrence of the same one or two motives in multiple movements.

Consider the minuet-trio pair from a Haydn string quartet shown in Example A.17. On first glance, it is clear that the minuet and trio are highly contrasting. Not only are there dynamic and key changes (from C major to A minor), but the trio is more sparse in texture than the minuet, with the first violin given the lion's share of melodic material and the lower instruments merely punctuating the tune with the occasional chord. However, a more detailed look reveals important connections between the minuet and the trio.

EXAMPLE A.17   Haydn, String Quartet in C major ("Emperor"), op. 76, no. 3, Hob. III/76

A.   Menuett: *Allegro*

B.   Trio

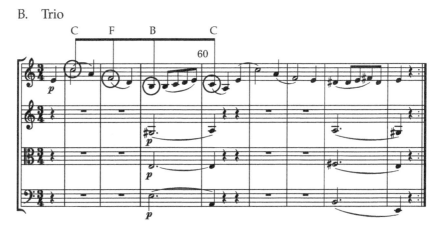

The minuet opens in C major, with the angular violin falling by ever-increasing large intervals: a sixth, a seventh, and finally a ninth. The other instruments imitate the first violin's jaunty contour, but the cello line (C–F–B–C) is particularly exposed. The opening of the trio reveals a barely hidden repetition of the earlier cello figure in the first violin, even though the trio is cast in the relative minor.

EXAMPLE A.18   Chopin, Mazurka in A minor, op. 17, no. 4

Continued

Example A.18 shows the opening A section of a Chopin mazurka in A minor, a section that contains a nested small ternary form (*aba*). After an ambiguous four-measure introduction, a wandering melody enters at m. 5. The opening melodic notes of the right hand (B–C–D) help to explain the function of the introduction, where the middle voice moves with this same three-note figure, almost as if it were lying in gestation before flowering into an expressive melody at m. 5.

Measures 8–11 are filled with chromaticism, including the descending line E–D♯–D–C. The mood remains somber, such that we crave relief. It arrives in mm. 37–42, as a more sprightly tune unfolds over a dominant pedal—this is the *b* part of the nested *aba* form. Despite the contrast, we see a compressed repetition of the chromatic line from mm. 8–13 recur in mm. 37–42 (Example A.19).

EXAMPLE A.19   Chopin, Mazurka in A minor, op. 17, no. 4

Continued

Rondo

"Variety is the spice of life" and "There's no place like home" are two popular sayings that convey very different meanings. Although most of us desire new experiences to keep life interesting, we also need frequent returns to the familiar so that our lives don't feel they're becoming too chaotic. This balance of variety and return—so fundamental to human nature—is reflected in **rondo form**. Rondo, like ternary, is a **composite form**, constructed of multiple self-contained sections. The sections of a ternary form introduced variety (in the B section) and return (in the final A section). Rondo form continues the balance of variety and return as it incorporates more and more sections. We can think of rondo form as an extension of ternary form, or we can consider ternary as a small three-part rondo:

Ternary form (three-part):	A	B	A′			
Rondo form (five-part):	A_1	B	A_2	C	A_3	
Rondo form (seven-part):	A_1	B_1	A_2	C	A_3	B_2	A_4

Rondo form alternates sections of recurring material (A_1, A_2, A_3, etc.), called **refrains**, with sections of contrasting material (B, C, etc.), called **episodes**.

The Classical Rondo

Rondos in the late eighteenth century often occur at the end of larger, multimovement works, such as sonatas, chamber pieces, and symphonies. With themes that are often taken from folk or popular sources—or at least imitate those sources—they provide a light finish and a welcome contrast to the usually more complex first movements and serious slow movements. Moreover, rondos provide an opportunity to demonstrate a musician's ability to change style quickly between contrasting sections. We next explore the two most important types of Classical rondo: the five-part rondo and the seven-part rondo.

Five-Part Rondo

EXAMPLE A.20   Clementi, Sonatina in C major. op. 36, no. 3

Continued

Continued

Example A.20 is the final movement of a Clementi piano sonatina. Clementi articulates the beginning of each section with double bars: The refrain (m. 1) recurs in m. 47 and in m. 105 (in an abbreviated form). The B section (m. 25) contrasts with the refrain: It has a different key, mood, texture, and melodic contour. Measure 71 begins another episode that is different from both the refrain and the B section; this section is labeled "C." The following is a form diagram for Example A.20:

Measures:	1–24	25–46	47–70	71–104	105–119	120–end
Sections:	A_1	B	A_2	C	A_3	Coda
Key:	I	V	I	i	I	I

Coda, Transitions, and Retransitions

The final section of Example A.20 is not a refrain; it merely serves to confirm the home key and to provide a satisfactory ending. When extra musical material occurs beyond the final refrain—the point at which a piece could have ended—it is called a **coda**.

The preceding form diagram represents at the large scale how Clementi's five-part rondo is put together (ABACA-Coda), but it misses a lot of detail. First of all, rondo forms, like ternary forms, can have connecting sections that move from refrain to episode (**transition**) or that return from an episode back to the refrain (**retransition**). At the end of the A_1 refrain, there is no modulation and no new theme or thematic development, and the cadence in m. 24 serves as a strong close for the section; therefore, there is no transition section. Contrast this with the end of section B: There is a PAC at m. 40, and the remaining material is fragmented and leads back to the original key. Measures 40–46 form a retransition. A similar retransition occurs at the end of section C, beginning at m. 90, so that the form now looks as follows:

Measures:	1–24	25–40	40–46	47–70	71–90	90–104	105–119	120–end
Sections:	A_1	B	Retrans.	A_2	C	Retrans.	A_3	Coda
Key:	I	V	$\rightarrow$	I	i	$\rightarrow$	I	I

Compound Rondo Form

A second important detail missing from the form diagram involves nested forms. As with ternary form, rondo form can be a **compound form** with nested forms. In Example A.20, A_1, B, A_2, and C are in rounded binary form.

Measures:	1–24	25–40	40–46	47–70	71–90	90–104	105–119	120–end
Sections:	A_1	B	Retrans.	A_2	C	Retrans.	A_3	Coda
Subsections:	a–dig–a'	b–dig–b'		a–dig–a'	c–dig–c'			
Key:	I	V	$\rightarrow$	I	i	$\rightarrow$	I	I

Seven-Part Rondo

The seven-part rondo adds another episode and refrain to the five-part rondo. These two added parts create a symmetrical form, which some liken to a musical arch. The following diagram shows the symmetrical form and the typical keys for the seven-part rondo:

	A_1	B_1	A_2	C	A_3	B_2	A_4
Major keys:	I	V, i, or IV	I	i, IV, or vi	I	I or i	I
Minor keys:	i	III or iv	i	iv, IV, III, VI, or I	i	I	i

As in the five-part rondo, the sections of the seven-part rondo are often cast in rounded binary forms.

Because of its symmetrical construction—and because section C may be longer and distinct from the flanking ABA sections—the seven-part rondo can sound like a giant ternary:

Seven-part rondo: $A_1 B_1 A_2$ C $A_3 B_2 A_4$

Ternary: A   B   A'

It is possible to confuse a large ternary form with a seven-part rondo, especially if a ternary form contains its own nested binary form in the A section. Generally, the context will help distinguish between the two:

- Rondos were favored in the eighteenth century and ternary forms in the nineteenth century.
- Slow rondos are less common than spirited rondos.
- Seven-part rondos usually contain repeated, nested smaller forms, adding yet another level of structure that is sometimes absent from ternary forms.
- Note that seven-part rondos can be shorter than five-part rondos, because the latter often have lengthy C sections, transitions, retransitions, and codas that appear less often in seven-part rondos.

Further Characteristics of Sonata Form

Monothematic Sonata Form

Example A.21 illustrates one of Haydn's string quartets in which the opening of the FTA theme reappears in the STA. Haydn frequently used the same theme (although often varied) in both the FTA and the STA, to create a form called a **monothematic sonata form**.

EXAMPLE A.21   Haydn, String Quartet in A major, op. 55, no. 1, *Allegro*

A.   FTA

in A:
(I)

Continued

B.   STA (using FTA theme)

in E:
   (V)

The Slow Introduction

Some movements cast in sonata form contain slow introductions that touch on foreign harmonic territory and chromatic key areas and incorporate modal mixture. This is particularly common in large works, such as symphonies. Slow introductions usually begin on the tonic (although tonic is not well established) and eventually move to and close on a half cadence. Because the slow introduction wanders harmonically before moving to V, and because V is often extended in anticipation of leading to the tonic, the introduction can be heard to function as a hugely extended upbeat that resolves to the tonic "downbeat" at the FTA.

A brief look at the opening four measures of Example A.22 reveals Beethoven's game plan: Although the first sonority is a root-position C chord, it contains a seventh; as V^7/IV, it moves to F, conferring on this sonority apparent tonic status. Tonal clarification is not given in the following measure since the V^7 that appears (G^7) moves deceptively to vi. The following crescendo sets up the expectation of tonal stability, but yet again Beethoven thwarts our expectations by falling in fifths, as vi moves to V^7/V to V, where a seventh is added. Subsequent attempts to resolve V^7 are thwarted, and the closing cadential gestures in mm. 9–12 reinforce the dominant. At last, in m. 13, V^7 resolves to tonic, which signals the beginning of the exposition.

EXAMPLE A.22   Beethoven, Symphony no. 1 in C major, op. 21, *Adagio molto*

Other Tonal Strategies

- **False recapitulation.** Two harmonic anomalies frequently appear near or at the point of recapitulation. The first is the false recapitulation, where the theme from the FTA appears in the "wrong" key. The real recapitulation—in the tonic key—usually follows soon thereafter. Thus, false recapitulations are actually part of the development. The first movement of Haydn's Op. 33, No. 1 String Quartet contains a false recapitulation.

- **Subdominant return.** The other harmonic anomaly is the subdominant return, where the recapitulation begins not on I but on IV. Given the exposition's tonal model of root motion up a fifth (from I to V), and given that the STA in the recapitulation must appear in the tonic to prepare for closure of the movement, composers begin the recapitulation down a fifth (and move from IV to I). Mozart's Piano Sonata in C major, K. 545, is an example of one such work with a subdominant return.

- **Three-key exposition.** Three-key expositions are found in major-mode works where the STA moves to a diatonic third-related key before arriving on the dominant. Bruckner's Sixth Symphony in A major moves I–iii–V in the exposition, for example.

- **Extended third-related STAs.** A more dramatic tonal strategy is to postpone the structural dominant until the retransition and to remain in the mediant key for the entire STA. For example, Beethoven's Piano Sonata in G major, Op. 31, No. 1, begins in G major. The STA is in the chromatic-third-related key of B major (which changes to B minor for the rest of the exposition). The dominant D major appears later, in the development.

Glossary of Abbreviations

A	ascending; augmented
AC	authentic cadence
Ant	anticipation
App	appoggiatura
Arp	arpeggiation
BRD	back-relating dominant
C	consonance
CCP	contrasting continuous period
CF	cantus firmus
CL	consonant/chordal leap; closing section
CIP	contrasting interrupted period
CPP	contrasting progressive period
CSP	contrasting sectional period
D	dissonance; descending; dominant
d	diminished
dig	digression
DTr	dependent transition
EC	embellishing chord
EPM	embedded phrase model
Fr	French (augmented sixth chord)
FTA	first tonal area
Ger	German (augmented sixth chord)
HC	half cadence
IAC	imperfect authentic cadence
IC	imperfect consonance
IN	incomplete neighbor
It	Italian (augmented sixth chord)
ITr	independent transition
LN	lower neighbor
M	major
m	minor
N	neighbor
Ñ̃	accented neighbor
P	passing; preparation; perfect

$\overset{>}{\text{p}}$	accented passing
PAC	perfect authentic cadence
PC	perfect consonance
PCP	parallel continuous period
PD	pre-dominant
Ped	pedal
PIP	parallel interrupted period
PPP	parallel progressive period
PSP	parallel sectional period
R	resolution
RTr	retransition
S	suspension
SATB	soprano, alto, tenor, and bass
STA	second tonal area
T	tonic
Tr	transition
UN	upper neighbor

Terminological Equivalents

Notational Equivalents

	BRITISH	SPANISH	FRENCH
whole note	semi-breve	la redonda	la ronde
half note	minim	la blanca	la blanche
quarter note	crotchet	la negra	la noire
eighth note	quaver	la corchea	la croche
sixteenth note	semiquaver	la semicorchea	la double croche
thirty-second note	demisemiquaver	la fusa	la triple croche
half step	semitone	el medio tono	le demi-ton
whole step	tone	el tono entero	le ton entier
rest		el silencio	la pause

	GERMAN	SPANISH	FRENCH
C	C	do	ut
D	D	re	ré
E	E	mi	mi
F	F	fa	fa
G	G	sol	sol
A	A	la	la
B flat	B	si bemol	si bémol
B	H	si	si
flat	-es (except for B)	bemol	bémol
sharp	-is	sostenido	dièse
natural		becuardro	bécarre
major	dur	mayor	majeur
minor	mol	menor	mineur

Octave Designations

A0–B0	A_2–B_2	AAA–BBB
C1–B1	C_1–B_1	CC–BB
C2–B2	C–B	C–B
C3–B3	c–b	c–b
C4–B4	c^1–b^1	c′–b′
C5–B5	c^2–b^2	c″–b″
C6–B6	c^3–b^3	c‴–b‴
C7–B7	c^4–b^4	c⁗–b⁗
C8	c^5	c′′′′′

Cadences

authentic cadence	perfect cadence; closed cadence; standard cadence
half cadence	semicadence; imperfect cadence; open cadence
plagal cadence	Amen cadence; church cadence
deceptive motion	deceptive cadence; interrupted cadence
evaded cadence	interrupted cadence; irregular cadence
contrapuntal cadence	inverted cadence

Chord Qualities

major triad	M, maj
minor triad	m, min, −
augmented triad	aug, +
diminshed triad	dim, °, min(♭5)
major seventh chord	major-major seventh chord, M7, maj7, Δ7, Δ
dominant seventh chord	major-minor seventh chord
minor seventh chord	minor-minor seventh chord, m7, min7, −7
half-dim. seventh chord	dim.-minor seventh chord, ᵒ7, min7♭5
(fully) dim. seventh chord	dim.-dim. seventh chord, °7, dim7

Chord Inversions

I, I^6, I^6_4	I(a), Ib, Ic
$V^7, V^6_5, V^4_3, V^{(4)}_2$	V7(a), V7b, V7c, V7d

Harmonic Function

Major key:	I	ii	iii	IV	V	vi	vii°	vii
	T	Sp	Dp, Tl	S	D	Tp, Sl	Đ7	Dl

Minor key:	i	bII	ii°	III	iv	v, V	VI	VII
	t	sL	s̄7	tP, dL	s	d, D	sP, tL	dP

Applied chord: V/x	Secondary dominant: (D)x
V/V	DD (overlapping)

Other

applied chord	applied dominant; secondary chord/dominant/function
cross relation	false relation
Ger⅚ chord	doubly augmented fourth chord; Swiss/English augmented sixth chord
incomplete neighbor	appoggiatura or escape tone (échappée)
leading tone	leading note
measure	bar
modal mixture	modal borrowing; borrowed chords; modal interchange
neighbor tone	auxiliary tone
parallel minor	tonic minor
Picardy third	tièrce de Picardie
pre-dominant	subdominant
similar octave/fifth	direct octave/fifth; exposed octave/fifth
step-descent bass	lament bass
submediant	superdominant
tones of figuration	nonharmonic tones; nonessential tones
unison	prime
voice exchange	voice interchange

Ternary and Rondo Labels

ternary form	first rondo form
five-part rondo	second rondo form
seven-part rondo	third rondo form
refrain	principal theme; rondo theme; reprise
episode	contrasting theme; couplet; digression

Sonata Labels

first tonal area (FTA)	transition (Tr)	second tonal area (STA)	closing section (CL)

primary theme (P)
  theme 1 (Th. 1)
  A
	transition (T)	secondary theme (S)
		  theme 2 (Th. 2)
		  B
			closing section (K)

Listing of DVD Text
and Workbook Examples

Text Examples

Example 8.11 D
Example 8.12
Example 8.13 A
Example 8.13 B
Example 8.13 C
Example 8.14
Example 8.16
Example 9.1
Example 9.2 A
Example 9.2 B
Example 9.3
Example 9.4
Example 9.5
Example 9.6
Example 9.8
Example 9.10
Example 10.1 A
Example 10.1 B
Example 10.4 A
Example 10.10 A
Example 10.10 B
Example 11.8 A
Example 11.8 B
Example 11.9
Example 11.10 A
Example 11.11
Example 11.12
Example 11.16 A
Example 11.16 B
Example 11.16 C
Example 11.17 A
Example 11.17 B
Example 11.17 C
Example 12.1
Example 12.2

Example 12.5
Example 12.6
Example 12.8
Example 12.9
Example 12.10
Example 12.11
Example 12.12
Example 12.13
Example 12.14
Example 13.1
Example 13.3
Example 13.5 A
Example 13.5 B
Example 13.5 C
Example 13.6
Example 13.7
Example 13.10 A
Example 13.10 B
Example 13.10 C
Example 13.11
Example 13.15 A
Example 13.15 B
Example 13.17
Example 13.18
Example 13.19
Example 13.20
Example 14.1
Example 14.5
Example 14.10
Example 14.12
Example 14.13
Example 14.14
Example 14.15 A
Example 14.15 B
Example 14.15 C

Example 14.15 D
Example 14.16
Example 14.17
Example 14.19
Example 14.20 A
Example 14.20 B
Example 15.2
Example 15.3
Example 15.4
Example 15.5
Example 15.7
Example 15.8
Example 15.9
Example A1
Example A2
Example A3
Example A4
Example A5
Example A6
Example A7
Example A8
Example A9
Example A10
Example A11
Example A12
Example A13
Example A14
Example A15
Example A16
Example A17 A
Example A17 B
Example A18
Example A20
Example A21
Example A22

Workbook Exercises

Exercise 1.6 A
Exercise 1.6 B
Exercise 1.6 C
Exercise 1.6 D
Exercise 1.7 A
Exercise 1.7 B
Exercise 1.8 A
Exercise 1.8 B
Exercise 1.8 C
Exercise 1.9 A
Exercise 1.9 B

Exercise 1.9 C
Exercise 1.15
Exercise 2.1 A
Exercise 2.1 B
Exercise 2.10 A
Exercise 2.10 B
Exercise 2.10 C
Exercise 2.10 D
Exercise 2.22 A
Exercise 2.22 B
Exercise 2.22 C

Exercise 2.22 D
Exercise 2.31 A
Exercise 2.31 B
Exercise 2.33 Example
Exercise 2.33 A
Exercise 2.34 A
Exercise 2.34 B
Exercise 2.34 C
Exercise 2.34 D
Exercise 2.34 E
Exercise 3.1 A

Exercise 13.1 B
Exercise 13.1 C
Exercise 13.1 E
Exercise 13.1 F
Exercise 13.1 G
Exercise 13.3 A
Exercise 13.3 B
Exercise 13.3 C
Exercise 13.3 D
Exercise 13.6 Sample 2
Exercise 13.6 C
Exercise 13.9 A
Exercise 13.9 B
Exercise 14.1 A

Exercise 14.1 B
Exercise 14.1 C
Exercise 14.1 D
Exercise 14.5 Sample
Exercise 14.5 A
Exercise 14.5 B
Exercise 14.5 C
Exercise 14.11 Sample
Exercise 14.11 A
Exercise 14.11 B
Exercise 14.11 C
Exercise 14.13 B
Exercise 14.13 C
Exercise 14.16 A

Exercise 14.16 B
Exercise 14.16 C
Exercise 14.16 D
Exercise 14.21 A
Exercise 14.21 B
Exercise 14.22 A
Exercise 14.22 B
Exercise 14.22 C
Exercise 15.1
Exercise 15.3 A
Exercise 15.3 B
Exercise 15.5

INDEX OF TERMS AND CONCEPTS